SENTINEL
of the SEAS

ALSO BY DENNIS M. POWERS

Treasure Ship

The Raging Sea

SENTINEL
of the SEAS

LIFE AND DEATH AT THE
MOST DANGEROUS LIGHTHOUSE
EVER BUILT

DENNIS M. POWERS

CITADEL PRESS
Kensington Publishing Corp.
www.kensingtonbooks.com

CITADEL PRESS BOOKS are published by

Kensington Publishing Corp.
850 Third Avenue
New York, NY 10022

Copyright © 2007 Dennis M. Powers

All Kensington titles, imprints, and distributed lines are available at special quantity discounts for bulk purchases for sales promotions, premiums, fund-raising, educational, or institutional use. Special book excerpts or customized printings can also be created to fit specific needs. For details, write or phone the office of the Kensington special sales manager: Kensington Publishing Corp., 850 Third Avenue, New York, NY 10022, attn: Special Sales Department; phone 1-800-221-2647.

CITADEL PRESS and the Citadel logo are Reg. U.S. Pat. & TM Off.

First printing: August 2007

10   9   8   7   6   5   4   3   2   1

Printed in the United States of America

Library of Congress Control Number: 2007922606

ISBN-13: 978-0-8065-2842-7
ISBN-10: 0-8065-2842-7

To those who protected
the mariners over the years—
and their contemporaries who
now work to keep the history.

CONTENTS

Part IV. The Coast Guard and On

PREFACE

The rock-strewn turbulent ocean and terrible windstorms off Northern California had claimed over time countless ships and lives. In 1865, the large sidewheeler steamer S.S. *Brother Jonathan* struck a seething reef inside Dragon Rocks off that desolate coast and sank in forty-five minutes. In the West Coast's then-worst peacetime maritime accident, 225 people perished within hours in those raging waters. The front-page newspaper accounts across the country headlined the news of the great loss and famous personalities on board when that vessel went down. A remote lighthouse somehow had to be built and operated there in seas that unexpectedly rose stories high within a few hours.

I became enamored of both the *Brother Jonathan* and those deadly rocks and pored through the files in coastal research stacks to write *Treasure Ship*, a book about the life and death of that gold-bearing ghost ship. I found myself spending as much time, however, meandering through the files that existed on St. George Reef Lighthouse. Built in response to that tragedy at sea, this distant and dangerous station was constructed mere miles from the disaster site on a desolate wave-washed rock. The two stories about courage, hardship, and the changing of eras were intertwined.

When Alexander Ballantyne constructed Tillamook Rock Lighthouse, another engineering feat located off the Oregon coast, he proved the feasibility of building on such a challenging site twelve miles from the closest port. The U.S. Light-House Board next appointed him in charge of constructing St. George. From reading his diary, detailed notes, and reports on the construction of these structures, I realized he was one of the very few who was up to this difficult task. And hardships abounded from the beginning. A howling nor'wester with massive waves, shrieking winds, and stinging sheets of spray twice forced the first construction expedition to turn back to its San Francisco homeport.

After horrifying experiences with more monstrous storms during the first winter, Ballantyne and his crew learned to adapt to these deadly forces of nature. They had to. Each spring, the workers needed to rebuild what the tumultuous ocean had wrecked the winter before. Storms and seas washed men away, whether they were working, sleeping in quarters eventually built on the rock, or running to avoid rogue waves. From the explosive showering of blasted rock bits and drizzling rains to running out of food and drinkable water, the conditions these workers endured were hard and terrifying.

Ballantyne and his men had to be inventive in surmounting the elements—and they weren't always successful. Years passed before their efforts sufficiently overcame the hardships and they could complete the lighthouse, a massive medieval-looking structure that towered above the rocks. It was the most expensive and dangerous lighthouse ever built in this country.

I pored over the Del Norte County Historical Society's voluminous files about St. George Reef Lighthouse, including its historical, one-of-a-kind records. Once more, the folks at the Historical Society in Crescent City, California, were very helpful in pointing my research endeavors to the right places. This information was added to newspaper accounts from Portland, Oregon, to San Francisco and Los Angeles. From the San Francisco Maritime Museum and National Archives in Washington, D.C., to the U.S. Coast Guard Academy on the East Coast, maritime historians and librarians added to my growing stacks on this story.

I researched in depth the risky construction and the station's history, and I became captivated by the stories about the men who built and then operated a lighthouse on this dangerous wave-washed spit of rock. The construction was difficult enough, but then it had to be operated and maintained against the onslaughts of typhoons and windstorms. Marooned with other men in tiny rooms for weeks at a time, a keeper had to be mentally strong to overcome the close quarters, shrill ear-piercing foghorns, and sense of isolation, especially when the whistling winds powered the ocean into tower-high crests that battered the man-made structure and the men held captive inside.

Owing to the ever-present dangers, the Light-House Board did not allow families to live there, as distinct from nearly every other lighthouse. Located miles off the coast, supply boats had to bring fresh water, food, supplies, and medical equipment to the rock, and the only way to land or leave St. George was by a derrick and a stories-high, wind-swung ride. Though the seas could be rising or falling as much as fifteen feet, the operator had to hoist small launches by a hook onto the reef or lighthouse. Danger was always present. In the early years, keepers died and others became seriously ill. Among the eighty men who served over a forty-year period between 1891 and 1930, sixty-seven resigned or transferred to another station.

Coast Guardsmen had to land on the reef to physically remove more than one keeper who suffered a nervous breakdown. Accounts maintain that one or two lookouts simply disappeared after the seas crashed over the reef or became unaccounted for. During one storm, a monstrous 160-foot-high wave surge crashed over the lighthouse, totally inundating it and the men inside, pouring ocean inside while shattering windows in the uppermost lantern room that was fourteen-stories high above the reef.

The courage of these keepers—and their tales while on this prison-like fortress—stood out. Whether they were painting a railing or traveling to the lighthouse by small boat, risk to life and limb lurked in performing the simplest tasks. As important, the warning fortress on St. George is a testimonial to the historical times in our country that came and passed.

This book is about eras that our grandparents and even parents lived, knew, and read about. But the lives of those who built and lived in that lighthouse inside Dragon Rocks were very different.

ACKNOWLEDGMENTS

From a writer's perspective, each book has its own distinct rhythm and lyrics. *Sentinel of the Seas* came together owing to the assistance of different maritime experts, researchers, and historians, all blending their insights into the stories of courage and fortitude that span from the late 1800s into the new millennium. I wish to thank them for their gracious help, suggestions, and information.

The Del Norte County Historical Society in Crescent City, California, provided valuable help with their old pictures and extensive files on the St. George Lighthouse. A longtime helper and researcher, Sandy Nuss, deserves special mention for her suggestions, work, and ideas. Linda Cox, David Gray, and Linda Ging, then director of the Historical Society, also provided appreciated help for this project. Brian O'Callaghan is the new director and has also given needed support.

Special thanks go to Sandy MacLean Clunies, who provided very valuable historical and genealogical research. We had fun working together during our hunt which spanned from the National Archives in Washington to the Mormon genealogy records in Salt Lake City, for the information and background on the elusive Alexander Ballantyne, the brilliant builder of two of the most dangerous lighthouses constructed. Thanks, Sandy!

Maritime museums and organizations deserve special recognition for their assistance in tracking down information about the builders, their ships, and maritime life during these times. Jeffrey H. Smith is the associate curator of the widely respected Columbia River

Maritime Museum, located in Astoria, Oregon, who opened his files on the ships used in this lighthouse's construction. Tricia Brown of the Cannon Beach Historical Society in Oregon, Richard Whitwer of the Oregon chapter of the U.S. Lighthouse Society, and the highly respected author Elinor DeWire gave helpful leads and information. The Humboldt County Historical Society in Eureka, California, also provided interesting background history.

The ex-mariner and researcher Colin MacKenzie, with his Nautical Research Centre library in Petaluma, California, provided helpful historical information on the building of St. George Reef Lighthouse, along with the notes of Alexander Ballantyne on both this lighthouse and Tillamook Rock. Special thanks also go to Bill Kooiman of the Porter Shaw Library in the San Francisco Maritime Museum and National Park, who also provided pictures and research assistance.

The U.S. Coast Guard provided excellent historical information and assistance. Richard Everett, the head of reference and instruction for the U.S. Coast Guard Academy in New London, Connecticut, deserves special recognition. He located valuable records about the heroics of the Coast Guardsmen in 1951 after a rogue wave roared in and capsized their launch, as well as historical records on the building of both lighthouses. I appreciated the suggestions of Dr. Robert Browning, the Coast Guard Historian in Washington, D.C.

The informative and well-regarded maritime author Jim Gibbs provided ideas on Alexander Ballantyne's background, including what life was like on these lighthouses. As part of this, I thank John Gibbons for the generous amounts of time, information, and accounts about his days on St. George Lighthouse, more than any other Coast Guardsman ever spent. He not only told great stories, but was such a fun person to know. My time with Floyd Shelton was equally rewarding and I thank him specifically as well.

Experienced librarians are a key in any research. Anna Beauchamp is the coordinator of interlibrary loans for Southern Oregon University and was very helpful in my tracking down old publications and records.

Pam Selig is the librarian for the *Medford Mail Tribune* in Medford, Oregon, and found links that led to my contacting the descendants of wickies who worked on the Battery Point and St. George Lighthouses.

In historical research, pictures are as important as diaries. Inspecting old pictures of the construction, workers on site, ships used, equipment provided, and first keepers gave more accuracy to this story than any of the tales—and some contradictory—written or told much later. Jeff Gales is the executive director of the U.S. Lighthouse Society in San Francisco, California, and he generously supplied pictures and articles from the Society's publication, *The Keeper's Log*, which opened up what lighthouse life was like. Chris Havern is in the United States Coast Guard Historian's Office, and that facility helped provide more interesting photographs from that era. Tim Harrison and Dee Leveille at *Lighthouse Digest* generously provided more photographs, old articles, and lost information about the lighthouse. Kraig Anderson, the creator and owner of the well-constructed and informative Lighthousefriends.com, supplied digital images of various lighthouses across the country, as well as helpful suggestions.

I flew out to see St. George on the first helicopter flights allowed in two years. From the friendly people at the tiny airport to those on the caisson deck, the St. George Reef Lighthouse Preservation Society and its volunteers deserve special recognition. To fly over the ocean to a lighthouse where waves crash thunderously from all sides, land on a forty-foot-wide stone deck, and feel the ocean's power is the experience of a lifetime. Guy and Alice Towers, Peggy Thomas (communications), David Everson (our pilot), Bill O'Donnell (filming the station's video), our guides (Susan Davis, Jim and Marilyn McLaughlin, Terry and Nick McNamara, Rick Hiser, and Guy Towers), and others deserve our commendations. Each provided helpful information in writing this book.

John Ford is the park ranger at Yaquina Head Lighthouse in Oregon, and he helped answer my questions. My good friend, Chris Honore made various suggestions about this project and the manuscript. Guy Towers of the lighthouse society also reviewed parts of the manuscript with helpful input. Also, no thanks would be appropriate without my special mention of the editor-in-chief at Citadel, Michaela Hamilton, for her continual positive attitude, insights, and professional suggestions. I truly appreciate my literary agent, Jeanne Fredericks, who has been with me throughout the years and has always been supportive. My wife, Judy, accompanied me again on numerous trips involving this book project, and, without any question, made the difference in it becoming a reality.

The number of individuals who journeyed with me made this trip fun and interesting. Their help allowed me to create this book with all of its history and insights. I thank them all.

PART I

BALLANTYNE'S CHALLENGE

CHAPTER 1

Into the Dragon's Lair

The raging seas rose high and engulfed *La Ninfa* as it smashed into another tumbling wind-whipped wave in the shrieking nor'wester off Northern California. The harsh thud against the schooner's bow threw people below to wet wood floors or against bulkheads, and the sounds of the ocean hissed over the ship. Pulled by an eight-inch hawser from the steamer that slogged ahead, the two-masted, 126-ton vessel emerged, only to slam again into another large, frothy swell. Tons of cold seawater rushed down its decks and coursed into every non-watertight compartment, as heavy raindrops splattered against the ship. The blustery gale shredded sailing flags and forced the few men who ventured outside into protective crouches. The date was April 8, 1883.

With dark smoke billowing back toward *La Ninfa*, the wrecker *Whitelaw* bucked down one seething wave, then skidded sideways, as the vessel's harsh lurching carried forcibly back to the boat that it was towing. From the schooner's bow, the tow-ship disappeared behind the rolling swells, as the cable suddenly became taut and the towed ship surged forward. The skies were darker, as what once had been day was soon to become an even more threatening night.

With the ominous skies and seas boiling around him, one man in a worn sealskin coat remained on *La Ninfa*'s deck and scanned the horizon. When the cruel winds finally cut into his face and body with a chill that seeped into his bones, Superintendent Alexander Ballantyne turned from the deck to head below. As he watched a wave build up higher than the gunwales, Ballantyne braced himself against the bridge for the impact. The foam-covered roller slammed into the vessel, as dark gray-green ocean surged noisily over its sides.

Once inside, he stood next to a seaman who stared expression-lessly out a port window. Ballantyne still felt upbeat about this trip's chances. He had come to know this ship during the past several days, and although it continued leaking, he felt confident that the schooner would make its destination this time regardless of the conditions. Despite *La Ninfa*'s skittishness due to her recent refurbishment and bad trim or sailing abilities in harsh weather, Ballantyne was optimistic—but, then again, he was always that way.

The vessel's pumps were still keeping pace with the ocean's immersions, and he hadn't yet seen any major cracking in the hull from the ocean's constant pounding. Constructed six years ago, the squat wooden schooner was eighty-six feet long with a twenty-five-foot beam and was in good seaworthy condition. At least this was what he told his men. Although some of them were still fearful and most not used to ocean travel, Ballantyne knew they had accepted his assurances—so far.

He felt the same way about the steamer that was pulling the schooner. Nearly one hundred feet long, the *Whitelaw* was twenty-five feet wide and had a gross weight of 176 tons. Newly built in San Francisco the year before, the ship had been constructed as a wrecker: a sturdy vessel used in the salvaging or refloating of ships that the sea had claimed. It had been built to tow ships like this one, although he wasn't sure under what conditions.

This was the third time the *Whitelaw* had tried to forge through this windstorm with *La Ninfa* in tow. The expedition was trying to reach North West Seal Rock inside St. George Reef at the farthest point of California, located a few miles south of the Oregon border.

If the men could ever get to that rock, they were to start building a massive lighthouse there. The constant pummeling from the near-typhoon conditions, however, had forced the expedition to turn back to San Francisco the first two times. Not a good omen, Ballantyne thought, because building such a structure in the ocean even under good conditions would be a difficult challenge.

St. George Reef was the peak of a submerged volcanic mountain six miles off the northern extreme coast of California. Rough weather with howling winds and crushing waves could create mists that obliterated the peaks with great risks for mariners. In 1792 the British explorer George Vancouver had dubbed the reef-strewn area "Dragon Rocks," and over time the reef became known as St. George Reef, in the hopes "that the dragon might one day be slain." One after another, ships and their men met disaster on the rocks off this severe coast.

On July 30, 1865, the gold-bearing sidewheeler S.S. *Brother Jonathan* ran into a similar nor'wester before these conditions forced her to turn back and head for a safe port. The vessel struck an uncharted reef in the heavy seas inside Dragon Rocks close to land and sank in forty-five minutes. In the West Coast's then-worst peace-time maritime accident, 225 people perished within hours from drowning and hypothermia. The ship carried important figures who died on board, including General George Wright, the past Commander of the Pacific for the Union forces; Governor Anson Henry of the Washington Territory (later, the state) and close personal friend of President Abraham Lincoln; and James Nisbet, the well-known author, editor, and part owner of the *San Francisco Evening Bulletin*, to name a few.

Newspapers from San Francisco to New York City headlined the loss. The wreck of the *Brother Jonathan* was such a national calamity that it prompted the later passage of laws protecting passenger safety on steamships and the eventual authorization to construct the light-house that Alexander Ballantyne was to build. After various delays, the U.S. Light-House Board finally decided to build the station on

North West Seal Rock at the far end of this collection of rocks and small islands.

Since this reef was located six miles off the coast and thirteen miles from the closest port of Crescent City, California, housing the workers and supplying this large construction project would be a major undertaking. N.W. Seal Rock was relatively small and low in the ocean, making the towering waves that infested this area a constant danger. Ballantyne knew that he couldn't safely erect living quarters on this ridge of rocks until after his men had finished blasting and cutting the foundation into place. Quartering the men in Crescent City wasn't an option either, as too much valuable time would be lost taking men back and forth in this area's uncertain weather conditions.

He had selected the topsail schooner, *La Ninfa*, and had her initially outfitted to accommodate twenty-five men, including cooking, dining, and sleeping areas. Once construction began at the site, the numbers housed would need to more than double. The ship's refurbishment included enlarging the forecastle (the upper deck located at the bow but ahead of the foremast) by building new bulkheads, which gave more space for eating and cooking, and installing iron tanks with a carrying capacity of six thousand gallons of fresh water. Although built originally to carry copper ore on the west coast of South America, *La Ninfa* was a former sealing ship and had most recently been used as a makeshift lightship marking the wreck of the *Escambia* on the San Francisco Bar. Ballantyne considered the ship as being "strongly built," which the present gale conditions were severely testing.

On April 3, 1883, the working party boarded *La Ninfa*, which he had chartered along with the *Whitelaw*, for its first attempt on making the northward voyage. Ballantyne had already convinced several of his best workers who had toiled with him two years before in building Tillamook Rock Lighthouse—located over three hundred miles to the north off the Oregon coast—to join him in this new quest. And what an adventure this had already turned out to be.

As *La Ninfa* was to be permanently moored off the reef, a second vessel had to tow it and haul construction materials. The *Whitelaw* pulled the schooner and its men, tools, fresh water, and provisions toward N.W. Seal Rock. On board were the crew, quarrymen, stone-cutters, and even a blacksmith who would repair broken tools. *La Ninfa* also carried one, six-ton and three, four-ton "mushroom sinkers" for its mooring, along with four spar buoys, "two hundred fathoms" (or approximately 1,200 feet) of two-inch-thick chain, and a two-ton ship's anchor for the aerial tramway that would be constructed to transport men to and from the rock. Depending on the depths, the mooring plan called for up to eight rope-cables to be strung out in a spidery network from the quartering ship to the large buoys and anchoring heavy sinkers.

The ships immediately sailed into very bad weather, later reported to be just an "unseasonably" late storm. Worried after learning about the first storm reports, the captain of the Office of Light-House Engineers for the Twelfth District, A. H. Payson, in San Francisco, wrote a personal letter to the Crescent City (Battery Point) Lighthouse keeper. Captain Payson penned that he was "very anxious" to be kept current about the state of affairs and safety of *La Ninfa* and the expedition. He wrote that since his only communication with Ballantyne and the schooner would be "twice a month or so," he implored the lighthouse keeper to send "by every mail" a report as to what he knew about the construction force. Payson wanted to know that the schooner had been seen and the men were all right, concluding, "Of course, I shall be glad of any information regarding her or her party which you may be able to send me."

After the storm turned the expedition back for a second time, Ballantyne and Payson discussed whether they should simply wait another week. Weather reporting of today's caliber didn't exist in the

1880s, so whether a voyage was successful or not could simply depend on luck. The gale continued with such force on this third attempt that Ballantyne worried that the *Whitelaw*'s captain might decide once more to turn back. Such an act would subject his plans to more "interminable" delays, and he was concerned about his workers. Although Ballantyne had been on ships before under these severe windstorms—and more than a few times—most of his workmen had not.

Within an hour after the vessels again ran into stormy seas, *La Ninfa*'s plunging once more caused many of Ballantyne's "freshwater sailors" to become seasick. The noise of vomiting resounded from within the schooner's quarters and the acrid smells overcame even the hardiest. Despite the cold spray and saltwater that poured inside, some opened portholes or took frigid baths when stepping outside to gasp in fresh air.

When this occurred on the first attempt, the sick men could barely eat and stayed inside their close quarters toward the ship's stern. They remained there until the *Whitelaw* finally turned around and hauled *La Ninfa* back into San Francisco Bay's gentler waters. After a day of waiting for the weather to clear, the *Whitelaw* built up steam again, pulled the cable tight, and gently edged the schooner into the ocean on its northward journey. After sailing again into the queasy swells and pounding roller-coaster waves—compounded by the connecting hawser pulling taut as a steel cable and then dangerously slack—seasickness again overwhelmed those who hadn't yet developed their sea legs. Depending on the conditions, even the most experienced seamen can become seasick, and numbers of the men had bouts of nausea on all three trips.

People afflicted by seasickness, or motion sickness, claim that only a mercy killing can relieve their problem. Punctuated with wracking vomiting, headaches, and cold sweats that can continue for days, the person lies in a general state of malaise. Seasickness is a balance problem that comes about when your brain receives conflicting messages: one part of the balance-sensing system (your inner ear and sensory nerves) screams that your body is moving, while your eyes don't sense that motion.

Although passengers today use the patch and antihistamine drugs like Dramamine, seasick voyagers then had to rely on home-spun remedies. They ate saltine crackers and water, tried drinking bitters (a couple tablespoons of Angostura Bitters mixed in a half-glass of water), chewed ginger, drank liquor, lay down, smelled fresh sea air, stopped eating or drinking, avoided strong odors, and used whatever remedy they had heard about. Whether anything worked, however, depended on fate.

Until darkness completely overtook their murky surroundings, anxious men stared at seas running "mountains high," and as the ship creaked and groaned at seemingly every joint, it seemed as if she couldn't hold together any longer. The great combers that arose with their crested heads seemed like living sea monsters; they swelled ten feet over people's heads, acting as if to finally swallow up the ships and everything inside.

One ugly towering wave approached *La Ninfa* with sharp hissings and slammed into it with near overwhelming force. The sea inundated the dwarfed ship and drenched the schooner's interior. Cold saltwater leaked through the overhead decks, drained around timbers, poured through cracked hatches, and surged through portholes thrown open for air. The ship was waterlogged, and what once was well secured now floated inside or on the deck. The schooner heaved to one side as the men inside swore oaths or fervently prayed. Although she nearly lost her steerage, *La Ninfa* eventually righted herself.

The seas raged during the night's blackness, while the *Whitelaw* tossed myriad swirling sparks into the air that the winds quickly extinguished. The steamer's smokestacks at night looked as if fireworks were spewing from its very insides. As *La Ninfa* bucked the ocean, the wind whistled outside with spray and foam smacking against the ship's sides. The vessel moved slower and slower as one monstrous wave after another plowed into the boat. When the hawser went slack, the ship stood still and wallowed in the seas, but it then suddenly plunged forward when the rope pulled tight, nearly out of control and heaving from side to side.

Manning the pumps, the crew struggled to keep the ocean at bay; however, their efforts could only keep the sloshing ocean from completely overtaking the ship. Vessels could leak as much as one foot of saltwater per hour under these conditions, and the crew was hard-pressed to keep up with this flooding. These conditions eventually forced the workmen to leave their cold, smelly, flooded quarters to look anywhere else for warmth and dryness, braving a rocking, rolling, crashing passage. Unfortunately, no place was dry or warm.

A few men tried to stay in the dining area, as this was better than being cooped up in their tiny berths, slammed against walls, or pinned near upside down with water sloshing below. However, these facilities were toward the bow and took the brunt of *La Ninfa*'s collisions with the high waves. The whale-oil lamps gave off surrealistic shades of black and white, as the crashing of furniture, moaning and motion of the ship, and near overpowering smells overtook the senses.

One of the mates grabbed a sounding rod and shoved it into the pump well. He discovered that inches of water still remained inside. The ocean had so saturated the vessel that the pumping rate had to be increased. A rotary crank attached to a heavy flywheel worked the ship's pumps, and the two pumps threw water equal in volume to that shot from a fire engine. After a few hours, this worked.

The storm continued to whip the ocean into its agony. The extent of a wind's severity is directly related to the surrounding wave conditions. A wind at ten knots per hour (one knot equals 1.15 miles) creates waves two feet high. At twenty knots per hour, the winds create eight-foot whitecaps. At forty knots per hour (or forty-six miles per hour), the waves have well-marked streaks and reach twenty feet. Once the winds hit fifty knots per hour (or fifty-seven miles per hour), the seas are white with overhanging crests that are twenty to thirty feet high. This condition existed now and for what was a slow, unbearable amount of time.

Seemingly in the midst of the confusion, *La Ninfa* then stopped moving ahead. The sounds of the heavy chain anchor thumping wildly over the ship's side reverberated throughout its interiors. The schooner still pitched heavily in the seas but didn't experience the same heavy impacts due to the lack of movement. Owing to the darkness, storms, and howling winds, the men didn't know where they were or what was happening.

The workers stared at Ballantyne with anxious or uncertain looks from the shadows of their quarters and half-light of the lamps. He told them that the ships had finally come to the reef. Before nightfall, the ships were supposedly only a few hours from the rock, but that time period had more than passed. Without anyone needing to mention it, one fact stood out: if *La Ninfa* was where it should be, then the ship was now anchored during a raging storm inside the deadly Dragon Rocks.

When the first rays of the sun broke through the darkness, the pink streaks of dawn blended into the horizon's grays. Although the seas still ran with high waves that encircled *La Ninfa*, the ship's rolling and pitching had lessened somewhat from the night, and the shrieking winds had settled to gusts. As daylight sharpened the awesome sight of the flecked carpets of high seas that surrounded them, the ocean's spray still flew over the gunnels from bow to stern. The deck was deserted but for the few needed to keep watch.

When the men took their first look at North West Seal Rock, they were aghast at the sight of rolling swells and spray that completely covered the rocky point with violent surges of hissing whites. They had heard that the reef in places was no more than fifteen feet above sea level. Those who cautiously ventured outside received a drenching from the spray in return, and the morning air was chilly; they soon stepped down the hatchway for the protection of the ship's quarters. As Ballantyne assessed the way the waves crashed up fifty-four feet to the reef's highest point, he realized that getting his men off that rock would be as important as getting them on it—especially since the plans called for excavations that would carve around that point by over one-half its height.

He would have a greater problem in supplying this construction effort than he had at Tillamook. Many lighthouses on the West Coast were on land or more easily accessible, and when building these stations, the workmen simply walked home for the evening or lived in nearby housing. Whether the work was at Battery Point Lighthouse in nearby Crescent City or Yaquina Head to the north in Oregon, people raised cattle for beef and milk, grew vegetables, and were self-sufficient—an impossibility on this wave-washed rock. These parts of the coast were not only heavily forested, lightly populated, and undeveloped, but the closest town then was Crescent City with its population measuring in the hundreds.

With *La Ninfa* still anchored, the *Whitelaw* hauled back its tow rope. After building up steam, the wrecker bobbed up and down as it made several attempts to lay the six-ton sinker and permanently moor the schooner. Although the heavy sea conditions made it difficult for the crew to position the large spar buoy, the workers with a determined effort were finally able to do so. As soon as the crew successfully anchored the ship, the weather turned worse. They were forced to abandon any attempts to set the remaining moorings, and the *Whitelaw* steamed away to "stand off to sea." Another furious gale quickly blew in from the southeast, and the huge swells and screaming winds blew for several days, reaching their heights on the morning of April 14, and then continued for two more days. According to Captain Payson's report to the Light-House Board, the schooner during this time was "holding on it (the mooring) in great discomfort and the steamer lying by in the offing."

Alexander Ballantyne spent the time working on his construction plans and calming his men. He counseled them that the first days of bad weather were always the worst for any project and pointed to his experience on Tillamook Reef a few years earlier. With a powerful build, confident eyes, and a heavy, trimmed "Van Dyke" beard, Ballantyne exuded strength and conviction. He was in his fifties, slightly shorter than the average man, and absolutely fearless. This man wouldn't order anyone to do anything that he himself wouldn't try. He commanded respect and gave it to those who joined with him to meet his project goals.

BALLANTYNE'S RELATIONSHIP with John Trewavas was the reason for his being here. Trewavas was born in England and became a stonemason, working long years during the construction of Wolf Rock Lighthouse. Built between 1862 and 1869 off the coast of England, this structure was based on the design of the third Eddystone Lighthouse. These plans relied on setting huge, interlocking blocks of stone into a mortared foundation that was fitted to the rock to withstand severe storms. The first design used strong, iron legs set into the rock to support the lighthouse that were intended to let the seas slide past; however, this initial design didn't work. A powerful storm reduced the first Eddystone Lighthouse with this design into twisted stubs of iron.

Born in Scotland, Alexander Ballantyne met John Trewavas on Wolf Rock and worked with him on the important stone and masonry work. Located four miles off the coast of Cornwall, England, this site is risky regardless of weather conditions because swells can surge over it due to the surrounding deep water. And Wolf Rock gained its name from the howling that sounds when the wind whips through its cracks. When they worked there with the lighthouse's builder, both men gained valuable experience in the type of construction best used with wave-washed rocks.

Trewavas was the first of the two to immigrate to the United States, where he continued working as a master mason in Portland,

Oregon. The Englishman married Mary Eudy in Clackamas County (Portland area), Oregon, in 1872. His wife was the daughter of William and Jane Eudy, whose father was also a stonemason from England. The Eudy family and three children, including Mary, had arrived in Oregon in the 1850s. Trewavas knew them in Cornwall, where both he and William Eudy were stonemasons. When he landed in Oregon, Trewavas looked them up, saw how grown up his daughter was, fell in love, and married her.

One year later, Alexander Ballantyne was aboard the steamer *Calabria*, which had left Liverpool, England, arriving then in New York City in May of 1873. The ship's register listed his age as forty-six and the estimated year of birth as "about 1827"; however, this was an approximation. Listed as accompanying him were four other stonemasons: Caleb and James Murray, ages twenty-six and twenty-eight, who were from London; Martin Burrell, age thirty-eight, from Yorkshire; and David Bentley, eighteen, who was living in Lancashire and whose father was also a stonemason. Ballantyne recruited these stonemasons from England, and more than likely they joined him in his later projects on land and sea.

A young female accompanied Alexander on the ship, and her name was Margaret Ballantyne. The register indicated her age as twenty, that she was a weaver, and born in England. One would assume that Margaret was Alexander's daughter, but there is no further mention of her once the group landed in America.

Alexander met up with Trewavas in the Portland area and took up residence in nearby Oregon City, which later became Oregon's territorial capital. He is listed as being from Oregon City, but staying at the St. Charles Hotel in Portland in July 1875. He and Trewavas not only knew each other in Oregon, but they quickly became business partners. The *Morning Oregon* issue of June 5, 1877, announced:

> The building of a mausoleum and chapel: Mr. D. Macleay is having erected in Lone Fir Cemetery a very handsome and

enduring structure in the way of a chapel and mausoleum. Excavation was commenced a short time ago. Its architectural style will be gothic, of the most elaborate design and finish. In cost and elaborateness of design, this mausoleum will not be surpassed. Mssrs. Trewavas and Ballantyne have the contract for erecting this expensive structure.

The cost of the mausoleum was "in the vicinity of $13,500," or about the cost then of an average lighthouse on level land—and half a million dollars or more in today's money to create such an exquisite, specialized structure with excavated, hewn, and finely polished stone blocks.

Trewavas and Ballantyne were the best stonemasons in the region. They were extremely busy, much in demand, and hired by only the wealthiest. The *Daily Oregon* for August 17, 1878, exclaimed that Mssrs. Trewavas and Ballantyne, "the well known stonemasons," had received the stonework contract to build a new brick and stone building, located at the corner of First and A Streets in Portland. They employed a "force" of twenty men who were engaged in shaping the stone. At the same time, they also had the contract for the stonework in building a large Catholic Church.

The State of Oregon transferred title to Tillamook Rock in August 1879 to the United States so that this lighthouse could be built. Knowing about Trewavas's extensive experience with lighthouse construction on the rocky coasts of Britain and the two men's work in the Pacific Northwest in stonemasonry, the U.S. Light-House Board asked Trewavas to supervise the construction of the Tillamook Rock Lighthouse. The Board talked with both men, but Ballantyne stayed inland to oversee the land arrangements and keep the partnership's projects running.

Both Trewavas and the Board wanted him to land immediately on the site so that the proposed project could quickly start. On September 18, 1879, a surfboat took Trewavas and a sailor named Cherry to the rock to conduct the survey. All went well at first and he quickly made the preliminary surveys. But in climbing up the eastern slope of Tillamook, Trewavas slipped and fell, sliding down the rock's face to a ledge where a crashing wave quickly swept him into the ocean.

Cherry did what he could to save Trewavas by leaping into the sea and swimming toward the struggling man, but the strong current quickly drew the Englishman under. The boat's crew quickly rowed to where Trewavas had been last seen struggling against the ocean. No one could reach him in time. The savage underwater currents swept him down and he disappeared into the depths. His body was never found.

This "most unfortunate disaster" prejudiced the public against any landings on this sea-swept rock, let alone building a lighthouse there. News of the disaster spread rapidly, and soon there weren't many workmen left who would venture over those waters to the risky islet. The Light-House Board held an emergency conference and acted swiftly. Not surprisingly, it chose Alexander Ballantyne, Trewavas's partner, to lead the construction as its superintendent. Considered to be a "robust, intelligent builder with leadership talent," Ballantyne quickly accepted and started looking for workers to join his construction crew.

Interestingly enough, the Board announced that it chose "Charles A. Ballantyne," which is the reason why later published accounts name him "Charles." In 1883, archives list Ballantyne as an employee of the Engineer's Office for the Twelfth District of San Francisco: "A. Ballantyne, Superintendent Construction, born Scotland, appointed California, employed San Francisco, salary $250/month." He signed later documents that show the "A" stands for "Alexander."

As with St. George now, Alexander Ballantyne had great difficulties landing on the rock at first due to bad weather. Despite the heavy seas, he and the first four workmen finally landed on Tillamook Rock one month later with supplies and a temporary shelter. Cherry was the first one to scramble up the wet rock, followed in turn by a quarryman.

Being twice as high as N.W. Seal Rock with a broader base and located one mile from land, Tillamook Rock was an easier site on which to build a lighthouse—although it also was a wave-washed rock where the ocean hit from all four sides. The men first had to fight off numbers of sea lions and seals that took exception to their invasion. A strong windstorm next blew for three days, leaving the men with wet blasting powder, soaked food, and brine mixed with their fresh water. After a difficult time of risky experiences, Ballantyne and his men finally prevailed in completing this station's construction.

On January 21, 1881, the lighthouse's bright light beamed over the ocean for the first time. It took 575 hardworking days and cost $123,493 for Ballantyne to complete the building of Tillamook Lighthouse (or "Terrible Tilly"). There was no loss of life after Ballantyne took over. His construction of Terrible Tilly in one and a half years and under the original estimate and appropriation of $125,000 was the reason why Congress finally approved the building of St. George Reef Lighthouse. Two years later, Alexander Ballantyne was supervising its construction, but from the start this lighthouse's location was more difficult and dangerous than any other in the United States.

WHEN THE WEATHER moderated sufficiently on April 16, 1883, the men on board the *Whitelaw* readied to set the remaining three moorings. As with the first one set one week before, these buoy were large square, built-up platforms of "solid sticks" resembling telephone poles that floated on the surface. They were attached with long chains to mushroom sinkers (these being four tons) that anchored them into the bottom. The wood boxes were built in various shapes—from poles to squares—but for these depths a pyramidal base was used. Holes were drilled through the bottom ends and lined with heavy castings to which the loop of the anchor chains was attached. Two holes for the ship's attaching hawser were strengthened by cross-bolting and set at right angles on the floating section.

The original plans called for five buoys to be set: one each for the breast, bow, and stern lines when the ship was anchored close to the rock; one for an "outer" or bad weather mooring (the six-ton sinker) when lying farther from the reef; and a fifth for mooring the outside end of the tramway. Depending on the number of available buoys, the men either attached the tram to the mast or dispensed with the middle or breast buoy.

With the sinker holding the mooring buoy tight, a ship was secured to it as the heavy float became an anchor. However, strong storms could still pull the ship away with its mushroom sinkers dragging along the bottom—even rip the hawsers from a vessel or snap them away at weak links. To keep the ship reasonably secured when storms swept in, four buoys were placed around this vessel and the ship was tied in turn to each one. If held by only its anchor, the winds and swells of a bad storm could easily pull La Ninfa away and splinter the vessel on the nearby rocks.

Captain Payson still was concerned that the schooner, which he thought was not "especially built" for this purpose, could be secured at the rock this way and be "beyond all risk" of breaking away or forced during a bad storm to be cut loose from the moorings. Other than the obvious danger to the men, such a calamity would also mean the end of that work season.

When the crew on the Whitelaw slipped the first buoy into the water and strung out its anchor, they watched the structure barely float above the ocean's swells. These moorings didn't have enough buoyancy to offset the heavier lengths of chain needed to reach the deep bottom. The sea here had unfortunately proved to be deeper by eight to ten fathoms (or some sixty feet) over what the first soundings had indicated. The remaining spar buoys that had been brought were far too small and light for use at these greater depths.

Ballantyne had doubts about these depths as first determined, since the only data available was from soundings taken two years earlier. He had argued to no avail that a second depth-sounding was needed before the expedition began. Unfortunately, he was right. The depth was actually thirty fathoms (about 180 feet), not the twenty fathoms (120 feet) as first assumed. Although the schooner remained secured to the bottom during the recent storm by its one heavy mooring, Ballantyne didn't trust the weather conditions in these waters. He felt that even stronger storms like the ones he experienced on Tillamook Rock would rise and drag the schooner onto the fatal rocks. He decided three larger moorings were needed like the buoy that now secured the six-ton anchor.

He turned around to find larger moorings that would support the heavier chains. Leaving *La Ninfa* anchored to its strong mooring, the men on board the schooner transferred to the *Whitelaw*. The wrecker steamed that day for Humboldt Bay, which was a seventy-five-mile trip south and where the port city of Eureka was located. With San Francisco as its prime hub, the U.S. Light-House Service had decided that Humboldt Bay would be the supply center for the project's equipment and materials. Other vessels or even lighters (small ships that delivered supplies over short distances) would haul the materials, tools, and supplies from there to the construction operations.

The men had to wait in Humboldt Bay, however, until loggers could cut down the larger "sticks," or trees, and haul them from the woods to construct the larger buoys. Although the original iron strappings from the old buoys were still useable, the wait for the larger timber and another windstorm outside the bay delayed their departure. The driving rains caught the workmen before they could complete the moorings and forced them to seek shelter until the storm subsided.

During this time, Ballantyne met with Captain Payson, who as the Light-House Board's district engineer, was the titular "project manager" for St. George's construction. Although Ballantyne was under a chain of command and formally "reported" to Payson, there is no question that Alexander had Payson's total respect and support. Ballantyne's experience and leadership unquestionably made him the decision maker—and later developments proved this.

Under the Light-House Board's organizational chart, each light-house district had its own engineer, supplied by the U.S. Army Corps of Engineers, and an inspector, who was on active duty with the U.S. Navy. Each district engineer recommended major decisions to the Board's engineering secretary, who in turn referred the most important decisions for final authorization by the entire Light-House Board in Washington, D.C. Alexander Ballantyne's original design of the St. George Reef Lighthouse in 1883 was what the Light-House Board ultimately went with, although minor changes were made to those plans when Major D. P. Heap, the engineer secretary of the Board, gave his final approval.

Ballantyne's men were fellow immigrants, migrating to the West Coast primarily from European countries such as Finland, Denmark, Norway, France, Germany, and England. The California Gold Rush in the late 1840s and 1850s had attracted hundreds of thousands to seek their fortune; they in turn convinced family and friends in their homelands to join them, and this migration continued over time. Ballantyne's crew was a melting pot of different customs, languages, accents, and experiences—and he was their leader.

Some had worked in Oregon and California as cannery workers, lumbermen, or even fishermen, but most had taken this job because they needed the money. Working on this dangerous, isolated rock was not what someone generally chose as an occupation. Like most work during these times, a high school education was rare and not essential. These jobs generally required using one's hands, whether it was farming, manufacturing, mining, fishing, canning, building, or constructing a lighthouse.

Most were rough, give-and-take men. They were usually single, and saloons of "vice and sin" became more numerous in these towns than churches. The men who had labored with Alexander Ballantyne on Tillamook Rock Lighthouse knew what was ahead. While working hard, long hours and living under cold and wet conditions, these workmen endured colds, pneumonia, deep cuts, abrasions, and broken limbs. Over time, the workers' oilskin jackets, floppy hats, suspenders, flannel shirts, heavy boots, and trousers became stained, torn, and frayed.

While his crew waited for the storm outside Humboldt Bay to dissipate, Ballantyne worked patiently on the bidding specifications, pored over plans, conferred with Payson, and decided on the additional materials and provisions that the *Whitelaw* needed to transport back with *La Ninfa*. While he looked over the steamer again, he also communicated with the owner about its and the schooner's seaworthiness. The owner of both ships was well experienced in his own right and the wreck steamer bore his name.

Captain Thomas P. H. Whitelaw was born in Scotland, went to sea at the age of twelve, and wound up in San Francisco. In 1868, at the age of twenty-one, he began working in the ship-wreckage business. Owing to his business shrewdness and abilities, Whitelaw successfully raised valuable vessels, including the steamship *Constitution*, which in 1878 entered San Francisco Harbor on fire. When the crew couldn't extinguish the flames, the captain scuttled the ship and sank it in Mission Bay. Whitelaw's salvagers made the hull watertight, pumped out the seawater, and refloated the ship.

Whitelaw eventually became one of the larger ship owners on the West Coast, including the *Whitelaw* and *La Ninfa*. His knowledge of seamanship, ship carpentering, and engineering allowed him to become a success in his business, and Ballantyne conferred with Whitelaw about his ships and their use.

SHORTLY AFTER WORKMEN BUILT the last large buoy, the weather finally cleared. When the first ships sailed back into Humboldt Bay, the sailors reported that the seas were still high but manageable. Bal-lantyne assembled his men on the *Whitelaw* and oversaw the loading of the buoys, extra chains, and additional provisions. Ten days had passed since they arrived in port, and Ballantyne was anxious to get back to the reef and start work.

Although the ocean swells were high when they started, the jour-ney proved to be uneventful and took less than a day. The *Whitelaw* arrived by the reef on April 28, 1883, with clearer weather and calmer seas. Ballantyne and the ship's captain scanned the horizon with their spyglasses as the steamer cruised toward the area where *La Ninfa* was moored and waiting. They soon would be able to start the site preparation and commence the long-awaited construction.

Once they came to the spot, however, no one could find the large schooner. As his men stared at the ocean or at each other with bewildered looks, no wreckage, lumber, or any item associated with the vessel was seen. Ballantyne was not pleased by this unpleasant sur-prise, but he kept his emotions in check.

The seas were calm, the sun was bright, and the ocean at North West Seal Rock calmer than ever before—but *La Ninfa* had simply vanished. It was as if the schooner had never existed.

CHAPTER 2

The Ghost Ship and
the High-Wire Act

The *Whitelaw* steamed around the rock islands and spits that comprised Dragon Rocks, its men hoping to find some evidence that would give a clue as to what had happened with the mysterious *La Ninfa*. Smoke spiraled from its stack with the sails on its two masts not unfurled, as the *Whitelaw*'s crew worked behind the cabins and pilothouse toward the stern.

Ballantyne had told the captain to drop "dragging lines" (weighted ropes with iron hooks at their ends) into the ocean and commence the search for some sign of the ship or its large anchor mooring. The large grappling hooks swung in arcs deep beneath the sea as the ship motored around the obstacles, but nothing out of the ordinary became visible. Men pulled hard on the oars of the surfboats lowered from the steamer's davits, and the small boats circled around Northwest Seal Rock. The seamen were careful to avoid coming too close to the currents and being swept onto the sharp rocks, but no sign of the schooner ever appeared, not one shard of wood, metal shred, or ripped canvas.

Despite not knowing what had happened to the ship, Ballantyne gave orders for the crew to take the three large moorings on board and set them in place. Regardless of the schooner's fate, some ship would need to moor off the reef so the project could move ahead. All he could do was hope that while in port, the strong storm that suddenly blew in had caused the winds and strong currents to snap the mooring and cause the crewless *La Ninfa* to drift away. Otherwise after all these years, the elements had claimed another ship before construction could even start on the vital warning light and fog signal.

Although its loss certainly would not help his reputation, Ballantyne's dogged construction of Tillamook Lighthouse had brought him worldwide fame—and he was not afraid of using this card to charter another vessel if need be. Dealing with Captain Whitelaw, however, would be another consideration. Whitelaw had a deserved reputation of being shrewd and rugged in the barroom brawls of his business.

Ballantyne returned with the *Whitelaw* to Humboldt Bay. Although his report states that he consulted with the lighthouse engineer, Captain Payson, there is no question that he was also in contact with Captain T. P. H. Whitelaw. Although a wire-telegraph existed in Humboldt Bay, the port was close enough to San Francisco to confer in person. As Ballantyne and Payson were assuring Whitelaw that any losses would be made whole, Ballantyne's men were fanning through the small harbor port to ask the returning sailors if they had seen anything odd. At the same time his men located another six-ton mooring.

The seamen on the brig *Josephine* finally told one crewman that they had spotted a schooner like *La Ninfa* during a gale off Cape Mendocino on April 30. (Cape Mendocino is located fifty miles south of Humboldt Bay.) As soon as Ballantyne coaled the salvage steamer and loaded the large buoy aboard, the expedition quickly steamed away to search for the missing ship. They immediately sailed into choppy waters and another squall.

As the *Whitelaw* churned in the general direction of where the seamen said they had spotted a ship like *La Ninfa*, the sea conditions improved and the frothy waves lessened. The captain of the ship and Ballantyne scanned the horizon with their spyglasses for anything that resembled a two-masted ship—but saw nothing. Day after day went by, while the ship and its crew tracked back and forth trying to find the missing vessel.

Although the storms by now had powered overland, they had left gray, foreboding skies that prevailed until a blanketing fog eventually settled in. Nearly one week had passed when one crewman shouted that he had seen something move inside the fog to the starboard side. When the steamer turned toward that area, no one could see anything inside the cold mists. They concluded either the man was fantasizing or something other than a lost ship was out there. A few whispered that *La Ninfa* had disappeared again because it never had been real. On the eighth day out, another crewman shouted through the disquieting silence that he saw a silhouette of a ship moving toward them.

Ballantyne wheeled around and trained his glasses toward the location where the seaman pointed with jerky movements, but saw nothing in the thick fog. The crewman continued to shout that he had indeed seen something, then another sailor yelled that he saw it, too.

With all hands staring out where the seamen were pointing, a colorless-looking vessel emerged from the haze with whips of fog spiraling around its masts and rigging. The surreal-looking schooner showed no signs of life as it eerily slipped back inside the mists. The captain ordered "full-steam ahead," and soon the wrecker was in close vicinity to where the vessel had disappeared. Once there the *Whitelaw* slowed down, thick black smoke pouring from its stack. Disappointment again reigned with nothing visible but enveloping curtains of cold mists. The ship turned and slowly came back, and the captain ordered the pilot to cut the engines. It drifted in the fog. The waves slapped noisily against the hull in the unsettling silence.

A high-pitched voice cut through the quietness, "There it is. She's upon us." The men turned in the direction of the man's alarm. Rocking back and forth in the swells, a drifting schooner loomed ahead. As both ships headed directly at one another, the captain ordered his wheelman to turn the still-moving *Whitelaw* hard port to avoid the drifting schooner.

The empty *La Ninfa* silently passed by. Although no one was supposed to be on board that ship, the vessel's appearance without a crew brought shivers to a few. Once the steamer had maneuvered close to the schooner, crewmen quickly lowered a surfboat and rowed toward it with Ballantyne. The wooden ship creaked and groaned while the small boat approached the large ship. As the vessel rocked noisily back and forth in the waves, a seaman threw a grappling hook over the side, sounding with a dull thud on the wood deck.

The man quickly pulled himself up and threw a rope ladder down to the waiting crew. Ballantyne climbed up the swinging cord steps and boarded *La Ninfa* with the other men following close behind. The ship seemed cold and foreboding. What once was teeming with men and bustling action, now was dripping wet, creaking, and smelling like rotting fish. Rigging, spars, and once-furled canvas were loose and disjointed or laying at weird angles to the deck. Part of the gunnels were splintered and decay had already started in parts of the water-logged ship.

The superintendent soon found the evidence he was searching for: The schooner's anchoring hawser had parted during the gale, the ripped part protruding out from where it had once been attached. The storm that imprisoned everyone inside Humboldt Bay had also ripped *La Ninfa* from its mooring and blew it away. He finally had located her on the morning of May 6, twenty-five miles to the southwest of Crescent City.

For two weeks, the two-masted ship had drifted miles away to the south of Crescent City at Trinidad Head. Another storm blew in from a different direction and then drove the schooner miles north—

after the *Josephine*'s men had spotted her off Cape Mendocino. She had been drifting for days up and down the redwood coast.

Ballantyne decided that the powerful winds and waves had savagely rocked *La Ninfa* back and forth as the ocean smashed over ship and mooring. The extreme conditions finally snapped the vessel from its anchor and the new eight-inch hawser holding it to the wood buoy, driving the vessel away during the night of April 22. The surging currents and heavy weight of fifty fathoms (three hundred feet) of chain attached to the mooring spar sank the "stick" buoy to the bottom, including the twenty fathoms of the hawser that led from the ship to the buoy. The gales drove the ship for miles in different directions on its strange odyssey opposite the California redwoods until Ballantyne finally caught up with the derelict.

THE REDWOOD COAST of California stretches from the Golden Gate of San Francisco to the Oregon border. For over three hundred miles the shore is wild, isolated, and dangerous. The heaviest fog on the Pacific coast, savage storms and shrieking gales center here, lasting days, even weeks at a time. There are few harbors and little shelter along this rocky coastline with towering mountains that plunge to the sea. The ports are usually ringed by heavy surf and the offshore rocks create a special hazard. Heavy rainfall up to 125 inches per year occur in this area, and the need for lighthouses was apparent, especially given the rough weather, hard terrain, and dangerous coastline.

After the discovery of gold in Northern California at Sutter's Mill in 1848, the Gold Rush brought about one of the greatest migrations of people and commerce experienced in U.S. history. Miners first traveled by ship around the Horn or trans-Isthmus through Panama or Nicaragua, followed by settlers crossing the prairies in covered wagons. The intercontinental railroad was not complete until 1869, and this route consisted of only one track when officials drove in the golden spike at Promontory, Utah, that joined the two

coasts. Ships even carried the locomotives manufactured on the East
Coast to the West Coast in building these railroads and track net-
works. Maritime commerce and its countless ships meanwhile brought
the people, supplies, goods, vegetables, fruits, and everyone's needs
up and down the western coastline from California to British Columbia.
Along with this ever-increasing, massive coastal navigation, however,
came the need for guiding and protecting lighthouses.

After the tragedy of the *Brother Jonathan* with its large loss of life
and subsequent national outcry, the Light-House Board knew that a
light and fog signal had to be built inside Dragon Rocks. This chain
of sunken rocks, reefs, and barren rocky islets was six and a half nautical miles long and from one to one and a half nautical miles wide.
Depending on the winds, currents, and tides, some of these obstruc-
tions were submerged, while others were above water, but the conditions could change overnight. The largest islands form a rough chain
that projects in a generally northwesterly direction from Point St.
George on land, which is located midway between Cape Mendocino
in California and Cape Blanco in Oregon.

In rough weather, parts of the reef were said to "smoke," as the
savage crashing of strong ocean currents against the rocky outcroppings
produced a thick smokelike mist of spray that obscured and made
the rocks difficult to see. When the Spanish explorer Vizcaíno first
discovered and noted the reef in 1603, he named it "Cabo Blanco de
San Sebastian," or the "white cape (end of land) of San Sebastian."
The traditional home of the Tolowa Indians, the English explorer
George Vancouver finally renamed the hazardous rocks "Dragon
Rocks" and the land point off the reef for the patron saint of England,
St. George, perhaps hoping that one day St. George would slay the
dragon.

The reef comprises nine visible rocks and many barely submerged ledges. The U.S. Coast Survey first showed the reef and some
of the rocks in an 1850 sketch of the U.S. West Coast. The first light-

house built in the area was the station constructed in Crescent City in 1856. Named the Battery Point Lighthouse due to its location, this light proved helpful for the harbor and vessels approaching from the south. However, the lighthouse was located thirteen miles from Dragon Rocks' outermost point, and the hills of Point St. George completely hid the beacon when ships sailed or steamed down from the north.

The public outcry over the *Brother Jonathan* disaster forced the Light-House Board into action. Ten months after the disaster, it requested in May 1866 for the General Land Office to reserve certain lands for lighthouse purposes in the area, including "that portion of Point St. George which remains unsurveyed." Eight months later in 1867, President Andrew Johnson signed the formal reservation to use those lands. It wasn't clear, however, where the best location would be to build such a lighthouse.

Two years after the loss of the *Brother Jonathan*, the Light-House Board requested funds for the construction of the St. George Reef Lighthouse. With the costly Civil War having ended just two years previously, Congress, due to the extensive reconstruction efforts, was unwilling to allocate the large sums needed to construct such a light station on that exposed reef. The federal government allocated funds at the time generally to rebuild lighthouses that had been destroyed or damaged during the war, and as these wave-swept outcroppings were considered too difficult, risky, and expensive on which to build a station, the Board looked at alternate sites in the area over the years.

In 1875, the Board decided that despite the higher costs, it might be more effective to locate the lighthouse on one of the outlying rocky islets, such as North West Seal Rock. The U.S. Coast Survey in Los Angeles, however, responded that although a light on N.W. Seal Rock would benefit shipping, the exposure of the rock to the "full force of the sea would make establishing a foundation on it very difficult." While different sites were being considered, the Light-

House Board recommended to Congress that the station be constructed on a site "at or near Point St. George." From 1874 to 1879,
its Annual Report contained the same statement:

> This [Point St. George or its "vicinity"] is one of the impor-
> tant points for a seacoast light on the coast of California.
> The bluff point is about 130 feet high, with level land for
> some distance back of it. Off the point, extending some six
> or seven miles, is a very dangerous reef of rocks, quite a
> number of which show above water, and many are awash at
> low tide; others have from three to four fathoms [eighteen to
> twenty-four feet] of water on them. The passage between the
> outlying rocks of this reef and Point St. George is quite wide,
> and is used by coasting steamers. The steamer *Brother Jonathan*
> was wrecked on this reef some years ago during a fog [sic],
> and many lives were lost; among them General Wright and
> staff, with the families of himself and several of his staff. A
> light-house and fog-signal should be erected here. An appro-
> priation of $50,000 is asked to commence the work.

The Board members later rejected building onshore as impractical, being located too far from the hazardous reefs. Since vessels
steamed well out to sea, they felt it was mandatory for a lighthouse
to be placed on a reef and not far from where the *Brother Jonathan*
sank with such a high loss of life.

This cluster of rocky islets, pinnacles, and sunken rocks fanned
out like the spine of a submerged dragon from Point St. George,
which was four miles north of Crescent City. Inside the reef was a
broad and deep channel used during northwest stormy weather by
northern-bound steamers, but only in daylight, clear weather and
"probably at some risk from sunken dangers not shown on the
charts," as stated by the Light-House Board.

With its mid-location between the Cape Mendocino, California, and Cape Blanco, Oregon, lighthouses, the area was considered to be a "suitable location for a first-class light (the largest of the light-house Fresnel lenses)." The difficulty in any such construction was that tiny Crescent City with its port was reported as a "small and iso-lated settlement, distant by difficult mountain roads one hundred and fifty miles from the telegraph and more than three hundred miles from a railway." Supplies, materials, and equipment would need to be shipped from San Francisco to Humboldt Bay to the north, then continue on another seventy-five miles to the reef.

North West Seal Rock was positioned farthest from the coast on this chain of rock islands, and it was considered to be the "outer-most danger of St. George Reef." South West Seal Rock, the infamous Jonathan Rock, the reef which the *Brother Jonathan* fatally struck, and then Whale Rock swept from there toward land. Hump Rock and Star Rock were next in line, followed by Castle Rock that was closest to shore.

After further review, the Board decided that the only two practi-cal sites on the offshore rocks were Star Rock, which was closer to shore, and North West Seal Rock, located two miles from its closest neighbor, South West Seal Rock. The Light-House Board finally set-tled on building the protecting light on N.W. Seal Rock—over fif-teen years after the ship disaster—due to its proximity to shipping lanes.

The continuing offshore haze, or fog, forced most vessels to steam away from the point by ten miles. Since the strongest foghorns had a useful range of six miles, and the reach of a first-order Fresnel lens under this dense haze would be rarely seen, the Board decided that the farther away a lighthouse could be positioned from shore, the more effective it would be in warning and marking ship posi-tions. In its 1881 annual report, the Board emphasized "the necessity for constructing a first-order light-station on North West Seal Rock, off Point Saint George, to the northward of San Francisco."

This small rocky spit was three hundred feet in diameter, slightly over an acre in size (46,000 square feet), and six miles away from land. Captain Payson reported to the Board: "It is a mass of meta-morphic material, varying considerably in character, extremely hard to drill, and brittle under the action of explosives, but offering almost the resistance of glass to the erosive action of the sea." Its smooth water-worn surfaces indicated that the sea swept over its fifty-four-foot high point; moreover, the planned excavation by itself would have the workers carving down and around that point to where the reef was a scant twenty-four feet above calm seas. During their site inspections, the surveyors experienced the unpredictable gales that suddenly arose to whip heavy seas over the rock. They dis-covered that the winds could suddenly thrash a glassy calm to where the ocean roared over the "topmost surface of the rock" inside three hours.

One of the most isolated, risky places—and the most inaccessi-ble lighthouse site in U.S. history—had to be chosen. Even after the recommendation, doubts remained as to whether a lighthouse could be built at a reasonable cost at any location in those stormy seas. The experiences with past stations at such wave-swept locations, such as the first Eddystone lighthouse in the English Channel and the first Minot's Ledge station off Massachusetts, was that storms could rise and demolish the structures with loss of life. Accordingly, Con-gress was not willing to go along with such a gamble for several years.

WHEN ALEXANDER BALLANTYNE was able to successfully build Tillamook Rock, Congress became finally convinced that construct-ing a lighthouse on an exposed wave-washed rock in that ocean would be possible. Located one mile off the coast between the coastal towns of Cannon Beach and Seaside, Oregon, toward the Washington border, Tillamook Rock was a prime lighthouse site due to its proximity to the mouth of the Columbia River and its treacherous sand bars. The Columbia River was then and still is an important watercourse now for maritime commerce on the West Coast and Pacific Northwest.

Native Indians wouldn't go near this site in the old days, because they considered the rock to be the domain of powerful, evil spirits. Even on calm days, landing by sea was difficult. Bounded on three sides by steep cliffs, the one-hundred-foot-high "islet of bold basaltic rock" was extremely treacherous to approach. In 1878, Congress appropriated $50,000 to start its construction, twenty miles to the south of the Columbia River's mouth.

Due to the circumstances of Trewavas's death, Ballantyne had problems at first finding anyone to work on the rock. Eventually he convinced eight men who were unfamiliar with the death, or didn't care about the details, and sequestered them at an old lighthouse keeper's dwelling at Cape Disappointment (across the Columbia River on the Washington side) to keep "idle talk" from frightening them away. Some of the workers undoubtedly were from his work crews in Portland and those who traveled with him from England to Oregon.

Ballantyne had great difficulties at the beginning in landing on the rock due to bad weather. Despite the heavy seas, he and the first four workmen finally landed on Tillamook Rock on October 21, 1879, with supplies and equipment. Using the heavy rope rigged between a ship's mast and the rock, Ballantyne moved his men and materials to the island. The men transferred hammers, drills, iron ringbolts, a small stove, provisions, and a supply of canvas from which they would make a temporary shelter. Five days later, the rest of the quarrymen joined them, and the men assembled a small derrick to haul up the heavier equipment.

For the first fifteen days, the men worked to offload materials, build level areas, and construct tents for the workers, supplies, and explosives. As the rock had no deep recesses into which they could seek refuge from the driving rains, Ballantyne had his men cut up their canvas to make A-frame tents, which rope lashings held down to ring-bolts driven deep into the rock.

One of the lessons Ballantyne learned there and took to St. George was that on Tillamook the men didn't have a dry place to fully shelter themselves from the elements. The men constructed a storeroom and on the very day when they first started blasting, winds and rains overtook their rock station. Camping out in a confined tent while working outdoors had definite disadvantages. Ballantyne wrote into his log for November 2, 1879:

> It was rather disagreeable in our tent, it being six by sixteen feet with a horizontal ridge pole about four feet six inches from the ground. The tent just holds ten men. We always do our cooking on the lee side, shifting according to the direction of the wind.

Despite horrendous gales and crashing seas, Ballantyne's band of fifteen men struggled against the elements to carve out the rock and commence building the lighthouse. Traveling during these times was difficult, especially when hauling the heavy equipment, supplies, blasting powder, iron, and lumber needed to build these stations at such remote places. Cars and roads were nonexistent, railroads had not been built in these areas, and even stagecoaches had to ford swollen rivers and avoid mountain passes during the winter. The land was relatively unpopulated with scattered settlements, thick forests, and mountainous terrain.

Ballantyne leased schooners, steamers, and eventually a steam tug to move his equipment and supplies on this expedition. The nearest supply point was Astoria, Oregon, located "thirty miles distant, on the harbor twelve miles inside the bar, at the entrance to Columbia River." The supply depot and vessels for Tillamook generally operated from Astoria during the Tillamook construction period.

Lewis and Clark stayed near Astoria during the winter of 1805–1806 and built nearby Fort Clatsop for shelter. It is the oldest U.S. settlement west of the Rocky Mountains, and members of the Pacific Fur Company, owned by John Jacob Astor, arrived in March of 1811 and established Fort Astoria. The first U.S. Customs House was established there in 1849, but it wasn't until the later 1800s that Astoria's salmon canneries, lumber mills, and shipping industries brought commercial development. Its seafaring nature and location reminded immigrants of the countries they had left behind. In seeking a new life, they had immigrated here primarily from Finland, Scandinavia, England, and other coastal European countries, especially when their fishing industries declined due to over fishing. The population of Astoria grew to 7,500 people by 1890, which made it a large city for Oregon coastal communities. The average rain in the area, however, is seventy-five inches per year, making this a very wet and windy climate.

Once arriving off Tillamook, the supply and equipment vessels moored to buoys built of layers of Oregon spruce, forty-five feet long and two and a half feet in diameter. Securely attached by one-inch iron bolts, the mooring chains were "forty to fifty fathoms" long and attached to a heavy sinker at the bottom. Alexander Ballantyne used the same basic concept at St. George.

Ballantyne's log was very detailed for Tillamook, although he didn't maintain one as detailed for St. George. These daily reports give a strong glimpse into not only the man, his crews, and the obstacles, but what was also used to construct it and the next lighthouse project at North West Seal Rock. When completed, the Tillamook station consisted of a square tower on top of a one-story dwelling with rooms for each keeper, a kitchen, and a storeroom. The stone structure was forty-eight feet by forty-five feet, with an extension under the same roof that was thirty-two feet by twenty-eight feet and which housed the foghorns.

From the center of the main building, the sixteen-foot wide, square tower rose forty-eight feet in the air. The crews built a structure to hold coal and a landing wharf with a tramway. Carved deep into the rock, a cistern collected rain for the station's water supply. The specifications for this lighthouse—as with St. George—were extremely exacting. These detailed rules covered every aspect from the stonework, foundation, water table, and walls to the bricks, mortar, plaster, and paint. For example, the walls were detailed as following:

> The walls will consist of first-class ashlar [stone] masonry laid in courses, one-foot rise, as headers and stretchers, with a full bed of fourteen inches. The headers will run through a full twenty-four inches from front to rear, and have a bond with the brick lining; the rear faces will be rough hammered to a smooth surface. The headers will have a face measurement of twelve-inches square, and the stretchers will not be less than three feet nor more than four feet long; the outer faces will be smooth hammer-dressed.

On January 21, 1881, Tillamook's bright "First Order" Fresnel lens beamed over the ocean for the first time. With the worldwide fame that Ballantyne gained from the techniques he used to construct Tillamook under its budgeted $125,000, no loss of life after he took control, and in a reasonable time, Congress finally approved the funding to build St. George. The benefits to maritime commerce were now for the first time seen to be greater than the difficulties and expense of building on that site. In August 1882, Congress appropriated the long sought after $50,000 to start its construction, which was supplemented with another $50,000, approved six months later in February 1883. The Light-House Board's debate had started during President Andrew Johnson's term, then continued during President Grant's two terms, through Presidents Rutherford B. Hayes and James A. Garfield, then into Chester Arthur's second year.

The Board estimated then that it would cost $333,000 to build the structure, or nearly three times what it took to construct Terrible Tilly. This by itself would make the St. George station one of the most expensive lighthouses ever built in that time. The second Minot's Ledge off Boston cost $300,000 to build in 1860 and was the lighthouse most associated with St. George Reef and Tillamook Rock, as all three were wave-washed rocks, where the ocean hits the station from all sides.

Northern California's history was already replete with stories about the wrecks that littered this coastline. Beginning with the ships *Paragon* in April 1850 and *Tarquin* the following January, the coasts of Del Norte and Humboldt County in this area were the scene of maritime disasters. While on her way in 1855 from San Francisco to Puget Sound, the paddlewheel steamer *America* anchored on its regular stop in Crescent City Harbor. As this port was located midway between the commercial centers of San Francisco and Portland, it was an ideal place for ships to re-coal, offload goods destined for the interiors, and take on new passengers. However, a fire soon broke out and by the next day, only the charred, smoldering hull remained.

Ten years later, the large sidewheeler *Brother Jonathan* left Crescent City on its stop and tragically smashed into barely submerged Jonathan Rock. The delays in building the lighthouse on St. George Reef meant that Crescent City had burial grounds filled with shipwreck victims. From the period of 1878 to 1881, vessels named the *California*, *Wall*, and *Elvenia* crashed or grounded near Crescent City. A savage storm pared the moorings of the schooner *J. W. Wall* in 1881 and blew her ashore at Crescent City. Five years later, the schooner

Restless wrecked there. All of these disasters showed not only the continued need for a lighthouse, but also that the weather conditions in this region were inhospitable at best.

The first Congressional appropriation allowed Ballantyne to visit St. George Reef and survey North West Seal Rock. A surveyor later landed on the rock, but the seas rose so quickly that he was forced to flee for his ship's safety after spending only one hour on the reef. This was an inauspicious start. However, he was able to obtain a "few rough measurements and sketches of the rock."

On April 8, 1882, Ballantyne and a civil engineer traveled to Crescent City to land on the reef and take surveys. Although he was in the best weather season with a crew of men who had actually hunted sea lions there, Ballantyne was only able to make three successful landings on the reef during his four-week stay. This experience gave him a firsthand look at the terrifying gales that arose here, even during supposedly good weather times with a group of seasoned men. However, he and his engineer were able to complete a decent survey, and, upon their return to San Francisco, the engineer constructed a model of the rock on a scale of fifteen feet to the inch with three-foot contours.

Congress authorized in 1883 an additional sum of $100,000 to commence construction. In that same year, Alexander Ballantyne drew up his plans for building the massive lighthouse on N.W. Seal Rock that eventually were approved, and then left with his men to construct it.

ONCE HE HAD finally tracked down *La Ninfa*, Ballantyne's crew attached a large hawser to the schooner, and the *Whitelaw* cruised back to North West Seal Rock with the vessel in tow. Ballantyne and his men were again ready to start. Once at the site, he ordered his men to tether *La Ninfa* to the four larger mooring buoys—350 feet away from the reef. The workers secured the schooner to two high parts of the rock, so that the buoys and rock points circled to pin the schooner at its anchorage. If one hawser gave way, then the others kept the ship in place. The vessel then could serve as the barracks and mess hall for the construction crew.

His men tried for two days to find the sunken six-ton buoy with the *Whitelaw*'s special dragging equipment. When their search for the lost mooring proved unsuccessful, the *Whitelaw* steamed back to San Francisco. A contract then was entered into for the use of another vessel to supply the expedition. About every ten days, the *Crescent City* steamed out with needed supplies, men, and messages from Captain Payson, leaving with broken tools, garbage, injured workers, and Ballantyne's reports and replies. In making these regular trips, the small coastal steamer journeyed from San Francisco to Crescent City and back, but swung by Humboldt Bay and Seal Rock on its way.

The ocean surges, however, continued to create unwanted dangers whether getting on or off the reef. Building up within a couple of hours in what was once a calm sea, the swells threatened to break entirely over the reef—and the men knew this from the beginning. On one earlier survey trip, bad weather suddenly blew in, created fifteen-foot waves, and the surges caused Ballantyne and his seal-hunter guides to cut their time short.

The reef was steep with an irregular oval shape like a rough Indian spear that had been chipped away on its sides. It had a ridge running from east to west, sloping gently to the north, but steeper on the sides; to the west was a "prolongation," or small rock islet named "Little Black Rock." When the ocean rose to crash against the reef, its shape took the crude form of a heart with two, small rock spits at the top. Its approximate size of an acre wasn't even that large, owing to the contours, rock spits, and parts underwater during storms. With the plans calling for excavating thirty feet down from its top, the men would be toiling only some twenty feet above what was a very capricious sea level.

On top of this, the blasting and excavation work meant that permanent quarters would be impossible to build until the five-story foundation was constructed—not to mention that the small rock offered little space for sheltered storerooms or quarters to be even built. The 1884 Light-House Report noted that:

> There was no space available on the site where even the temporary security of men or material could be assured, and the frequency and quickness with which all parts of the rock became untenable much exceeded in experience any previous anticipation.

On May 9 the men made their first landing on the rock with their equipment and supplies, and they quickly drilled in ringbolts, anchored tools, and cached food, water, sleeping gear, and canvas for tents. The next day the workers managed to move their blasting powder ashore and began drilling later on the north side to begin the site preparation in constructing the high, underpinning concrete pier.

Any landings on the reef were dangerous, regardless of the ocean's conditions. The slippery rocks, strong undertow, and constant undulating ocean rocked boats and their men precariously as they tried to unload tools and provisions.

For the workmen who came with Ballantyne from Tillamook, their experiences were surprisingly similar to what they saw when building that lighthouse a few years earlier. Their first efforts met with tragedy or difficulty. At Tillamook, the first superintendent, Mr. Trewavas, unfortunately drowned and disrupted the construction's timetable; at St. George, they lost time and money when *La Ninfa* disappeared. As before, families of sea lions and seals took an exception to their invasion of N.W. Seal Rock. Long a favorite residing spot for hundreds of these animals, they weren't very happy at the first sights of these strange invaders and charged them; eventually the seals retreated and retired to rocky resorts not as close. At Tillamook, a gale blew over the terrified men three days after their landing with high winds and waves, leaving the group with soaked provisions and wet explosives. These intense storms continued over North West Seal Rock with the same effects—but these storm surges proved much higher with disrupting effects.

One of Ballantyne's most important decisions in this construction was his innovation in moving men back and forth on the reef. When the weather began to worsen with higher waves and winds, landing by a small boat onto the rock became dangerous and nearly impossible. Stormy seas created the danger of large waves suddenly surging over the tiny reef and sweeping the launch, men, and provisions away. Barren of caves, overhangs, or ledges, the reef could not provide the barest of shelter, as the workers prepared to start chipping, chiseling, and blasting away.

With *La Ninfa* moored off the rock, men first moved to the reef by rowing a small boat across the choppy ocean through very cold water, turbulent seas, and powerful currents. With the boat rising and falling with each swell, any leap onto the slippery rocks was risky. Once on the rock, workers had to walk and move like billy goats, due to the steep, wet rock that swept upward. From afar, the undulating rocky reef's outline showed a twenty-degree incline, sometimes more; but once on that small spit, it was a desolate place—one difficult to move about—and barren but for the scattering of supplies and tools being provisioned.

As boat landings became so difficult due to the seas that surged against the sea-swept spit, Ballantyne created an aerial boat-to-island tramway. This idea had worked before at Tillamook Rock, when the two-masted schooner *Corwin* anchored off the construction site. He had a cable stretched between the reef and ship, and a series of pulleys hauled the water kegs, lumber, and supplies in a net from a hook that ran over it. This rocky islet, however, was quite higher than Seal Rock and had problems, so he had to improvise to use the Tillamook system here.

In his log, Ballantyne wrote that he directed his workmen to rig a long "traveler of 2½ inch wire rope" and make this fast to a ring-bolt skewered into the rock's pinnacle. The workers then stretched the cable from the reef to *La Ninfa*'s masts over one hundred yards away, between them, and attached it to a spar buoy moored thirty feet behind the schooner's outer side. If sufficient buoys weren't available, Ballantyne had his men connect the rope from the rock to the schooner's mast. He had the "fore and main throat halyards hooked onto the wire to take out the sag" and used a traveler block to run up and down the endless line of cable. An enclosure for the men was attached to the moving block.

The traveler block was constructed of two pieces of boilerplate that were bolted together and formed the bearings for the axles of four grooved, gun-metal wheels. These wheels held the cable tight between the upper and lower pairs of wheels, keeping the wire rope from binding or twisting, even when the ocean twisted the traveler block around. Depending on the surging of the vessel and the hal-yard's control, the crew on board the schooner raised and lowered the cable wire as it became necessary.

His workers attached a four-foot-diameter horizontal iron ring to the overhead traveler, from which ropes were suspended and then attached to a boilerplate platform. Four to six men crowded on to the cage at one time and held onto the ropes, as the apparatus traveled between the moored *La Ninfa* and the overlooking reef. For the first few months, laborers strained to pull the cable back, which inched the platform slowly up the line to the rock. Gravity then sped the cage back. Once a donkey or steam engine was installed, the platform scurried upward to the reef. When moving down to the moored workers' quarters, the engine wasn't needed due to the transit line's steep decline and rapid, amusement-ride-like descent.

The cage ferried men between *La Ninfa* and the construction site. The enclosure traveled between three hundred and three hundred fifty feet—depending on the seas, currents, and moorings—starting on the rock end where the cable was sixty feet above the sea. When released from the rock, the cage ran down the slope at "great speed" and the lowest point of the line wasn't higher than fifteen feet above the ocean; this meant that in stormy seas, the ocean could rise above and engulf the lower portions of the cable or its cage.

This apparatus allowed the workers to be transported to the rock and work, and then quickly return to the mother ship when a storm suddenly blew in. Ballantyne calmly watched the weather conditions around him. When the seas built up and threatened to wash over the reef, he yelled out the command to "Quit." This order caused the workers to quickly lash their tools to iron rings hammered into the rocks and ride the platform quickly back to La Ninfa's safety.

When the weather and ocean conditions permitted, the men traveled back and forth to the site in the surfboat. Not only did some men prefer this to the high-wire ride, but not using the tramway saved on costly water, coal, and equipment wear and tear. The donkey engine used scarce fresh water to build the steam for its engine, and using the boat saved on the downtime when the cable equipment broke down or needed repair. As a new wire had to be strung if any weakness on the existing line was seen, owing to its constant use, the entire cable needed to be changed at least three times during each work season. When worn by use and pressure, pulleys, hooks, blocks, ringbolts, and halyards needed replacement. La Ninfa's movements caused its mooring lines that led to the rock to often part. As there was no "give and take" as with the anchoring buoys, these lines snapped when the swells moved the ship and had to be replaced.

The cage technique used at St. George, however, was a substantial improvement over what was employed at Tillamook. A single cable powered by men and pulleys moved workers and equipment there. Ballantyne utilized a breeches buoy—basically a pair of pants cut short at the knees and within a life ring—to ferry people one at a time over the line. Although a crewman made the suggestion to use a heavy rope rigged between a ship's mast and the reef's top in moving people, it was Ballantyne who worked out its application and personally proved to his men that this could be used safely and efficiently.

One of the Terrible Tilly tales involved Mr. Gruber, a corpulent quarryman (also the cook), who weighed three hundred pounds. Frightened by any thought of being ferried upward on the swinging breeches buoy, he refused to leave the steamer. When his friends' catcalls pushed him to try the buoy, the men discovered that Gruber was much too large to even fit inside. Ballantyne suggested that his workers lash Gruber to the breeches buoy, but the oversized man refused and stayed on the ship. The superintendent, however, came up with the idea of using a jumbo-size cork life preserver and lashed this to a boatswain's chair. After Gruber's friends made so much fun about his refusal to try even this, the man declared to everyone that he would go to the rock even "if it killed him."

Ballantyne waited for calm water with no wind and the best weather conditions before ordering the transfer made. Due to this approach and those who oversaw every move detail, the overweight man reached the rock not only safely, but the only one who apparently ever got there without getting wet. Gruber arrived, however, "white as chalk." After that trip, the portly, good-natured German cook never ventured out again on that perilous buoy. He stayed on that rock during its construction and operation for sixteen years—until the day he died.

With Tillamook's transfer system, the winched pulley could haul up only one man at a time. On St. George, the steam engine powered a cage that moved up to six men. To avoid the tedious and constant need to reposition the schooner when men transferred, *La Ninfa* was positioned close to the rock to allow the wire cable to be tight and workable. These improvements were quite necessary, as the conditions at St. George were more dangerous than at Tillamook with multiples of men and equipment needing to be moved.

The workers also had to get used to their conditions and this by itself was difficult. The reef's dangerous section was the northern part, only twenty-five feet above the sea, and the ocean's sprays continually drenched the men, who had to quickly leave when the seas rose higher. The workers were understandably afraid at first about these big waves and stayed toward the top of the rock. Soon they became braver, no matter where they labored, and would work even when the white foam and saltwater splattered them and the reef. Ballantyne's men adopted his example: they didn't think of leaving their work until the sea began to continuously surge over their working level. Men didn't leave individually—they left in groups.

The laborers during this first season typically only worked for a few hours at a time, because as the waves grew higher, they had to fasten their tools quickly to the ring-bolts so their equipment wouldn't wash away. As the four-foot cage carried four to six men, depending on size and who was there, moving the workers took a number of trips to bring the full complement of twenty-five to thirty-five laborers back to the floating hotel. Although gravity carried the cage swiftly down to the schooner, the donkey engine required three minutes to move it back. With a complete trip taking five minutes, up to one-half hour could elapse before all of the workers were safely away.

Even Ballantyne was impressed, however, at the way his men jumped inside the cage and held on to lifelines on their trip down, as the large waves rose and fell fifteen feet or more—and the rope-pen with its occupants dipped as wildly. These rides were like riding a bronco over the heaving ocean, not to mention that the operations involved delicate timing. When the large waves threatened, the surges rose over the lower portion of the cable, requiring good judgment on the best time to push the enclosure down. Reportedly this "rather alarming method of retreat" had the men and their cage skiing swiftly downhill to catch the boat as it lifted above the swell.

The wire cable worked well, although the line snapped one time. As the men were jumping into it from the rock, the enclosure suddenly swayed and plummeted with a loud crash to the ground. The heavy seas had swelled over the rope by the ship, and that extra weight with the cable's tautness caused it to snap. The trapped workers were very fortunate: their fall was only a few feet and little injury occurred but for some bruising. This was an unsettling experience, not to mention what could have happened if the cable had snapped several stories above the ocean or the rocks.

With this accomplished, the need to replace the large, bad-weather mooring still remained, as a strong storm could rip away the smaller moorings and sweep the schooner onto the rocks. The *Whitelaw* was chartered to return with the needed buoy. Leaving on June 2, the steamer immediately ran into another violent nor'wester and was delayed for eight days. There was little doubt by now that the seething ocean and weather were as great a deadly obstacle to this project, as the isolation, difficulty of supply, and complexity of construction.

When the steamer finally reached the reef, the conditions were so bad that the bad-weather mooring couldn't be set. As *La Ninfa* was again in danger, Ballantyne ordered the steamer's crew to attach the tow hawsers to the schooner and for *La Ninfa*'s men to slip the mooring lines. While the seas tossed white spray over the ships and crew, these tasks were finally completed. The *Whitelaw* then towed the ship south of Point St. George to the safety of Crescent City.

At the port, the men waited out the gale and loaded on board the donkey engine, supplies, and more water and coal. The steamer eventually headed back to North West Seal Rock with *La Ninfa* in tow for the third time and reached it on June 14. The crew finally was able to position the bad-weather mooring, and the steamer towed the vessel closer to the rock. After stretching out the slack from the buoys, the *Whitelaw* left the schooner for the last time that season as it rocked in the swells one hundred yards from the reef.

From this point forward to September, the excavation work commenced in earnest and without material interruption, although the aerial tramway was in constant use due to the continuing storms.

The workers had to hastily get off the rock, even after they had just arrived—but in spite of "many narrow escapes and some dangerous accidents," no one died. There were much parting of the lines and tackle, including ringbolts pulled straight from the reef, but the workmen continued to persevere despite injuries and a few taken to land hospitals. Despite the ocean swells constantly drenching the rock with cold spray and high water often breaking over the ledge, everyone held their ground until the last possible moment.

Alexander Ballantyne's plans called for the reef's top to be cut down into successive layers of broader levels that looked like an ancient, conelike temple rising from the sea. Depending on the rock strata and the blasting, the levels eventually became six-sided and then roughly circular toward the bottom—but each one was crafted into sheer levels so that the huge underpinning stone blocks could be set flush on each one.

As the mother ship tugged at her moorings off the reef, the workers swarmed over the rock and began to chisel and blast out the foundation's outlines. As approved by the Board, Ballantyne's design called for an elliptical caisson of large squared-stones that encircled the layered rock knob, starting at the very bottom. These interlocking huge stones eventually would rise five stories from its base with rock-fill packed between the cut blocks and carved rock. Cavernous rooms for a water cistern, boilers, coal storage, and storerooms were to be excavated and constructed toward its top with stone flagging cemented in place at the "roof." Although the walls would be nearly fifty feet high, most of the pier would be block, rock, and mortar cement.

The design was creative and called for the cutting of the large horizontal terraces around the scaled-down peak to the foot, or bottom, of the outer wall of the caisson or pier. The huge mass of rock would remain within the walls of the pier with enough room for the cistern, equipment, and storerooms. Once Ballantyne's men had built the huge caisson, it would support a seven-story lighthouse tower that would rise from there. With the height added of the reef, lantern room, and lens cupola on top, its light would flare out to the horizon at fifteen stories above sea level. This placement was at an optimum level, so that from twenty miles away, mariners could see its constant warning.

St. George is classified as a "wave-swept" lighthouse, or one that is exposed to the full force of the seas from all sides. Ballantyne's design kept in mind several important criteria that he had learned at Wolf's Rock and Tillamook. The structure's mass had to have a low center of gravity to prevent large winds and waves from moving the tower, with little dependence on horizontal joints or dovetailing stone blocks to keep the structure together; the lower tower walls exposed to direct wave thrusts were to be constructed with vertical faces; the upper walls were either battered (not smooth faced) or continuously curved to deflect the ocean's strength; masonry towers were preferred due to their strength; and the tower had to be high enough to avoid the surf or spray so that its light wasn't obscured.

The tower's foundation had to be deeply embedded in solid rock with interconnected stones that anchored the lighthouse, so that the thunderous surges couldn't wash over and break it apart. The lesson learned over the past was that the only way for men and their structures to survive at sea was to construct them "one with the rock."

CHAPTER 3

Guarding Lights Over Time

D uring the earliest days of sea travel, ships usually sailed only by day and close to coastlines. These mariners navigated by landmarks in the sea, on land, the stars, sea currents, and wind direction. To avoid known hazardous reefs and underwater conditions, fires were lit on land for nighttime traveling, but these lights needed continuous tending and weren't visible during fogs or storms. The Greeks built the first recorded fire beacons in the fifth and sixth centuries BC to mark the harbor entrances to their cities. In the seventh century, shore fires at night guided the Phoenicians, who prospered on the Mediterranean coast in what is now Lebanon and Syria, on their regular voyages to the coasts of England. Over time, navigators created maps and charts, which showed the water depths as measured by lead lines and rope anchors, and mariners improved upon crude compasses, sextants, and even light-warning structures.

The first lighthouses date back to ancient times. The Greeks built the giant bronze Colossus on a promontory that overlooked the harbor to the Mediterranean island of Rhodes in Greece. Holding a continually fed fire in one huge open hand, this statute of the sun god Helios was 125 feet high. The construction took twelve years and was finally completed in 280 BC. Fifty-six years later, a powerful earthquake devastated Rhodes, badly damaging the city and breaking the Colossus at its weakest point—its knees. One of the Seven Wonders of the World, the statue was never repaired.

The Ptolemies constructed a huge lighthouse on the island of Pharos that was also built in the third century BC and was nearly four hundred feet high. This towering structure marked the entrance to the port city of Alexandria, and it was the guiding light for sailors who approached the Egyptian coast. A long-vaulted ramp led to the entrance of the Lighthouse of Alexandria, and a lengthy spiral stair-case worked upward to the tower's many chambers, where a huge bonfire burned at its summit. Another one of the Seven Wonders of the World, this magnificent structure lasted seventeen centuries until an earthquake destroyed it in the mid-fourteenth century.

The Romans built more than thirty lighthouses along the coasts of Europe to mark the courses for their ships, before the destruction of their empire in the fourth and fifth centuries. The Tower of Hercules is probably the only ancient Roman lighthouse still in use. It was built in the first century, located on a peninsula one and a half miles outside the city of La Corunna, Spain, and a Phoenician tower may have originally occupied the site. Monks also lit and kept fires going along the coastal areas of France and England to help guide ships and warn them of hazards.

The development of the prototypes for today's lighthouses didn't start until over one thousand years ago after the fall of the Roman Empire and its civilization. After receiving a "patent" from officials to extract dues from passing ships to cover their costs and a profit, private citizens then constructed these guiding lights. For example, Eddystone Rock had always been a dangerous area for ships entering the English Channel off Great Britain, and for cen-turies vessels continually smashed or grounded onto those rocks. This barely submerged set of three reefs lies fourteen miles off Ply-mouth, England.

An accomplished artist, engraver, inventor, and designer of playing cards, Henry Winstanley was quite interested in mechanics. He
also was a very wealthy man and the owner of five ships. By the end
of 1695, however, he owned only three vessels, because two of them
had wrecked on the dangerous Eddystone Rock. Winstanley as a private citizen commenced construction of the first Eddystone Lighthouse in the same year that William the Third was King of England.

Henry Winstanley was eccentric, to say the least. If someone care-
lessly kicked at what appeared to be a loose slipper in one room of
his rambling mansion, a ghostlike figure seemed to rise from underneath the floorboards. If a guest sat down in a chair apparently
placed there for convenience, its arms immediately grabbed the startled person, who couldn't free himself without the help of an attendant. Resting by an arbor on one side of a canal that ran through his
estate's spacious grounds, people soon found themselves floating in
it and not able to return to shore without the owner's help. The
design of this lighthouse reflected his whimsical manner.

The Royal Navy aided him by lending boats and men, and Winstanley's crew in the first year of construction drilled twelve large
holes into the rock, as well as fastening huge iron stanchions in each
to anchor the structure. Workers poured molten lead into the holes to
seal the legs inside the reef. The crews in the second year built a
solid, twelve-foot-high round pillar that was fourteen feet in diameter and made of Plymouth granite. The pillar was later increased to
sixteen feet in diameter and its height to eighteen feet—all anchored
to the reef by the inside iron legs—and the structure swept up continuously from that point.

England was then at war with France, and an English warship
anchored nearby to protect Winstanley and his men. One day in
early summer when the ship didn't show up, a watchful French privateer sent a boat that captured Winstanley and took him to France
as a hostage. When King Louis XIV heard about this, he loaded the

smiling Winstanley with valuable presents, punished the privateer, and returned Henry to England with a message. It read: "I am at war with England, not with humanity."

During the third year, his crews built the hollow lighthouse tower, and the workers could live inside its confines, now eliminating the time-consuming daily trips of the workmen to land. Winstanley and his men soon completed the eighty-foot-high wood structure with a weather vane perched at its top, and in November 1698, it began operating with its lantern glowing from burning tallow candles. This was the first lighthouse built on an isolated wave-swept rock that was exposed to the full force of an ocean like the Atlantic.

Winstanley's quirky nature was part of the tower's architectural design, which had a jutting bay window (from which people could fish), open gallery in the tower's middle, and unique windmill-like ornamental details on the walls. The structure was painted a deep red with armlike ramparts sticking out toward its top from which a large flag flew. When Winstanley later inspected the site, however, he saw that the ocean's waves and spray often blew over the lantern's top. He consequently strengthened the foundation, took down the building's upper part, and raised the tower to twelve stories above the sea. Although mariners still worried that the tower wouldn't stand up to a truly bad storm, Winstanley laughed those concerns away, saying confidently, "I only wish that I may be in the lighthouse in circumstances that will test its strength to the utmost."

He had his wish. Winstanley left Plymouth five years later with his men to carry out needed repairs on his lighthouse. When the weather became stormy and worsened, he decided to spend the night. Then the "great storm" came. This terrible gale destroyed buildings, houses, trees, and church spires, killing over one hundred people on land and causing over one hundred shipwrecks with thousands of sailors drowned.

No one knows exactly what happened that night, except that on the morning of November 27, 1703, people looked out at the rock and discovered no trace of the lighthouse. The rock was barren. The huge storm had swept away the entire structure, including its designer and the keepers. Two nights after the ocean had destroyed Winstanley and his work, a merchant ship plowed into the reef and foundered with all but two of her crew perishing. The vessel was returning from America and the men, ironically, were still celebrating that they had survived the recent terrible storm.

A wealthy silk merchant undertook the next construction of a tower on those rocks. John Rudyerd's men started building the lighthouse on Eddystone three years later. He tripled the number of anchoring irons and used different techniques to set the molten lead into the anchoring holes. The wood and stone constructed station contained living quarters, storerooms and a lantern room; it was not as high as Winstanley's but was broader. Once completed in 1709, its twenty-four tallow-candled light beamed out its warning. This station stayed in operation for nearly fifty years before the candles overturned and set fire to the wood lantern room. The blaze burned each floor down to the granite foundation, where the granite blocks, one by one, dropped into the sea. The badly burned old lighthouse keeper soon died of his injuries.

Originally a maker of odd, intricate scientific instruments, but later also a mechanical engineer and often regarded as the "father of civil engineering," John Smeaton then built what's called the third Eddystone Lighthouse with a much sounder design. It was the first lighthouse built in the form of a solid stone structure, and Smeaton came up with the necessary conclusion that the stones had to be held together by their dovetailing, not by quick-drying cement that the ocean's constant pounding eroded and chipped away. This time, the men built the structure with massive tied-together stone blocks on foundations that were secured to the rock. His idea was that the lighthouse would be a continuation of the rock on which it was built. This concept became the approach used with later wave-swept lighthouse locations, such as Minot's Ledge, Tillamook Rock, and St. George Reef.

During a three-year construction period, nearly fifteen hundred large, granite blocks were interlocked and secured with thousands of marble plugs, wedges, and trenails (or pegs). A seventy-foot tower was secured onto a thirty-five-foot stone foundation, which contained the men's quarters and storerooms inside. A chandelier of twenty-two candles provided the light for the lamp, and this lighthouse became operational on October 16, 1759. It stood for years as a monument to Smeaton's design. In 1877, workers determined that the heavy storm surges against the structure over the decades had undermined the rock under the lighthouse. They selected a new site on the Eddystone and constructed another tower which became operational in June 1881.

One lighthouse known for the fame of its builder and associated with the two poet/writers is Bell Rock, built on a sunken reef on the northern side of the entrance of the Firth of Forth, Scotland. Robert Stevenson, the father of Alan Stevenson—also a lighthouse builder—and the grandfather of Robert Louis Stevenson, the novelist, constructed this station.

When the Stevensons built Bell Rock Lighthouse on Inchcape Reef, their Scotch workers labored despairingly owing to the chilling North Sea waves that often washed over them. Stevenson told the story about how his men watched the next waves bearing down every few minutes, as each wondered if this was the one that would wash him away. At the time, it was said that a sailor on board the work ship played "sweet" music on a German flute, which somewhat cheered the drenched workers. Before long, the iron rods were fastened into the reef to hold the tower's levels of stone blocks, and a crane lifted the first stone into position. When this was finally secured in place, the workmen—ragged, chilled, and exhausted from their struggles—cheered wildly, "like soldiers just over the crest of an enemy's fort."

Remembering his lighthouse roots and experiences, Robert Louis Stevenson wrote the following poem:

The Light-Keeper

As the steady lenses circle
With frosty gleam of glass;
And the clear bell chimes,
And the oil brims over the lip
    of the burner,
Quiet and still at his desk,
The lonely Light-Keeper
Holds his vigil.

Lured from far,
The bewildered seagull beats
Dully against the lantern;
Yet he stirs not, lifts not his head
From the desk where he reads,
Lifts not his eyes to see
The chill blind circle of night
Watching him through the panes.
This is his country's guardian,
The outmost sentry of peace,
This is the man
Who gives up what is lovely
    in living
For the means to live.

Poetry cunningly guilds
The life of the Light-Keeper,
Held on high in the blackness
In the burning kernel of night,
The seaman sees and blesses him,

The Poet, deep in a sonnet,
Numbers his inky fingers
Fitly to praise him.
Only we behold him,
Sitting, patient and stolid.
Martyr to a salary.

THE EARLY LIGHTHOUSES in the United States were constructed of wood or stone. Understandably those built of wood ran a high risk of fire—and all eventually had the experience. Bound together by mortar, the stone lighthouses were actually towers built by piling one stone on top of another, tapered as each rose that allowed the base to support its height. The higher the lighthouse, the thicker the base had to be.

Built by local residents in 1673, one of America's first lights was the beacon off Point Allerton, Nantasket (now called Hull), Massachusetts, which consisted of "fier bales (fire balls) of pitch and ocum." Concerned that the shipwrecks on offshore rocks deterred commerce, colonial merchants encouraged the building of Boston Light from 1715 to 1716 on Little Brewster Island at the entrance to Boston Harbor, the first lighthouse built in the United States.

Construction of the tall lighthouse took little over one year. Tallow candles hung in the lantern of its stone, cone-shaped tower, and the country's first fog signal also took place there, when the keepers began firing a cannon as their warning for ships to stay clear of the rocks. Two years after the first keeper, George Worthylake, was appointed, he, his wife, daughter, and two men drowned in November 1718, when the boat in which they were returning to the lighthouse capsized in rough seas.

The use of candles in lanterns was an ineffective device, given the continual need to replace the candles and ease in being extinguished. Tallow candles over time gave way to burning whale oil and then lard in lamps, as clanging bells replaced cannons for the station's fog-warning devices. In 1762, a successful lottery raised enough money to build a nine-story, eighty-five-foot tower at Sandy Hook, which was the fourth lighthouse built. Twelve lighthouses had been built in the United States when the control of these stations passed in 1789 from the states to the federal government. No two were constructed from the same set of plans and all were built with local materials. When stonemasons learned how to cut blocks of stone to fit precisely together, taller and stronger towers were able to be constructed.

As the government began emphasizing these maritime protective structures and their signals, the U.S. Light-House Establishment in 1822 called for nine new lighthouses each year, and this increased the number from 70 to 246 such structures over a twenty-year period. They also maintained thirty lightships and more than one thousand buoys by that time, and these numbers ever increased each year.

The bulk of the country's lighthouses for many years was centered off the New England coast. Given the maritime industry's concentration in this region, some two-thirds of all lighthouses were located in 1825 between New York City and West Quoddy, Maine, less than six hundred miles apart. As other coastal sections of the United States demanded their share of these stations, lighthouses began to diversify along the East Coast.

These stations were part of this country's history. Boston Light became a center of the hostilities between the English and Colonial forces during the Revolutionary War. Each side tried to gain control or destroy the lighthouse so that the other couldn't benefit from its use. Before leaving Boston, the British fleet in 1776 finally blew up the tower; seven years later, the state rebuilt it and erected a seventy-five-foot-high stone structure.

The lighthouse on Cape Florida in 1836 became involved in the Seminole Indian War. As a band of Indians surrounded the station, the head keeper, assistant, and Negro servant fired rifles to keep them at bay. After incurring much loss in lives and injuries, the Seminoles piled wood around the tower's base and first-level room and set them afire. The raging blaze soon drove the keepers up the tower and into the lamp room. The Indians continued their return fire, killed the Negro, wounded the assistant keeper, and pinned down the third man inside the burning tower. A federal cutter arrived off the lighthouse just in the "nick of time" to rescue the one man still alive.

Even in the early 1850s, lighthouse construction still hadn't started on the U.S. West Coast. The prime reason was that the United States didn't acquire Oregon until its treaty with England in 1846 and California until the end of the Mexican War in 1848. At that time, not a single station or lighthouse existed from Southern California to northern Washington. This quickly changed when a dense fog caught the U.S. Coast Survey's own cutter, the *C.W. Lawrence*, and the blinded vessel in 1853 smashed onto rocks in the Golden Gate off San Francisco and quickly sank. Constructed in 1854 in San Francisco Bay, the first American-built lighthouse on the West Coast was Alcatraz Lighthouse, which was built on the rock that would hold its infamous prison. Since maritime transportation and its industries were one of the most vital and strongest components of the U.S. economy until the mid-1900s, within fifty years lighthouses, lightships, and Coast Guard Lifesaving stations dotted the coasts of California, Oregon, and Washington as they did on the East Coast.

In the 1850s, workers constructed screw-pile lighthouses for the first time. The Light-House Board constructed lightweight, wooden towers on iron stilts with cork-screw-like flanges that tipped the legs. Before building the towers, the workers screwed the leg-tips into the soft bottom of quiet protected waters, such as bays and sounds, and constructed the supporting base. This approach allowed lighthouses to be built on sandy sites too soft to support the weight of a heavy stone tower. These stations quickly gained popularity, so that within thirty years one hundred of these screw-pile lighthouses had been constructed, principally offshore the Carolinas and Chesapeake Bay.

Bricks towers were also constructed in the 1850s with nine of these towers built over 160 feet high on land by the end of that decade; six more were constructed after the Civil War. These towers were nearly always conical shaped, and their walls of solid brick were structurally stronger than other designs, although much more expensive. All fifteen of the towers were constructed along the Atlantic coast—from Fire Island, New York, to Florida—and nearly all of these lighthouses are still standing. The Cape Hatteras lighthouse at 193 feet is the tallest in the United States. By this time, the Fresnel lens from France began to replace the much less efficient reflector system, and this is discussed later.

Whether lined with brick or not, cast-iron construction of stations began in the 1840s. This construction was relatively light-weight, as contrasted against lighthouses built of stone and brick, and cast iron was inexpensive, strong, watertight, and had a slow rate of deterioration. By the close of the nineteenth century, cast-iron towers proliferated throughout the United States. The Light-House Service had also by then initiated the construction of lighthouses from Texas to Florida, wrapping them around the East Coast to the Northeast, in the Midwest and Great Lakes, and along the West Coast.

The traditional method of constructing a foundation in the northern United States was by laying and interlocking a bed of large stones underwater that weighed from three to five tons each—but this method proved time consuming and expensive. A hollow cast-iron shell, however, could be sunk to the seabed in water up to thirty feet and then filled with sand, rock, or concrete. A cast-iron light-house was typically constructed on the top of this supporting caisson. The Board constructed some fifty of these caisson lighthouses by the late 1870s. However, as Ray Stannard Baker wrote over a century ago in *McClure's* magazine:

> A stone-tower lighthouse bears much the same relation to
> the iron-pile lighthouse that a sturdy oak bears to a willow
> twig. One meets the fury of wind and wave by stern resis-
> tance, opposing force to force; the other conquers its diffi-
> culties by avoiding them. For southern waters, where there is
> no danger of moving ice-packs, iron-pile lighthouses have
> been found most useful, although the action of the saltwater
> on the iron piling necessitates frequent repairs. More than
> eighty lights of this description dot the shoals of Florida and
> the adjoining states. Some of the oldest ones still remain in
> use in the North, notably the Brandywine Shoal, in Delaware
> Bay, but it has been found necessary to surround them with
> strongly built ice-breakers.

The later use of reinforced concrete turned out to be in many
ways superior to iron and steel. This approach was stronger, cheaper,
and required much less maintenance owing to the corrosive effects
of saltwater. As this construction was stronger, lighthouses built in
places susceptible to earthquakes were made of reinforced concrete.
Hence, most of the major concrete towers are located on the West
Coast.

THE INITIAL STEP in the selection of any site was to determine the
"portee," or the approximate distance from which the light should
be seen. This calculation determined the height of the tower that
was needed for a given distance. For example, owing to the earth's
curvature, a light at one hundred feet above sea level would be seen
for thirteen miles (depending on its size and illumination), whereas
at five hundred feet above sea level, this visibility distance doubled.

The engineer needed to be careful when determining the heights, as dense fogs could form at these higher levels and drastically curtail the light's distance; foghorns and bells would be more important in these circumstances.

In the early 1800s, a different lens was developed that would better magnify the lamp's light. In 1822, the French physicist Augustin Fresnel invented a lens that revolutionized the lighting of these stations. He designed a system of optical lens that resembled a huge beehive, where prisms at the top and bottom bent light into a magnifying glass in the middle that concentrated the light into a brilliant beam. Fresnel's revolutionary design became the standard for lighthouses around the world, whether on the coasts of Asia, Europe, or America. What was even more impressive is that Fresnel made all of the important calculations—including the design of the delicate light magnification, bending, and focusing system—without having the benefit of computers or handheld calculators.

If a site was important and needed the farthest light visibility, such as off a rocky coastline, the first-order lens was available. This lens was the largest and emitted the most powerful light. The smallest was the sixth-order lens for use in harbors, and this lens was one-sixth the size of the much larger first-order optics. Different gradients, or orders, built down in size from the first-order lens to the sixth order.

Starting with the Egyptian 400-foot tower on Pharos, the earliest lighthouses burned wood. This meant that most workers spent their time finding, chopping, and carrying wood for the fire. Coal was later tried but this fuel burned too hot and created too much heat without as much light. The problem was trying to find some type of fuel that would build a bright light, not burn too hot, and be convenient to use.

John Smeaton found the answer with his mid-1700s design for the third Eddystone Lighthouse, which included a lamp that relied on a bowl of whale oil with a series of wicks that rose from the middle. Although this approach worked, its prime drawback was that the oil created a bad smell and thick smoke. In the 1860s, lard oil replaced whale oil, and the lard was stored in huge drums in a fuel room at the base of the tower, where a fireplace kept the temperature hot so that the lard stayed in a liquid form. By the end of that decade, lard oil fueled all large-order U.S. lenses. Coupled with the Fresnel lens, these lamps kept a "good light" four times as powerful as before, but only consumed one-quarter of the amount of whale oil.

Although kerosene had basically replaced the use of liquefied lard by the 1880s, the wick-burning-era keepers still needed to trim the wicks regularly, to keep down the smoke and darkening of the lens and glass. The "wickies" had to climb out and clean the windows every sunrise to keep sea scum from marring the light's clarity; during the day, the keepers painted and polished the brass fixtures, among other duties. Kerosene, however, still had a propensity to smoke, and the use of this "earth oil" didn't prove to be a saving change.

Electricity was first successfully used to illuminate a lighthouse when the Statue of Liberty was lit in 1886. (The Light-House Board had the responsibility for the statue at this time.) Before electricity, a system of weights suspended from the lantern room kept the lamp rotating and oil or kerosene fueled the lamps. The Board began converting lighthouses to electric service in 1900, but the conversion progressed slowly due to the limited access to power lines. Most areas were without the necessary grids and stations for generating electricity, and years would pass before transformers and poles were built in the isolated areas where most lighthouses were standing—especially on the U.S. West Coast in remote areas on its coastline.

Electricity also had its drawbacks when first introduced in densely populated areas in the 1890s. First, the lighthouses needed to be located close to an electric power plant, which didn't happen with most of the land-locked or wave-washed stations. Second, the power wasn't consistent with the technology still new and the problems still needing to be worked out. For example, one lighthouse built at Hell's Gate in the East River of Manhattan cast such weird black shadows that the mariners became confused; the entire equipment needed to be removed. Another problem was the difficulty of finding experienced workers who would accept the low pay that the Light-House Board offered, when they could make much more money in private industry.

As to foghorns, the development of fog signals dated back to Boston Harbor's Great Brewster Island. In 1719, the keeper heard several cutters firing small-deck cannons to announce their location at night. He located a working cannon, and the keepers fired it every half-hour during times of bad visibility when the fog rolled in. When dense fog occurred at other stations, the lighthouse keepers banged on pans, rang bells, or lit explosives that they threw over the rocks.

Stations into the mid-1800s, however, still fired cannons to warn shipping during their foggy times. This technique ran into problems over the long run, as gunpowder was expensive, not to mention the continual need to load the cannons and fire them during bad weather. Fogbells eventually replaced the use of cannons, and in 1820 the first fogbell was placed in use at the West Quoddy Lighthouse at Lubec, Maine.

Huge fogbells were eventually cast over time and installed at America's lighthouses. One weighed over one and a half tons, and this was erected in 1885 at Ediz Hook Lighthouse in Puget Sound. Rung every fifteen seconds by an automated striker, a bell house enclosed the clockworks and suspended weights that powered its striker. Workers needed to wind the works every few hours, but when the huge bell struck, parts of the lighthouse vibrated while rocks and dirt slid down around the tower. The Service constructed even larger bells, such as the two-ton bell installed at the Trinidad Head Lighthouse in Northern California. The weights for the bell were so heavy that in 1900 the cables snapped from the continued stress, and the massive weights held over a cliff crashed down into the sea.

Experiments were conducted on using guns, gongs, bells, rockets, whistles, sirens, and even trumpets to produce the needed warning sound. By the 1870s, the Light-House Board decided that steam-operated diaphone horns offered the best advantage. This apparatus drove compressed air through the diaphone, and a loud warning noise sounded through long, large megaphones. Large coal-fired boilers created the steam that forced the compressed air through the sound equipment. The problem was that in long fog spells, the coal required to fuel the furnaces could consume more than what was on hand and even resupplied.

Workers constructed a huge "Zylophonorous Trumpet" at Boston Light in 1894. This huge trumpet had an opening that was two stories in diameter and through which blasts of sound emanated. This understandably proved to be impractical over time, so the diaphone with its steam engines and machinery came to be the long-running fog signal. Although lacking in designing lens and adapting electricity to lighthouses, U.S. engineers did lead in the development of foghorn designs and devices, including the steam-operated diaphone horns. In fact, engineers traveled from England to study these developments, and U.S. specialists headed overseas to learn about lenses and wave-wash lighthouse construction.

Ringing bells had definite limitations as to range, and the use of whistles and diaphones quadrupled these distances. The ten-inch locomotive whistle at Cape Elizabeth, for example, was heard for thirty miles, even in northeast snowstorms. The problem was the quantities of coal and water that were consumed when producing the steam required to drive the foghorns. Lighthouse tenders typically delivered the coal in two- or three-ton lots to the station. From there, the men had to move the coal up in wheelbarrows, buckets, or by crane. The water was stored in cisterns; however, during droughts the number and duration of foghorn blasts had to be drastically reduced.

Locomotive-type whistles were generally used at remote stations, and it generally took half an hour to fire up the coal furnace and generate enough steam from cold water to blow the whistle. The machinery carried from forty to sixty pounds of pressure and consumed an average of seventy-five pounds of coal and 125 gallons of water for each hour of operation; as can be imagined, a great deal of steam was used with the constant blasts. When foghorns were in use for long periods, such as off the coasts of Maine or California, these precious resources were consumed in great quantities, requiring constant monitoring, cutting down blast lengths, re-supplying supplies in bad weather, and even eliminating the wickies' weekly shower.

The real problem for the keepers was the constant loud blasts of the foghorns. One engineer in the 1900s said, "At short range, it would be difficult to find anything more blood-curdling than the long drawn out, trumpet-like howl emitted by one of these machines." Although keepers and their families had to find some way to adapt to the noise-rendering horns, the continued blasting sounds and exhausting work needed to keep them operating properly didn't appeal to many prospective wickies. When the sirens blasted for protracted periods of time, the continual noise seemed to stun keepers, forcing some into zombie-like states. When you think about being subjected to such continual, yet intermittent, loud howling so close for hours at a time, adapting to this would be a real challenge. An answer was never found, other than wearing earplugs, as the mariner who was lost in the fog gave his thanks when hearing the warning blasts.

As to communication, Marconi didn't receive his patent for the wireless telegraph until 1896. Three years later, Marconi demonstrated his new technology during the America's Cup yacht race at Newport, Rhode Island. A transmitter was set up on a ship and a receiver at the Navesink Lighthouse in New Jersey. When the operator sent detailed messages that averaged fifteen words per minute, Congress authorized and the Light-House Board began installing the wireless equipment on isolated lighthouses and all lightships. This process, however, took time to be adopted by all stations.

AFTER THE FEDERAL GOVERNMENT assumed the construction and operation of America's lighthouses, presidents and other high officials oversaw the lighthouses. These duties soon passed to the Secretary of the Treasury and other offices, until in 1820 they became the responsibility of the "fifth auditor" of the U.S. Treasury. The problem was that the fifth auditor, Stephen Pleasonton, was a cost-oriented bookkeeper, who for over thirty years cut costs unmercifully. These actions resulted in the United States becoming a second-class lighthouse operation, according to historians, with numbers of ships wrecked and lives lost simply owing to the deterioration of these stations and their operation.

In response to the growing criticism and investigations that indicated this lack of safety, Congress passed legislation in 1852 to establish a nine-member U.S. Light-House Board, in place of the one-man, fifth auditor. This law carved the nation into twelve lighthouse districts, the First District starting at the St. Croix River in Maine and the Twelfth District encompassing the U.S. West Coast. Each district had an inspector (a naval officer) who was charged with overseeing the building of the lighthouses and their operation. When these inspectors became overloaded with their responsibilities, a U.S. Army Corps engineer was appointed in each district to watch over the construction of the stations, while the U.S. Navy inspectors ensured that operations were conducted in compliance with procedures and dealt with operational problems.

The role of the local Collectors of Customs, who could recommend keepers, and their political control over lighthouses consequently declined. In time, all duties over the "aids to navigation" were taken away from them and handed to the Light-House Board as it struggled to eliminate politics from these activities. The organization slowly became a professional career agency and introduced advanced technology with new types of lighthouses, buoys, fog signals, and lenses.

Dominated by the military, the legislation mandated that seven of the nine members be from the U.S. Navy or Army. This setup proved to be beneficial because career officers were committed to their jobs and responsibilities with military precision. The Light-House Board even set up central supply depots to control the supply efforts to the lighthouses and light ships on both coasts.

In 1878, the U.S. Life-Saving Service began building another chain of stations to aid shipping in addition to the lighthouses and ships. These locations were life-saving stations whose objective was not to prevent maritime disasters, but to rescue the passengers and crew when one did occur. These stations were constructed at dangerous reef-swept areas and equipped with line-running guns, breeches buoys, surfboats, and self-righting, self-bailing lifeboats, among other equipment. Lightships had already been in use for decades, and these floating sentinels were stationed by the rough water where lighthouses couldn't be constructed.

The U.S. Life-Saving Service was organized similarly to the Light-House Board with the United States divided into regional districts. Its largest district was on the Pacific coast and comprised California, Oregon, Washington, and Alaska. Each life-saving station had a keeper (the officer in charge) and between six and eight surf men.

By the 1890s, there were 1,100 lighthouse keepers in the United States with their pay ranging from $100 to $1,000 per year, depending on the complexity, size, and isolation of that particular spot. In the early 1850s, the salary for East-Coast lighthouse keepers was $400 to $600 per year; while the first assistant keepers received one-half that amount. On the U.S. West Coast, the average for keepers at that time was set at $1,000 and the first assistant at $650 per annum. Owing to the allure of gold and silver on that coast, the salary had to be higher to attract wickies. The average pay for all wickies nationwide stayed at $600 per year well into the twentieth century.

This pay was low by any standard. Despite this, the Light-House Board held every keeper responsible for equipment loss due to their negligence. In fact, one hapless Point Loma lighthouse keeper had the cost of a boat deducted on a monthly basis from his salary at fifty dollars per month due to such a determination.

The Civil Service Commission made appointments based on the recommendation of the district inspector and as endorsed by the Light-House Board and Secretary of the Treasury. The Board had enacted regulations calling for on-site inspections four times a year at each lighthouse, and each district had its chief engineer (U.S. Army Corps) and chief inspector (U.S. Navy) in charge of their separate functions.

Mechanically minded individuals were necessary to man the lighthouses now since the lights and equipment had become more complex. Workers were needed to keep the finicky boilers operating by keeping the boiler fires properly stoked, the steam pressure at the right level, and the equipment in good working order. The lens and lamp apparatus were more complicated with the use of precision, clocklike weights and bearings. As lighthouses became more mechanized and intricate, stations needed more people with the right engineering or mechanical background to construct, maintain, and repair their warning systems.

The need for skilled machinists grew so strong that the U.S. Light-House Board in the late 1800s established specialized groups in each lighthouse district. These people were all-round craftsmen who could install a replacement boiler, mend a steam engine, and even anchor a buoy as they worked on navigational aids, lightships, and lighthouses. Although their background was as an engineer, carpenter, or blacksmith, this group had to be versatile in their ability to fix whatever came up.

Regardless of where they were stationed, these specialists needed to work whether the weather conditions were good or bad. One

machinist who worked in the New England group in the 1890s
wrote:

> They must go at call for lives depend on their arrival or non-
> arrival. They must drive over snow-bound roads in the winter,
> pull a mile or two in a leaky dory, arrive at the station in the
> dead of night, and, though half frozen, go at once to the whis-
> tle house, work forty-eight hours incessantly—all this falls to
> their lot.

These specialists didn't just work on lighthouses but also on
lightships, buoys, and tenders. In 1900, about thirty lighthouse tenders—vessels from twenty to five hundred tons—existed that carried
up to fifteen men. These tenders carried supplies to the lighthouses
and lightships, serviced the buoys, transported construction materials and workers, and carried inspectors and engineers on their inspection rounds. The custom was for keepers to ring their lighthouse bells
in salute of the tender, and the ship blasted its whistle in response.

Some 4,300 floating iron and wood buoys existed on the U.S.
coasts and rivers in 1900. Usually long sticks of cedar, ten to sixty
feet long, were built in layers to form the wood floats, which the
service then shackled to anchors and moored. Three classes of iron
buoys were used, consisting of nuns (or a frustrum: the base that's
left when a pyramid top is sliced off), cans (almost conical), and ice
buoys (long and tapered).

Although most of the floating devices in use then were floating
day marks, not visible or of any use after daylight hours, non-automated
whistling buoys were used to mark rock spots both day and night. As
the buoy rose and fell with the rolling waves, a compressed reservoir
of air formed within the device. The air rushed through a locomotive
whistle attached to its top, which emitted a distinct, short groaning
toot with each passing wave. Although these buoys had a short warn-

ing range, particularly dangerous areas in busy harbors used gas buoys that burned continuously and were resupplied every two months.

Where electric plants were located close by, electricity could light buoy lamps through cables connected to the generators. At the same time, lighthouses were also ringing the coasts of Europe and Asian countries such as China and Japan. In 1900, an incandescent lamp was placed on spar buoys that marked the Gedney Channel in New York Harbor—but this was a definite exception. St. George Lighthouse was in too remote a location and far from shore, however, to benefit from these developments for some time.

Although Alexander Ballantyne was aware of these technological changes in the United States and their potential, his mission was to build a massive lighthouse on a remote and very dangerous location. This would involve trade-offs: although technology was improving for operating lighthouses, the construction still required workers who toiled under hardships and severe conditions. No assurances existed that this one could be built or that lives wouldn't be lost in the process—and everyone on this project was at risk.

CHAPTER 4

"Hunting Holes Like Crabs"

The crews set off powerful explosives in blasting away large chunks of the summit to carve out the huge caisson's outlines. As on Tillamook Rock, the men worked directly on the rough, slippery rock or suspended themselves from ring bolts hammered into its top, from which they swung down the steep side to their assigned level. If fastened to a boatswain's chair—formed by securing ropes to the end of a short board—the workman struck a short hand drill against the rock and laboriously hand-cranked the tool. Once the time-consuming effort to drill that area's blasting holes was complete, another laborer swung down and packed small, one-pound cartridges of black powder into the small openings. If the incline wasn't too steep or slick, completing this task was easier although still dangerous.

The blasters typically drilled and packed shallow "breast holes" that were one and a quarter inches in diameter and about one and a half feet deep. As the face of the excavation became vertically shaved, later holes were driven in ten feet deep or more, up to three inches wide, and packed with charges of one hundred pounds of explosives. By this method, 200 to 250 cubic yards of rock were broken up.

The men worked in crews of three each, one to work the hand

drill, and two to make the strike, with a blacksmith on hand to repair the drills and laborers to remove the rubble. Notwithstanding their constant exposure and discomforts at Tillamook, Ballantyne wrote, "The little party of honest, courageous quarrymen labored diligently throughout the winter, and no complaint was made of hardships endured." The same happened on this project, although the conditions were tougher.

After lighting the fuse to the explosives, the men ran pell-mell for cover, regardless of weather or ocean. Ballantyne wrote later about his men on St. George, "At my cry of 'fire in the hole,' they would have to hunt for their holes like crabs." The men scurried around to their rock pockets and hunkered down to protect themselves from the flying rock fragments that showered over the area. As the daily blasting continued, large pieces of rock flew around like shrapnel in a grenade battle. The rock was not only hard, but, unfortunately, the explosions could shatter the brittle rock into showers of smaller pieces that whistled about.

Ballantyne directed some of his men to construct a magazine of wood timbers on a high part of the reef. As the high-explosive powder in use had to be stored on the rock, Ballantyne had these men blast away a large hole and build a square magazine from heavy timbers. Once that was accomplished, the men wrapped canvas over the beams and built a rain-tight roof. They tightly criss-crossed a web of four-inch ropes around the canvas roof and structure and then tied them securely to ringbolts set into the rock. He instructed the laborers to wrap the powder carefully in thicknesses of tarred canvas to reduce the risk of explosion if they were jarred. Despite the four-inch rope netting and strong construction, when the seas surged over the rock and smashed against the magazine, the ocean's pressure twisted the structure around at the summit's carved top.

As the wood structure held six hundred pounds of blasting powder, the men were constantly packing in, taking out, and handling the unstable explosives. For ease of use and reducing the danger of a catastrophic explosion on the quartering ship, the decision was made to store the powder on the reef. The close proximity of the storage shed, however, with its continued exposure to the blasting and fragment showers, was a constant concern. The use of these explosives was inherently dangerous over time, especially since the glycerin powder used was unstable. This problem was lessened when the explosive manufacturer, the California Vigorit Company, began using wood pulp as the absorbent in the glycerin powder. This product proved to cause an explosion that was apparently as strong but far less sensitive to premature concussion firing, as evidenced by the blaster's need to use a stronger, special detonation cap.

The blasting was "distinctly" heard along the coast, and these operations even affected local residents that were miles away on land. One Captain Green became quite upset when he had to give up his usual seal hunting in the "neighborhood" of Point St. George. As the continual sharp noises of the explosions had driven those seals away, the poor captain had to move his camp closer to Crescent City.

The soaring rock fragments battered *La Ninfa*, even occasionally whistling over the masts of the schooner moored over three hundred feet away. The workers' quarters "bore many scars" on its bulwarks and decks, including one massive rock that crashed down and crushed the deck house. Ballantyne reported that no further serious damage happened to *La Ninfa* "save her appearance."

Spraying around like fireworks of rocks, the shrapnel of fragments caused frequent cuts, bruises, and injuries. Unless an arm was broken or a head bashed in, the laborers continued to work while nursing their wounds and pain. Given the constant dangers from sudden winds, high seas, and the blasting on a small rocky point, it is remarkable that no one was killed during the blasting operations.

From his experiences at Tillamook, Ballantyne improved upon the efforts at St. George. On the first rock, he used a sixteen foot by sixteen foot (and six and a half feet high) canvas tent that wood propped up and was attached to eye bolts drilled into the rock. He and his nine men first lived under this tent until a more permanent structure was able to be built on the reef. Block and tackle moved a cable that ran from the ship's mast to the rock's pinnacle, and a hook attached to a breeches buoy moved one worker at a time. At St. George, he leased the entire schooner *La Ninfa* as the living quarters until a better structure could be built. A steam-engine-powered cage brought more workers at one time to the site. The magazine built was stronger, bigger, and safer. Although the present construction had many more complexities, Ballantyne had learned his lessons well.

MINOT'S LEDGE is the lighthouse most associated with St. George Reef and Tillamook Rock, as all three are wave-washed rocks. Located two and a half miles from shore, Minot's Ledge is an almost invisible outcropping of rocks off Cohasset, Massachusetts, south of Boston, and as early as 1695, a schooner crashed on that reef, quickly sank, and left no survivors.

Captain William H. Smith of the U.S. Topographical Department, who designed the first lighthouse on Minot Ledge, said:

> Minot's rocks lie off the southeastern chop of Boston Bay. These rocks or ledges had been the terror of mariners for a long period of years; they have been, probably, the cause of a greater number of wrecks than any other ledges or reefs upon the coast.

During low tide when the sea was calm, the Indians in the earliest times paddled out to the ledges and offered trinkets, ornaments, and beads as sacrifices to appease the "Wicked One," called "Hobomock," who lived beneath the rocks and created the bad storms. When a well-known Boston merchant, George Minot, lost in 1754 a valuable ship due to those rocks, the reef was called from then on

Minot's Ledge. With numbers of wrecks over time, over eighty ships and four hundred lives were lost in these waters over a one-hundred-year period after the 1750s.

The ocean covered the "bold, black knob of a rock" at high tide, and if the seas were calm, only "a smooth, oily, treacherous eddy" evidenced its location. At low tide, a glistening mass surfaced only a few feet above the surface. In the thirty years before the lighthouse's construction, at least forty-three vessels had crashed onto that reef, of which twenty-seven were a total loss.

Although designers believed that a tower similar to the third Eddystone Lighthouse was the best approach, Captain William H. Swift, an engineer in the U.S. Topographical Department, decided on a different approach with an iron structure on top of spindly iron legs drilled into the rock. His design called for nine iron pilings that were cemented five feet into the submerged rock; the lamp house and keeper's quarters were built on top of the pilings. He reasoned that the small iron legs—as opposed to a solid block and cement mass—would not present as tempting a target to large ocean swells.

The first Minot's Ledge station cost $39,000, took three years to build, was the first wave-washed station constructed in the United States, and was placed into operation on January 1, 1850. The octagonal skeleton tower was cross-braced with the structure perched on top of its iron posts. In his book *Cape Cod*, Henry David Thoreau described passing Minot's Ledge Light in 1849:

> Here was the new iron light-house, then unfinished, in the shape of an egg-shell painted red, and placed high on iron pillars, like the ovum of a sea monster floating on the waves. When I passed it the next summer it was finished and two men lived in it, and a light-house keeper said that in a recent gale it had rocked so as to shake the plates off the table. Think of making your bed thus in the crest of a breaker!

The first keeper was Isaac Dunham, and his life in the lighthouse proved to be precarious. The keeper's quarters and its lamp above were perched seventy-five feet above the ocean, and in a storm of any severity, the station whipped back and forth, hurling dishes to the floor. Dunham's pet cat became the first casualty of this station, which swayed so severely (some say as much as two feet) during a storm that the panicked animal jumped to its death. He believed the structure was inherently unsafe and wrote into his log book three months later in March 1850: "The wind E. blowing very hard with an ugly sea which makes the light reel like a Drunken Man—I hope God will in mercy still the raging sea—or we must perish. . . . God only knows what the end will be."

Due to these fears, Isaac Dunham quit after ten months. The second keeper, John Bennett, believed at first when he took the job that Dunhan was flat wrong. Over time, he discovered that the storms hammered at the connecting cross-braces between the tower's spindly legs and caused them to require continual repair work. Bennett, too, came to believe that the lighthouse wasn't at all safe. In October 1850, he wrote, "Much remains to be done to secure it from accident." Six months later, a fatal storm began building on April 14, 1851. Within two days, these conditions had increased to a hurricane. The towering waves buried the tower so completely that a group of watchers on the Cohasset shore could rarely see the structure through the ocean surges and spray.

During a brief lull at the storm's outset, keeper Bennett rowed across to Boston and disappeared, but his two assistants, Joseph Wilson and Joseph Antoine, stayed in the tower and feared for their lives. At nightfall, people on land saw the light still burning "fitfully" until ten o'clock when it couldn't be seen; a towering wave had crashed apparently over the station and extinguished the lamp. Wilson climbed up the iron ladder to light the lantern, but found it impossible to return to his living quarters.

At one o'clock that night, people heard the violent tolling of the lighthouse bell over the storm's howling, and until then the gale's shrieking had dominated all sound. Five hours later, a chair from the tower's watchroom washed ashore. When the storm died down and residents could later take a boat to the reef, they found only a few stumps of the iron legs remaining in the rocks. The pounding surf had swept everything else away. The ocean in its final sweep over the parapets had sharply rung the bell that sounded the death knell that people had heard.

Two days later a Gloucester fisherman discovered a bottle with a final message from the keepers: "The beacon cannot last any longer. She is shaking a good three feet each way as I write. God bless you all." The body of Joseph Antoine washed ashore later at Nantucket.

Joseph Wilson managed to reach Gull Rock, apparently mistaking it for the mainland, but died there of exposure; all the while, keeper Bennett had been safe on shore. One month before, Wilson had walked into the editorial offices of the *Boston Daily Journal* to complain about the lighthouse. He described how the lighthouse shook so violently during past storms, including one time when he and Antoine huddled inside the lower storeroom for four days, praying that the tower wouldn't crash into the seas.

A lightship anchored off the reef from 1851 to 1860 while the work began in 1855 on a new lighthouse. General Joseph G. Totten of the Light-House Board generally received credit for the design, although there were modifications to his plans. The design called for interlocking granite blocks to be tied to foundation stones that weighed two tons each. Oxen hauled the cut granite from a quarry and then dragged the blocks to a ship that transported them to the site. Construction, of course, could only be accomplished at low tide when the sea was relatively calm.

General Totten and the Light-House Board appointed Captain Barton Alexander as the project superintendent. On his first visit to the reef, the rock was so slippery from the moss and ocean spray that Alexander couldn't keep his footing. The sea always seemed to cover a portion of the ledge with the remaining part—even at low tide—being above water for only three or four hours at a time. Alexander sent a crew to clear the rock of its weeds and cut level steps on which the workers could have a better footing. As the waves continued during their work, the spray splattered over the workmen.

If a storm suddenly blew in and the boats couldn't approach to take the crew off, the launch's boatswain simply threw out a line. The worker knotted the rope around his wrist and jumped into the ocean, as the sailors pulled him in like a "great clumsy cod." Owing to the weather, Captain Alexander reported that his men could only cut "four or five little foot holes in the rock during the whole of the season." However, in the second year the workmen constructed an iron platform that was twenty feet above low tide. They stretched ropes between the piles on which it rested, and when the waves were high, they held to the lines to keep from being washed into the sea.

In January 1857, a storm apparently destroyed the iron framework. Alexander and the engineer were very disappointed, of course, until a later investigation concluded that the surges had thrown a ship, the *New Empire*, against the platform and that collision caused the damage. As the impact also cracked the foundation granite blocks, the construction work had to start all over again. Six months later, the first granite block of this new phase was lowered into position.

Regardless of the precautions taken, sneaker waves still swept workers off the rocks during the construction. Alexander then hired only workmen who could swim and hired a Cohasset diver, Captain Michael Neptune Brennock, to be the lifeguard. A lookout would yell out a precaution as a wave approached, and the men learned to hold on tight to a steel bolt or rope until the sea passed. Although the waves could be high, the currents were apparently not as treacherous, because these precautions worked. No one drowned.

The men next constructed a sandbagged square or pen, after

which they bailed out the water and sponge-dried the enclosed cof-
ferdam. Next, they laid each stone on a piece of thin muslin that
was covered with mortar, and some commented that this looked like
a mustard plaster. The workers drew the edges of the muslin around
the top of the stone, and a crane lowered it into the inside of the
sand square. Each stone was "dovetailed" so that it fitted closely into
the block next adjoining it at that level.

The workers succeeded the following year in laying four levels
of stone block for the foundation; and in the last year, the six lower
courses of the tower were finished. After three more years, six thousand tons of granite supported a bronze lantern and the cone-shaped
tower was nearly one hundred feet high. On August 22, 1860, the
second-order Fresnel lens was lit and Minot's Ledge once again was
illuminated.

The total construction cost came to $330,000, which made the
second Minot Ledge the most expensive lighthouse built to that
time. Workmen dovetailed together nearly 1,100 blocks (over 3,500
tons) of Quincy granite that were reinforced with iron shafts. Except
for a narrow well, solid granite comprised the structure for the first
forty feet above the rock, and a storeroom, living quarters, and work-
space rose from there inside the tower.

In 1894, Minot received a new light with a characteristic 1-4-3
flash of different colors. When romantics decided that this flash
sequence stood for "I love you," Minot received the nickname of the
"I Love You Light." Called also the "Eddystone of America," this
lighthouse was well built and still stands. Although waves crashed
over the 97-foot tower and even smashed windows, the station sustained no major structural damage over the years. When severe winds
and waves hit the station, however, it swayed like "the trunk of a
tree."

The life of the Minot's Ledge keepers was difficult, as strong
storms not only menaced the lighthouse, but the unsafe conditions
cut access to the station for needed supplies and relief crews. How-

ever, being relatively close to land, the station was well stocked during non-winter months with food, water, medical supplies, and even new books and magazines to read. Henry Wadsworth Longfellow visited Minot's Light in 1871 and penned:

> We find ourselves at the base of the lighthouse rising sheer out of the sea. We are hoisted up forty feet in a chair, some of us; others go up by an iron ladder. The lighthouse rises out of the sea like a beautiful stone cannon, mouth upward, belching forth only friendly fires.

A reporter in 1900 visited Minot's Ledge and wrote in *The Chautauquan*:

> I had to be hauled up by a forty-foot rope, the height of the doorway above the rock, because the iron ladder was covered with ice. Meanwhile the crew of the rowboat in which I had approached the tower held fast to the guide-line to prevent my being swung against the structure. It was not exactly a pleasant sensation to find myself hanging between sky and stormy seas.
>
> I shall never forget the sensation when the first heavy sea struck the tower during my stay there. I had been told of the lighthouse being so completely buried in the ocean that the light was visible only at intervals, and of heavy seas striking the tower with such force as to send tons of spray high above the dome to crash down upon the lantern and stream over it like a waterfall to the parapet and into the ocean below.

Similar to Minot's Ledge is Spectacle Reef at the northern end of Lake Huron, Michigan, eleven miles east from the eastern end of the

Straits of Mackinac. This lighthouse was built not to guard against reefs and stormy seas, but against the ice packs, which can be two feet or more thick and cover thousands of acres. When these ice floes move, they generate a pressure force that cracks and crushes. In the spring of 1875, the ice piled up against the tower, whose base starts twenty-three feet above the lake, and the keepers needed to cut their way through the snow and ice before they could leave.

Spectacle Reef actually marks two shoals. Resembling a pair of eyeglasses in shape, the rocks of Spectacle Reef lie ten feet below the surface of Lake Huron. Numbers of vessels had run aground on that reef over the years, and with maritime commerce between Lake Superior and the lower lakes increasing dramatically in the early 1860s, the demands for a protecting lighthouse increased. It wasn't until 1867 when two large schooners ran aground and broke up on the reef that the Light-House Board went into action. In response to its request to build the station, Congress appropriated $200,000 over two years—but a grand total of $406,000 was spent. At the time, it was the most expensive lighthouse built. Constructed with limestone blocks, the tower stands ninety-three feet high and is an example of "monolithic" (massive) stone lighthouse construction.

The project supervisor was Orlando M. Poe, the chief engineer of the Upper Great Lakes Lighthouse District (and also General Sherman's "chief engineer" on his march to the sea). Work began in 1870 with the establishment of a base of operations sixteen miles northwest of Spectacle Reef at Scammon's Harbor. His plan consisted of constructing a ninety-two-square-foot wood crib with steel plates that was twenty-four feet high and had a forty-two foot open center. This huge structure was built on land and then towed to the reef.

Once in place over the rocks, the crib served as the working platform and the station was constructed within its space. When 1,200 tons of rock were piled up inside compartments of the crib, the wood square quickly sank into its place on top of the reef. Poe had his workers build their quarters on the pier, and with a temporary lens installed on one building's roof, the work on Spectacle Reef's tower could begin.

The engineer ordered his workmen to build a bottomless tub, forty-one feet in diameter with fourteen-foot-long staves, and this structure was placed inside the crib for the tower site. Similar to how a barrel is held in place, iron hoops were secured tightly around its perimeter. Divers then sealed the bottom of the tub with hay and Portland cement. After a pump emptied the tub of the water, the rock lay clean and bare, ready for the start of construction.

The stonecutters next leveled off the bedrock upon which the foundation would be constructed. Two weeks later, the first course of dressed stone blocks was bolted into place. As winter was fast approaching, the men worked long hours. They began work at three o'clock in the morning on shifts that lasted from eighteen to twenty-one hours, ate meals in minutes, and took little or no breaks. During the last days of the season, the waves dashed over the breakwater and constantly drenched the workers, as snow and sleet fell continuously.

The weather had turned bad, and the construction site shut down for the winter. When spring arrived, workers first had to hack away the solid ice surrounding the crib before the project could be restarted. Cut and dressed in the Marblehead Quarry in Ohio, granite blocks were shipped to Spectacle Reef. The stones were set with three-foot-long iron bolts placed through them into concrete as an anchor for each course (or level) of block.

Once the granite pier was complete, the workmen started construction of the limestone tower with its five floors. By the next summer, the first thirty-four feet of the tower had been built of solid masonry. Thirty-two feet in diameter, all of the stones were dovetailed firmly together with the irons bolts. Poe's men next built the final fifty-nine feet for five keeper rooms, one over the other, to complete the tower with all connected by a spiral staircase.

Construction was almost finished in the fall of 1873, when the winter storms forced work to be stopped once more. The laborers that following spring discovered that the ice had caked to a height of thirty feet and "considerably above" the station door. After spending days cracking away at the ice, the men finally worked their way inside the tower and completed the job. When the cast-iron lantern room and second-order Fresnel lens were installed, the station was operational.

The light glowed for the first time in June 1874. On these off-shore Great Lakes stations, such as Stannard Rock and Spectacle Reef, the keepers left their lighthouses at the close of the shipping season around the first of December when the ice began to close down the sea lanes. They locked the towers behind them and returned the following March to get ready for the busy summer shipping season. Each spring, they had to break their way through mounds of solid ice with picks and axes until they were able to open the entry door. More hours were then expended clearing away the winter ice from the lantern and foghorns.

The Board promoted Orlando Poe to different positions, and in 1883 he became the superintending engineer of improvement for the rivers and harbors on Lake Superior and Huron; he was responsible at this level for the construction of Falls Canal on the St. Mary's River between Lake Superior and Huron. He also receives credit for the "significant" improvements made to the Detroit River and shipping channels in Chicago, Duluth, and Buffalo.

Orlando Poe is generally remembered for his design and construction supervision during the 1890s of the lock at Sault St. Marie. With an eight-hundred-foot length and one-hundred-foot width, the new link was the largest in the world, and it allowed large ore-carrying vessels from the mining regions bordering Lake Superior to access the lower Great Lakes and Atlantic Coast. In recognition of his accomplishments, this passage was named "Poe Lock." As a major figure on the Light-House Board in the 1880s, General Poe reviewed

Alexander Ballantyne's plans for building the lighthouse on North West Seal Rock, signed off on them, and was primarily responsible at that level for any final construction decisions that were passed up.

ON BOARD *LA NINFA* in the cramped quarters, the four o'clock watch awakened the sleeping workers to start their day. The housing was Spartan in nature; Ballantyne had the former sealing ship outfitted with canvas bunks inside the holds, scarce furniture, and with not much storage for clothing and personal effects. He and a few of his closest aides bunked in the separate rooms of the adjacent, former officer's quarters. The facilities had sparse bathing and showering facilities, and the washrooms and toilets offered little privacy.

Although the expedition worked during the determined "non-winter" months from May to September, they were still working on a reef at day and living on a ship at night, all subject to nature's whims. Chilling, thick fogs rolled suddenly in, warding away the warming feelings of sunlight from mind and body. Winds blew, dark clouds came, and rains stayed with their cold, damp weather. Unless they used a handy bottle, the men had to get up in the darkness to find the bathroom, and then try to stay warm once they were out.

They had to get used to the boat's rocking and rolling from the ocean's swells. Although the moorings spread around the vessel like a clock's quarter-hands, these buoys were designed to keep the ship secured to its anchorage and not to stop the continual moving back and forth, up and down, and from side to side. When severe storms hit, the ship undulated savagely when the moorings slipped on the ocean's bottom and lost their tightness. Regardless of the time men had been on board the ship, seasickness was still way too common.

The coldness and dampness of their confined space greeted the waking men in the early hours. Dressing was a layering process. Wool sweaters, vests, and short jackets were worn over long-sleeve shirts and long-john tops. Long trousers of light gray or blue denims were in order, as were heavy boots and heavily laced work shoes. A clean-shaved man was an oddity; a rare picture of the forty-man work crew didn't show one worker without a mustache, beard, or both.

Wide-rimmed and placed tight over one's head, hats were worn for protection from the sun, rain, rocks, and dust. At times a bandanna was wrapped around a neck or an engineer's cap worn, but the weapon of choice was the broad-brimmed protection of a hat for face and ears. Once the worker moved around and warmed up, this layering brought on extra heat—especially after laboring continuously on the rock. The crews then jettisoned their coats and sweaters when the sun heated up or fog dissipated. Rain slickers were discarded as another storm pushed away.

Provided bad weather didn't prevent the scheduled ships from resupplying provisions, the cook and his assistant prepared an ample breakfast. Fried eggs, ham, bacon, griddle cakes, toasted bread, coffee, and fruits in season were heaped in mounds on the table inside the ship's eating quarters. However, if their provisions were low, then hardtack, old bread, canned goods and smoked or dried meats were the best that could be offered. The men afterward took out battered tin lids of tobacco and rolled cigarettes or thumped "tobaccy" into pipes. A haze of smoke soon filled the creaking room as the workers inhaled deep from sparking tips or drew noisily on their pipes during grunted conversations, and then moved about as they readied for the coming hard day's work.

The laborers soon meandered on deck, waiting their turn for the clattering donkey engine to winch their group up the long cable to the summit. This was a frightening experience at first because the bowed line ran from the mast three hundred feet over the ocean, stretching up five stories to the high rock excavation. As the series of pulleys slowly moved the men up inside the open-air, roped platform, the ocean waves caused La Ninfa to swell up or drop down,

the cable tightening or looping downward as the cage swung accordingly. After eating a big breakfast, this type of ride could quickly
become another unsettling problem.

If the sea was calm and allowed the surfboats to be dropped,
then the workmen rowed to the reef from the mother ship. As the
small launch approached the landing point, a man on land threw a
rope down to the boat. While holding the rope, the laborers
jumped—one by one—from the boat onto the rock. The sea could
be rising or falling over a man's height by the sea-glistened rocks,
but the men still left the boat. They had no other option.

If they timed their jump wrong, a rolling wave could catch them
in mid-jump, landing them in the frothy waters and slamming them
against the reef. The man on shore pulled hard to get the cold, sputtering laborer upright, next to the handholds, and onto the reef.
Either way, this was a risky commute—and before the hard labors
even started. One crewman stayed inside and rowed the surfboat
back to the schooner to pick up another group, and the process was
repeated.

Deposited at the top of the pinnacle while others swarmed
below with their chiseling, drilling, and packing of explosives, the
new arrivals stepped down from the cage and made their way to
their work assignments. The quarrymen were outlining the specific
places where the teams should drill and blast. They marked each
spot and the amount of glycerin or powder to use for each hole.
Determining what was to be blasted out and how much explosive
used was important, as the plans called for specific levels to be chiseled out with different rows of granite blocks set in precise locations
on those surfaces.

The dimension of the outside elliptical wall—sweeping five stories
straight up—had to be accurate with little room for error, because
the two-ton granite stones and outer walls would be quarried and
polished as precisely. On land, quarrymen later would mark each
huge block for its particular location on a predesigned grid.

As the cage delivered one group after another, the reef teemed with workers as they swarmed around the surface with their assignments. Depending on the weather, the reef could be warm with a bright sun and deep blue, white-flecked skies, as the gentle undulations of the sea washed quietly against the rocks. If a thick fog blanketed the reef, or a storm was bubbling up, the desolate and cold surroundings dampened the spirits of some, while everyone still carried on, heads hunkered down as they went about their business.

As one worker set his hand drill against a marked spot, another team worked to the side drilling or packing in explosives. Other men carried lumber, equipment, pickaxes, and shovels. The blacksmith replaced broken drill bits and tools, throwing the broken ones to the side where they could be repaired later. When holes were ready to be fired, Ballantyne or one of his supervisors personally inspected them, especially the large charges that fractured great amounts of rock, before the explosives were detonated.

Temporary shelters of canvas had been constructed to shield the men from the rains and used for storing food and water. The cook was landing coffee pots and provisions for lunch, then hauling them to their spots. However, when Ballantyne yelled, "Fire in the hole," everyone took their tools and raced away to find their safe rabbit holes. When the loud blasts sounded off with sharp bangs, a thick cloud of smoke, rocks, and dust raced up. Fragments of rock whistled through the air and splattered over the reef and backs of men. Particularly larger explosions rained dust, particles, and larger pieces that shattered onto the reef, crashed into the ocean with sea geysers, and sailed in a long arc into *La Ninfa*.

Men shouted instructions or curses at one another, while others grimly went about the task of carrying away the rubble and debris. Later, when the time came to fit the huge granite blocks into place, large wood-and-iron derricks (among other ways) hauled the heavy stones in their individual netting from the ships to the shore. Another derrick moved the blocks to their preassigned positions, and the layers of stone moved upward from the "zero" level. In time, Ballantyne and his assistants supervised numbers of constantly moving workers who were drilling, hauling, packing, excavating, and building that lighthouse from the foundation up.

When lunchtime finally came, the men took their food and ate by themselves or in small groups to talk, smoke, and try to relax their aching muscles. The cook had set out loaves of bread and meats for sandwiches, sliced tomatoes, cucumbers, and other vegetables, along with coffee, milk, fruit, and water. If the provisions were low or a bad storm had forced everyone to hunker down, workers dined on hardtack and dry biscuits again. If the sun was out and winds died down, the cook could fry up steaks, eggs, griddle cakes, and give more variety.

The work continued past the afternoon and into the evening— until Ballantyne finally gave the order to move off. The men grouped into the cage for their fast, downhill ride back to their quarters. Although tired and looking forward to sitting down, the grimy men still needed to be alert. This was not the time to take a misstep and fall off a path or from the enclosure as it started down the cable to *La Ninfa*.

Once on board, the exhausted workers tried to wash and clean up, but freshwater showers were near nonexistent and soap had not yet been invented that lathered well with saltwater. Shower facilities were usually reduced to saltwater pouring from an overhead wood container—and hot water was more than a luxury.

If the winds were quiet and storms absent, the men could look forward to a good meal. Fresh fish such as salmon, halibut, rock cod, ling cod, and snapper were abundant. The cook's crew served cooked meats such as chicken, beef, and pork, along with vegetables, bread, biscuits, pastries, water, milk, and the ever-present coffee. Depending on the season and availability, fruits such as apples, oranges, figs, and grapes graced the table.

Farming was the country's basic way of life now, and farmers by the coast raised cows, pigs, and chickens to join the kills of deer, elk, and even rabbit, the meat stored on land in iced-down wood lockers cooled by three feet of frozen sawdust. Waterwheels at river mills ground grain into flour, which the locals and bakers picked up in large sacks to bake into bread and pastries for home use and sale. Among other homegrown products, families traded corn and milk for flour and whey to feed their animals and make cheese.

The unique feature of the nineteenth-century American diet was not only the abundance of meat, but also the homegrown distilled liquor. Abundant land allowed the settlers to raise corn and feed it to livestock as fodder, and then convert much of the rest into whiskey. The only problem was that drinking on this job was discouraged. In frontier areas, the diet included potatoes, corn, and various greens (lettuce, spinach, and broccoli) with meals that included griddle cakes, grits from the South, and fried pork—and these were also making their way to the workers at North West Seal Rock.

The state of affairs on *La Ninfa* depended, however, on when the supply steamer or lighters (small boats) from Crescent City had last been able to visit the site; without electricity, blocks of ice cooled perishables, and when the ice melted, the food quickly spoiled. As long as the District had the money to pay the bills, food was not the problem—getting it there fresh and keeping it that way was the challenge.

After dinner, the tired workers played cards, sang songs on deck, or wrote letters under the light of the oil lamps. Others sat quietly on the deck by themselves, smoking a cigarette, thinking of loved ones, and dreaming about what they would do when their tour of duty finally ended. Soon, however, everyone was in bed with another long day of labor lying ahead.

This work was not an eight-to-five job, five days a week with time off for two-week vacations and holidays with benefits. These labors involved working long hours every day, except for some Sundays when the men had early-morning services and prayed. They were on call every day, every week, and every month of their tour. When bad storms hit, or Ballantyne knew they were falling behind schedule, the men worked extra hours until the calamity passed or the challenge met. Despite the dangers surrounding them, they received a set monthly amount that worked out to about one dollar a day, regardless of what they were called upon to do.

"Minor problems" such as sprains, cuts, abrasions, strains, and wounds weren't reasons for staying on board the ship. When a worker broke a leg or an arm, had a serious concussion, came down with appendicitis, or received an injury requiring hospitalization, he had to "grin and bear" it until another vessel could take him ashore. Once on land, specialized medical treatment was over three hundred miles away in Portland or San Francisco—and these were 1880s medical services.

Incurring a serious injury then didn't mean that the government sent a monthly check, such as workers' compensation, Social Security, Medicare, or having solicitous personal-injury attorneys come to your rescue. Quite to the contrary, disabling injuries meant that if you didn't have a caring and loving family, you were on your own in a backwoods wilderness trying to somehow survive. When Ballantyne sensed someone was cracking from the strains of the long, hard, desperate toils with tough men, or couldn't handle the isolation and hardship conditions, he shipped the person off with orders for one of his lieutenants to find a quick replacement. Unemployment compensation didn't exist.

Accompanied by heavy seas, the southerly winds that prevailed during April and May changed in early June to violent nor'westers, and the weather was the important factor as to how men and their work proceeded. Whether someone wore rain gear or not, working in the drizzling rain and slime, wind blasting into faces, slipping hard onto sharp rocks, and keeping weary eyes for death-dealing rogue waves was a challenge for anyone—not to mention that this occurred off and on for months. Back on the ship, the cold, wet, uncomfortable conditions continued. As the ship pitched and yawed, people gave nervous glances or words to one another about the gale winds and storm waves outside. The night soon became a leering blackness, and the winds howled with the mounting seas. Strong "thuds" against *La Ninfa's* sides slammed men around, and the ship rolled with the surrounding sounds of water washing overhead.

The thunderous waves in such a storm smacked against the ship, sounding tremendous thumps. As one noted long years ago: "People and furniture were rolling and tumbling, crockery breaking, doors creaking, and unaccountable noises heard on deck. After much fuming and fussing, we fell into an uneasy doze from which I was awakened by a lurch of the ship that upset a tray of clothes on me and disconcerted me."

As *La Ninfa* creaked, cracked, and moaned, the wind whistled outside with spray and foam covering the ship. Hour after disturbing hour went by. The noises inside and out the trembling ship echoed with a ghostly effect, unnerving and disheartening some. Cold saltwater leaked through the overhead decks, drained from cracks in the wood timbers, and poured through cracked doorway hatches. Seasickness would again quickly arise.

If the gales subsided enough, the men dressed in the early morning, ate breakfast if they could, and headed out again to the cage. Work had to continue, despite the elements. Ballantyne's final report stated succinctly that the weather change was so dramatic that "little progress was made until the first of July."

His workers made up for this when good weather finally returned and stayed. Toward mid-September 1883, however, an unexpected squall stormed in and the winds quickly picked up with blasts of gusting winds and huge seas surging against the reef's north side. As the operating conditions deteriorated, the superintendent and his assistants readied to give the command for everyone to pack up and leave. Although the rollers had not crested over the rock, the ocean's spray coated the lower areas.

Two quarrymen hurriedly tried to finish their drilling of a deep hole for explosives on the lee side, when a gigantic wave roared completely over the top and their area. Tons of ocean water swamped the ledge they were working on and washed the men from their perch. The sea currents hurled the rolling men down the steep southern slope, where they seemed to disappear underneath its foam.

As the hissing waters raced back into the sea with heavy rivulets crashing over the rocks, the others couldn't at first find their two companions. A cry cut through the confusion and directed their attention to a low point. The crew picked up the outline of the two men inside a large depression just before the reef dropped to the ocean; the rogue wave had swept them into its insides. The men clutched to the sides of the hole with outstretched arms. Without hesitation or second thought, others left their handholds at higher ground and carefully picked their way down over the wet, glistening rocks to the men. They managed to pull the severely bruised and bleeding workers back to safety.

After this storm and near loss, the weather for the next ten days toward the end of September turned out to be the finest weather of the entire work season. Motivated by the "ominous westerly swells, which set in from time to time" and wanting to end their long isolated term of work, the laborers worked so hard that they completed their season objectives by two in the afternoon on September 28.

By their long hours and determined efforts, the men had blasted and roughly formed the foundation benches that now only required the stonecutters' finishing touches. Additionally, the men dynamited a deep hole at the bottom of the carved knob that was estimated at 11,000 cubic feet and could hold 77,000 gallons of freshwater. When the last charge had been fired, the reef had a flat top and a series of ledges, "giving it the appearance of an Aztec pyramid." The different ledges provided a solid footing for each level of stone blocks that was to be set.

Ballantyne decided it was time to call an end to the first work season. The crew had nearly leveled a deep enough area to start the construction and its masonry, so he immediately suspended all further activities. The workers clutched their tools and cabled back to *La Ninfa*, but the superintendent's timing couldn't have been better. The weather changed abruptly the following day to a howling southerly gale, and the ocean swept mountainous waters over the reef.

Rain usually didn't accompany these types of storms. Typically, the winds built up, then the tumultuous seas followed—without precipitation. Sophisticated weather reporting didn't exist with the modern radar, maps, and understanding of wind currents we have today. Seafarers and wickies alike had to make instinctive decisions based upon their reading of the winds, currents, near obsolete reports, and their barometers.

Dating back to the early seventeenth century, a barometer utilizes the principle of a vacuum to measure the weight of the outside air's pressure, and the changes in this pressure are important factors in weather patterns. In general, low air pressure means rainy or cloudy weather, so when the barometer drops a storm may be approaching. High air pressure usually predicts clear weather, so that when the barometer rises, clear weather usually dominates. When the barometer quickly drops within twenty-four hours or less, then this shows that a strong storm is developing—and that is what happened. Ballantyne used that instrument and common sense in making his decisions.

However, the gale on September 29 was so strong that it snapped the ship's tethering lines to N.W. Seal Rock, one by one, leaving only the anchoring bad-weather buoy to restrain the *La Ninfa* from the reef's sharp teeth. The men stood by helplessly that morning, watching the gigantic, crushing combers smash into the rocky ledge where they had worked all season. They stared silently or muttered expletives as the ocean pushed away rocks weighing tons that the men had drilled from the lower north bench.

The white-and-green-flecked surges swept one-ton boulders away like a waterhose on woodchips, rolling them easily around the reef, and then left them deposited helter-skelter against the east wall as if a giant were playing marbles. Two weeks before, a gale had rolled the stones over the rocks to the west from where they had been lying; this typhoon then swept those heavy boulders over the reef's entire length back to its easterly side.

The gale continued that day and during the night, while the single outer buoy restrained the schooner from the nearby rocks. The winds fortunately began to diminish at midnight, and the storm started to subside. At daybreak on October 2, the relief steamer *Crescent City* appeared with Payson's instructions to close up work, which Ballantyne had already ordered.

The stormy conditions still made transfers and communications near impossible between the ships, but Ballantyne ordered *La Ninfa*'s crew to ready the schooner, raise her sails, cut her last remaining mooring line, and follow the steamer under the "lee of Point St. George." Once at a point where the seas calmed, he transferred his stonecutters and quarrymen to the *Crescent City* and set sail for San Francisco.

Although the heavy seas prevented the schooner from tying to the *Crescent City*, Ballantyne worried that the ship hadn't sailed in bad weather for some time, and he wasn't sure about its condition. Favored by a strong, northerly gale and a "sufficient crew aboard," however, *La Ninfa* ran behind the wind and made San Francisco in two days. The same storm made passage difficult for the steamer, which didn't arrive until three days later.

Before the reef was abandoned that year, Ballantyne had his men lash an additional spar to each mooring with chains. He wanted them to hold up until the next spring when new wood moorings would replace them, but still be able to use the same sinkers, chains, and anchorage. Once arriving on firm land, the men stored their equipment and tools on Yerba Buena Island in San Francisco Bay.

Ballantyne's decision to stop activities during the winter months carried forward to the following years. He limited the work period on the dangerous outcropping to the spring and summer months when the seas weren't as risky. Captain Payson agreed, knowing that as a general rule, the period between April and September gave the "smoothest" weather of the year. This didn't mean terrible conditions didn't arise during this time period. Gales stormed in at all times, generally from the northwest during the summer months and the south during the winter. This fact was underscored by the unanticipated late storms that had already caused delays.

Ballantyne then planned with Payson for the next construction season, and the issues ranged from deciding on the type and supply of building materials to how best to transport and store fresh water. Fresh, potable water was important for the men's drinking, mixing mortar or cement, and building steam for the lifting donkey engine. During the recently completed season, his records indicated that 16,000 gallons of water were consumed, of which the steam engine required 4,000 gallons (saltwater cannot be used) and the men drank, cooked with, or used the rest. The figures showed the workmen consumed an average of two and a half gallons every day. When the engine ran, it gobbled up twenty gallons each day—hence, the need to use the surfboat whenever possible to transport the men. The steam engine also used more water when it ran to tighten the numerous moorings and spring lines that anchored the ship.

The cost to ship fresh water from San Francisco in large tanks or barrels was ironically less expensive than filling the casks from Crescent City's water mains. This alternative required moving them by lighter to the schooner, hauling each aboard the ship, emptying them into its tanks, and then returning the empty casks back to the pier. Obtaining the water was less expensive in San Francisco and there was less movement involved with the barrels.

Whatever the need or requirement, a ship or lighter had to haul it a long distance and advance planning was the key to every aspect of this project. Nothing was left for chance, regardless of construction stage. There was no room for error.

PART II

THE YEARS OF CONSTRUCTION

CHAPTER 5

Mud River and Paysonville

A fter the first year's experiences, Ballantyne and Payson also
conferred about their engineering and construction plans
for the massive lighthouse. Based on Superintendent Ballantyne's time on the rock, unpredictable seas, and the thunderous
power of the ocean, both men felt changes to the first plan were
necessary. A letter in November 1883 from David P. Heap, the engineering secretary of the Light-House Board, to General Orlando Poe,
who was an important member on the Board, indicated this chain of
command. Once Ballantyne and Lieutenant Payson agreed to the
changes, Payson, as the head of engineering for the Light-House
Twelfth District (the West Coast), sent those changes for approval
to the engineering secretary of the Board. If the new specifications or
modifications were important enough, the Secretary in turn passed
on those changes to his superior or the entire Board for its approval.
The letter read:

> I send you herewith a revision of the plans of building NW
> Seal Rock Light as proposed by Payson. To my mind his
> argument against using concrete is conclusive [as recom-
> mended by Ballantyne and to employ "sandstone ashlar
> masonry" instead of concrete], and I have sufficient confi-

dence in his judgment as shown by the results already accomplished to agree to all his propositions, as the undertaking is a difficult one and so far has been successful. I am in favor of approving the change of plans, but would be very glad to have your review. Should the Committee of Engineering also approve, I want to so inform Payson at an early day, as time is of importance to him, without waiting to have a Board meeting or else call a meeting for the specified purpose. Until yesterday I was sick in bed or I would have sent you the papers sooner.

General Poe approved the new plan modifications, and his signature is on the accepted plans as indicating the Board's approval. At the same time, the men decided on establishing a depot on Humboldt Spit for the stonecutting, finishing, and shipping of the required granite blocks to be used in construction. The Twelfth District would purchase 10,000 cubic feet of dimension (foundational) stone in San Francisco and ship them to Humboldt Bay. At the same time, the district arranged for sandstone to be brought from a quarry located near Crescent City and used for the pier filling.

At an unused courtroom in the Appraiser's Building in San Francisco, Captain Payson's engineering office prepared the specifications for the materials and the details of the caisson design. After conferring with Ballantyne, his office drew a plan of the pier, foundation benches, the masonry, vertical steps, and special stones to be utilized in constructing the caisson. Allowing for a tolerance of only $3/16$th of an inch between each stone for mortar, they drew the exact pattern or footprint for each stone to be laid and cut that precise silhouette from zinc sheets.

In the fall of 1883 Ballantyne and Payson agreed on more plans, drawings, and specifications to be drawn for building a wharf, workmen's quarters, and a stonecutters' shed on the North Spit of Humboldt Bay as the depot to shape and dress (removing the rough

irregularities, including sizing and polishing) the stones before shipping them to the reef. When the Board agreed to these plans, the
Twelfth District asked for bids to construct the structures. James
Simpson of Eureka, California (close to Humboldt Bay and sixty
miles south of the lighthouse site), was the low bidder.

The depot consisted of the stonecutters' shed, a mess hall, bunkhouse, the wharf, and two large steam-driven cranes, one set at the
dock and the other in the stoneyard; a short, narrow-gauge track for
hand carts connected the two cranes. The plans called for the stonecutters' shed to be built of rough lumber, be 120 feet long, opened
in the front, but closed on the ends and the back side, with an office
at one far end. The men's quarters was eighty feet long by twenty-
two feet wide, included a storeroom, contained bunks for fifty men,
and was partitioned into rooms that housed four men each. The
mess house was forty feet long by twenty feet wide, built in an L shape,
and contained a kitchen, dining facilities, and storeroom. These structures were completed in mere months.

The wharf was built also in an L shape, and it was 150 feet long
and 20 feet wide. The building of the dock called for clusters of deep
pilings at both ends of the cross-head for mooring ease. As soon as
the wharf was completed, the men constructed a narrow-gauge railroad track from its outer end that led to the front of the stonecutters'
shed. The specs called for four railroad cars to haul the heavy granite blocks over the tracks.

The work didn't stop there. Owing to the "violent winds which
prevailed incessantly" on Humboldt Spit, Ballantyne and Payson
ordered the workers to build a high windbreak on the north end of
the stonecutters' shed and then floor the entire four thousand square
feet of building space to protect the finishers and their work from
the constantly wind-blown, shifting sands. They constructed a well
covered by timbers with a pipeline to the end of the wharf and installed
a secondhand windmill and tank. Finally, the donkey engine used
the previous season on the reef was brought from its storage to

power the derrick that would winch the stones onto the oceangoing
steamers.

When Alexander Ballantyne and Simpson were discussing the
details of the site construction in December, the contractor told him
about a recent discovery of a sizable granite deposit along the Mud
River near Humboldt Bay. The river was located five miles north of
Humboldt Bay, and the granite deposits had been discovered on the
face of a steep bluff that was a short distance from a railroad line.
When he learned that this railroad line ended in Eureka and close to
the spit, Ballantyne immediately traveled to the spot, realizing that
the problems in long-distance quarrying, moving, and shipping of
large blocks from San Francisco would be solved. He wrote in his
report:

> I, at once, visited the location and found a deposit of granite
> boulders of a good quality, and making a careful estimate of
> the quantity in sight, I thought we might get enough for the
> completion of the lighthouse. I, at once, communicated
> the information to the lighthouse engineer [Captain Payson].

Payson's inspection with Ballantyne proved that his assessments
about this deposit were not only correct, but that it was of excellent
quality and held more than enough for the project. The two decided
at once on the ways to transport the granite. Once quarried, railcars
and barge would move the newly discovered granite stones across
the bay to the north spit of Humboldt Bay, where the depot to cut
and finish the boulders and rough-cut rocks was then under construction. From there, the quarry workers would load the finished
blocks onto waiting ships.

The approach was well thought out. The price of granite excavated from the high Sierras, then hauled to San Francisco by wagon
train and rail, and then transported to Humboldt Bay, was high con-

trasted against quarrying them a few miles away from the finishing site—despite having to build more facilities at the Mud River quarry.

Payson contracted on behalf of the District to purchase the granite at four cents per cubic foot and for the local railroad to transport the granite from the quarry to the stoneyard at two dollars per ton. The agreement with the Mud River Railroad included not only transporting the stone by rail and lighters to the depot wharf, but also the cost of constructing needed extensions of the track and building a trestle for 1,200 feet from the granite hill to the railroad track. The contract included a guarantee for the railway to haul up to two hundred tons of granite each week.

A newspaper article at the time reported that the site contained "huge boulders weighing hundreds and thousands of tons, scarcely covered by earth." Such a find made it much easier to cut and dress the hundreds of required huge blocks, rather than having to cut them rough-piece by rough-piece from a solid deposit. The granite was "a darkish color of fine and very compact grain, somewhat resembling basalt, free of streaks and blemishes."

Ballantyne supervised the on-site construction work and solved the daily building problems, whether it involved clearing the ground, determining foundation placement, or deciding on the exact positioning of lumber joists. This construction was not easy, since the area's winter rains, chilling fogs, and muddy terrain complicated meeting the schedule. Building structures in sunshine is one thing; constructing them in the cold-winter rains is another. His workers again camped out and ate in tents if not fortunate enough to live nearby. Once the facilities were complete, the men could live on-site.

The task was not just coordinating the construction of the large shed, mess hall, bunkhouse, and wharf. These facilities required the installation of the large steam-engine-driven cranes by the connecting narrow-gauge rail tracks, along with putting in place bunks, stoves, washrooms, outhouses, storage places, repair areas, and medical facilities. People would be also living and working day-in, day-out at this facility.

During the spring of 1884, Ballantyne pushed the workers to complete the improvements on both ends of the spit so that a "few cargoes" of cut stone would be ready for shipment to St. George and break in the facilities. He and his assistants hired laborers to quarry, initially shape, and then transport the stones to the finishing site where skilled stonecutters cut and dressed the blocks.

Between the railway and the foot of the high-sloped hill of granite were 1,200 feet of flat-bottomed land. Workmen at the quarry removed the fallen trees and next cut down the standing large trees to open up the area. To haul the excavated boulders down to the level land and completed track extension and trestle, Ballantyne built a 400-foot long slide of heavy timber. This wooden incline split into a double track with two stone-sleds, and as the downhill land-toboggan slid down with heavy stones, the weight pulled up the empty one through a cable to the top. A powerful brake and windlass—a cylinder on a horizontal axle that's turned by a crank and rewinds the cable—regulated the speed of the sleds at that point.

Another derrick was used to excavate the stones. Its standard tripod design utilized two legs with a telephone pole–like centering piece. Depending on the slope and ground density, the center support was placed at an angle in front of the two legs, forming a pyramid-like structure. From there, a hoist boom was set in the ground in front of the supporting apparatus with ropes attached to pulleys. Workers tied ropes around the stone that needed to be pulled up, looped it over the pulleys, and pulled that back to the legs.

When the command was given, men, mules, or horses (instead of a clanking steam engine) pulled down the hill with their might to lift the stone up. Given the slickness of the slope, men had already placed wood planks on the ground over which the animals moved down. The crew then worked the windlass and double-track slide of wood and sleds to lower the stones down the steep hill. Once there on level ground, the workmen shaped the granite into rough blocks and smaller squares or rough fill.

Although the weather determined how fast stones could be quarried and ultimately finished, when the sun shone, the men reportedly worked like "gangs of human woodpeckers" at the quarry on the sides of the huge boulders. The techniques used at both facilities were basically the same. The cutters used small hand drills and hammers to peck the outline of the desired shape in a row of holes that were several inches deep. With tools called plugs and feathers, the stonecutters inserted two "innocent looking" steel wedges into each hole, the thin side to the outside. They then placed a large, heavy wedge between those two lips and strongly swung a hammer into the wedge. With a few blows of the hammer, an expert cutter began to split the boulder into the desired rough shape and dimensions.

Once the work started, the men worked day after day on the stones with most being shaped as they wanted and the unsatisfactory ones tossed to the side. However, even scrap rock had use. The crews hauled the growing mounds of small blocks and rubble to one depository. Later, railcar, barge, and steamer moved the smaller rocks to the reef where they were used as fill inside the caisson. This extra bonus meant that the rough-squared fragments, not large enough as foundation block, were used inside the caisson instead, and it was not necessary to build an expensive plant to create this fill.

After a cutter worked on a boulder at the level part of the quarry, a noisy steam-driven derrick lifted the rough stone onto a waiting railroad car. This train of stones then clattered slowly down the tracks to the first dock for the trip to the finishing site on the peninsula on Humboldt Bay. The rails led straight onto the wharf and a waiting scow, where the train operator parked each railroad car with its heavy load. The barges were large with the capacity to carry 150 tons of stone block and accommodate up to eighteen railroad cars.

A steamer or steam-tug then towed the scow with its "huge bins on wheels" teeming with granite blocks across the sea to the finishing site on the peninsula's other side. The powerful steam derrick there lifted each large block of granite, some weighing from four to seven tons, from the railroad cars to small handcars on the narrow-gauge track, and from the wharf these carts hauled the granite to the front of the stonecutters shed. With the work quarters, mess hall, and offices also located here, this site was the nerve center for the stone and block operations.

Once there, specialized stonecutters took over. These experts worked on the rough blocks and unfinished stones, using a variety of tools, including the plugs and feathers, wedges, planers, hammers, and chisels to shape the stone blocks and finish them. Using a gauge, stonecutters precisely cut each block to fit the space and location that it was designed to be set in the five-story caisson. Each stone block had a "tenon" at one end and a "mortise" at the other, insuring its fit into only the right neighoring block.

The tenon and mortise locking mechanism consisted of a joint that could only fit into the hole of the specified stone. A supervisor numbered each block for where it was to be set, and noted who worked on that stone and what was used to dress it. The stone polishers finished each block so that it could be laid with the allowed $3/16$-inch joint or margin.

With an average block weighing $2^1/2$ tons, men then wrapped a rope netting around each one. The second steam-driven crane lifted the heavy blocks onto specifically fitted ships on the ocean side of the bay. These large vessels steamed to the reef and moored close by, where the reef's construction derrick hoisted the blocks, equipment, and men to the site. As the noisy donkey engine powered the boom's cable, the crane lifted the blocks to their assigned locations.

When the blocks were assembled at the lighthouse site, the mortise and tenon locked each block to the precise stones that were to be adjacent. The construction workers inserted bronze rods (dowels) with a 2½-inch diameter and different lengths into predrilled holes to secure the blocks to one another or the rock. This use of inter-locking blocks of granite and bronze dowels gave needed strength to the structure so it could withstand the mighty storms that would rise up.

The "few cargoes" of granite towed down in early June from the Mud River to the finishing site on the peninsula weighed around 125 tons each. The entire cost of operating the quarry for 1884 was $17,000, slightly higher than thought due to the "incessant rains." The overall cost of building all of the structures and improvements to the quarry and finishing site, site preparation, and the cost of oper-ation came to $100,000. To construct a similar series today of improve-ments, quarrying, and operations—assuming someone could obtain the myriad of now-required environmental, planning, and construc-tion permits—would now be in the millions of dollars. Even then, the estimate to finally complete the lighthouse was set to be "several years."

Ballantyne was in charge of the quarry for one year, in addition to his other responsibilities. The U.S. Army Corps's Twelfth District Engineer, Captain A. H. Payson, was then placed in charge of the finishing site to shape the large stones. To do the best job possible, he imported stonecutters from Italy to complete the finish work on the rough granite blocks.

Working on the lighthouse was so important to Captain Payson that when he married in November 1883, the employees of the Light-House Department presented the "happy pair" with a model of the North West Seal Rock Lighthouse completely made of flowers. The model was seven feet high and constructed in an exact imitation of the building from the plans drawn in the office: a high, squat base with an ascending squared, tall tower. The main body of the model was completed with white flowers, then outlined with chrysan-themum and pink heliotrope and offset by colorful violets.

Born in December 1847, Albert Henry Payson lived in Massachusetts, and his father, Edward, was a cashier at a commercial bank. Once in the U.S. Army Corp of Engineers, Lieutenant (and then Captain) A. H. Payson eventually ended up in Oregon. Along the way, he met young Abby J. Parrott, whose father John was a rich and powerful San Francisco banker. In the 1860s, John Parrott was a founder and "potentate" of San Mateo, a wealthy suburb of that area.

At the time of his marriage in 1883, Payson was thirty-six years old and his wife was twenty-five. Payson was the district engineer at that time, but he then accepted a transfer in 1887 to oversee the important job of quarrying. Once Payson was on the site at Mud River and the quarrying of the granite commenced in full scale, the large finishing site became known as "Paysonville"—and this name for the place was used for decades. The children of Albert and Abby were born in 1886 and 1888, eventually marrying into wealth and international society, including one who married a viscount. After his work in the Corp of Engineers, A. H. Payson entered into San Mateo politics. When the city was formally incorporated in 1894, he was elected to the first Board of Trustees.

Credit should be given to the now forgotten men who worked to create the finest polished granite that was so necessary: David Chalmers, the foreman of the stonecutters; Thomas W. Brown, the supervisor of quarrying; Captain Payson, the Corps of Engineers supervisor; and, of course, Alexander Ballantyne.

David Chalmers was born in Scotland in June 1850, and came to the United States in the 1870s. He also knew Ballantyne through his stone-masonry operations in Portland. As foreman, Chalmers worked under Ballantyne as an employee of the Engineer's Office, and the Scottish/English stonemason connection continued between the men who knew and worked with Alexander Ballantyne. Chalmers married an English lady in Oregon in 1879, and they moved to California during the time he worked at the Mud River quarry in Humboldt County. He worked as a stonecutter or contractor his entire life and later moved back to Portland.

DURING THE FIRST OF MAY, the *Whitelaw* steamed into Humboldt Bay on another charter for the second work season. As the ship serving as the quarters and the steamer laden down with heavy blocks would often need to tie up at the same moorings, it was important that the buoys be materially strengthened each year. As workmen in Crescent City had shaped five new heavy spruce "sticks" (or moorings) to replace the old ones, the steamer headed to Crescent City with more heavy chains onboard and picked up the new sticks. The *Whitelaw* then set its course to the reef and set the new or repaired moorings in place.

When she returned to Humboldt Bay ten days later, however, the vessel only had the iron plate that once held its derrick in place. Due to the usual delays and problems of high winds and stormy weather, the steamer lost one of the new spars while towing it during a bad gale. After the crewmen anchored the other four buoys in place, they tried to winch up the lost one. Owing to the weight and the waves, the steamer's winch broke away in the operations. After carpenters made the necessary repairs and replaced the winch, the *Whitelaw* steamed back with fifteen of Ballentyne's men to help in the recovery efforts.

Once there, the crew used grappling hooks to locate and finally raise the lost mooring. As important, by working fourteen to sixteen hours each day, the workers were able to raise and install the large boom derrick used to lift the huge stone blocks from the carrying vessel. The mast of the derrick was fifty feet long and nearly two feet in diameter with a ninety-foot-long boom and slings; its two "stiff legs" were seventy-eight feet long. The legs secured the mast to the ground with its swinging boom used in lifting up the blocks.

After being refitted in Humboldt Bay with sleeping quarters, a mess hall, and water-storage tanks, the 178-ton schooner *American Bay* sailed to the site for use as the workers' quarters, since *La Ninfa* was not available at the time for charter. The Twelfth District also ordered a double-cylinder hoisting engine and a "suitable boiler" to power the large lifting derrick.

Word was then received that the economy-minded Congress had appropriated a scant $30,000 for the 1884 work season instead of the requested $150,000. (Note: funds authorized in one year would be spent over the next twelve months; for example, the money for the "1884 work season" would have been authorized in early 1884, but spent then from July 1, 1884, to June 30, 1885.)

When learning about this sizable cutback, Ballantyne immediately suspended work and discharged both vessels and their crews, as he and Payson estimated that they needed $15,000 for each month, or at least $75,000 for the entire work season. In today's dollars, this one-season sum would approximate $2 million dollars alone, but be in the multiple millions when one included the increased costs and delays from environmental impact reports, higher benefit (Social Security, unemployment, medical insurance, and the like) costs for workers, wildlife and habitat-mitigation studies, risk insurance against damage, and expensive courtroom legalities that didn't exist then.

With what funds were available, he optimistically contracted for nearly one year for a force of some "twelve to twenty" quarrymen and laborers, along with "six or eight" stonecutters, to continue work in cutting the large granite blocks. These efforts continued until the end of October, when the superintendent hired a watchman to stand guard. His workers also constructed scaffolding to guard the big derrick against possible damage by high seas and marked the caisson's outline with "brass bards" placed at the center of each "stone, header and stretcher." In retrospect, these decisions were well made, as instead of using the appropriation for one month's construction (with two weeks for starting up and then winding down the work), Ballantyne used the scarce moneys to inventory stone blocks and protect his valuable equipment.

Despite requests for $150,000 in annual funding during the next years, Congress authorized a disappointingly small $40,000 in 1885 and then nothing in 1886. During this time, work was limited to performing minimal maintenance at the construction site. The super-intendent chartered a steamer and sent a working force from Hum-boldt Bay to remove all the moorings in June 1885, except for one that was relaid and rebuoyed. The workers also constructed tempo-rary scaffolding for the "full height of the rock" and a light platform that covered the pier foundations.

The men marked the outline of the pier's levels on that platform, and then they carefully plumbed the different points for the various levels. Workmen drove brass brads into the rocks to mark the junc-tions of the different curves and centers, establishing the precise lines of each level upon which the huge granite blocks would eventually be set. They laid the zinc patterns (or templates) from the San Fran-cisco Engineer's Office for the blocks to be set at each level, and then marked those positions with lead plugs that indicated where each one would be set. To Ballantyne's great satisfaction, the stone pat-terns fit "satisfactorily" on each square level (or bench) of the shaped reef cone that the base would wrap around.

But that was all. When funding eventually became available, Bal-lantyne wrote he would need at least six weeks to set the moorings, place the derricks and engines, and ready the vessels before con-struction could be commenced, "leaving only six weeks or two months, at most, before the winter storms may be expected." The district engineer complained in his report that "it would be difficult to point out more clearly than has already been done, the useless-ness of beginning construction without enough money to push to the uttermost this difficult work during the short favorable season." However, once funding and the "preliminaries" were completed, they were ready to set the stone blocks.

WITH THE GREAT NUMBER OF PEOPLE perishing in the 1865 *Brother Jonathan* tragedy, including very prominent officials, construction of the protecting lighthouse still didn't commence until seventeen years later. This was after years of the Light-House Board's continual appropriation requests, and then the project ran into three years of drastic funding cutbacks after construction began. The location by itself was deemed too difficult at first on which to build a station, so the Board looked at alternate sites for several years. The first delays after the costly U.S. Civil War ended was due to Congress and the nation's citizens being too busy rebuilding the country. Reduced revenues and heavy economic problems later on contributed to the government's spending priorities. Then and for decades later, the federal government didn't borrow money in substantial sums to conduct its business as it does now.

Following an era of high prices and business activity after the Civil War due to the reconstruction activities, a severe financial depression in 1873 marked President Ulysses S. Grant's second term. A boom in railroad construction was then under way with 35,000 miles of new track laid across the country between 1866 and 1873, which doubled the railroad-track mileage in existence in 1860. The nation's largest employer outside of agriculture was its railroads, and this business required large amounts of capital in risky ventures. Speculators already had rushed in and invested large amounts of money, and this created in turn excessive growth and unused track capacity. President Grant's monetary policy then made the problem worse, when his administration decreased the nation's money supply. As businesses expanded with less currency in circulation, obtaining financing became much harder and set in motion the conditions for an economic crash.

Jay Cooke and other entrepreneurs had decided to build a second transcontinental railroad called the Northern Pacific Railway. His Philadelphia banking firm invested heavily in the railroads, and it was one of the great banking concerns involved in this consortium. When the firm became overextended and failed to meet its obligations, however, the company was forced to declare bankruptcy in mid-September and closed its doors. When Jay Cooke and Company went broke, strong institutions were brought to their knees and thousands of people financially ruined because these businesses were so intertwined.

The large firm's closure caused the economy of the United States to collapse in a domino effect. The New York Stock Exchange closed for ten days. One-quarter of the nation's railroads went out of business, and 18,000 companies failed between 1873 and 1875. Unemployment reached 14 percent by 1876, and the value of U.S. bonds plummeted. Peoples' savings became exhausted, and many banks were forced to close.

By 1877, wage cuts and poor working conditions caused workers to strike and kept the trains from moving. When President Rutherford B. Hayes sent in federal troops to stop the strikes, the ensuing battles between strikers and troopers killed more than one hundred people and left many more injured. The tensions between the country's workers and banking and manufacturing companies lingered on well after the depression itself lifted in the spring of 1879.

Some years passed before businesses regained their former sizes and employment levels, and this also meant that expensive government projects wouldn't continue unless there was strong patronage. Disgusted at the economic conditions, the Congressional acts, and the Grant administration, Americans in 1876 voted in President Hayes.

This constant changing of the guard also factored in to how Congressional approval was withheld on difficult projects. In the close election of 1880, Republican James A. Garfield prevailed, and the famous people who lost their lives on the *Brother Jonathan* were identified with Republican President Abraham Lincoln and Andrew Johnson (his successor). Brigadier General George Wright, the past Commander of the Pacific for the Union forces, and Governor Anson G. Henry of Washington, a close personal friend of President Lincoln, were among those who died. When officials in power remembered their friends, they were more likely to push for the construction of this difficult site.

At the time Congress in August 1882 appropriated $50,000 to start construction of the lighthouse "at or near Point St. George," the Board estimated that it would cost $333,000 to complete, which was indeed very expensive. Congress next authorized in 1883 an additional sum of $100,000 for its construction, deciding that about one-half of the anticipated costs was now funded.

The 1884 election, however, changed the criteria. In another close election, Democratic Party nominee Grover Cleveland won by a narrow 20,000 popular vote margin, but with a higher electoral vote count, in defeating the Republican candidate, James Blaine. Another party with different priorities swept into power, and this was during the great financial dislocations of 1884. Called Wall Street's most memorable nineteenth-century springtime panic, "Grant's Panic" broke out on May 12, 1884. This calamity is named after the former president, who was a co-owner in a failed bank that helped precipitate the chaos. The financial panic of 1884–1885 severely depressed the buying of new railroad cars, new business formation, revenues to the government, and the overall economy. A frugal-minded Congress appropriated a scant $30,000 for the 1884 work season instead of the requested $150,000. Funding was only improved by $10,000 for 1885, then totally lacking in 1886.

Once the nation's financial conditions improved sufficiently, Congress approved a sum of $120,000 for construction in 1887 and granted even more for the subsequent two work seasons. Ballantyne dryly observed, "In four years, only one working season of about one-hundred working days was utilized advantageously on the rock." These delays also meant that the costs of supervision continued without any construction accomplished, equipment on land deteriorated from nonuse, and repairs had to be made on work already completed on the reef.

This combined to "make the cost of public work excessive and correct estimates for it impossible," as the Board stated in its annual reports. When the Light-House Board made its requests for the

$150,000 appropriations, it argued that not only was $15,000 per month necessary to do the work, but that "a certain sum must be set aside to meet the casualties to which such a work is necessarily exposed."

Once funding was renewed, the Board found out how right that assessment was. The forces of nature paid no heed to the political squabbling and legislative decisions.

CHAPTER 6

The Angry Seas

Tillamook Rock Lighthouse had been operating since January 1881, with Alexander Ballantyne also keeping an eye on how it had been faring since its completion. He and his men from Tillamook understood the savage power of the sea, and these experiences gave them an understanding in building the much more difficult site at St. George. From time to time, gale winds and mountainous seas pounded the lighthouse at Tillamook.

In January 1883, high winds and surf tore rocks loose and blasted them high into the air. The heavy stones rained down on the iron roof of the fog-signal building and broke through in twenty places. The workmen repaired the holes temporarily with putty and later used galvanized-iron sheets in making the permanent repairs to the facility.

In mid-December 1886, another typhoon hit the rock and carried the landing bridge completely away. "The heaviest surf known there" to date had totally engulfed Tillamook. The surges crushed the roof on two sides of the fog-signal room, as well as another side of the main building roof. The pounding by rocks and sea had pulverized the galvanized chimney tops and smashed the plastering away in places. The sea carried away the brick parapet and concrete filling outside the fence at the southeast corner—estimated to weigh half a ton—and flung this one hundred feet over the fence into the station enclosure.

Keeping note of the winter storms, Ballantyne traveled to Tillamook from northern California to see what was happening for himself. Noting that Terrible Tilly's structures were built on a rock twice as high as what he was now working with, the superintendent knew that St. George had to be built even stronger. The good news was that Tillamook—despite the damage to its structures from flying rocks and the pounding surf—was standing strong and still immovable.

The distance from Crescent City to Tillamook, Oregon, is approximately 250 miles. Driving today over the coastline route takes five hours; then, such a trip could take days and the route wasn't as direct. Since railroads, automobiles, and paved highways didn't exist yet for that trip, stagecoach, horse, and steamer were the only alternatives to hiking this yourself. Whether riding by stagecoach or on horseback, wide rivers, huge rockslides, and land detours caused continual delays on land, not to mention the mud, floods, and landslides encountered during the rainy season. Once there, the traveler still had to get to the lighthouse, located 1.3 miles from shore.

A faster way to journey was by steamer from Crescent City to Astoria, Oregon, located inside the mouth of the Columbia River, provided the schedules met your timetable. Because there was no direct, serviceable road at the time to Tillamook Rock from Astoria, one had to travel by small boat back through the river's mouth and south for twenty miles. Whether travelers went overland to Portland and then to Astoria, or by steamer to the small port, they still had to cross the Columbia River Bar.

Traveling through the Columbia River's mouth and its sandbar was never an easy trip. The river's flow into the ocean is massive with a million cubic feet of water rushing into the Pacific every second. Owing to the strong river currents running out and the force of the ocean swells racing in, huge impacts of colliding currents slam violently together at the entryway. As the waves cross the Columbia

River Bar—a four-mile-wide stretch of sand that built up at the mouth—these surges can double in size when entering the area. The waves grow to twenty feet or more and break when they hit the river, becoming a raging sea like a dam bursting. Severe weather at the mouth worsens these conditions. Since records were first kept, they report deaths every year, as vessels large and small capsize by or at the bar.

Due to the proximity of Tillamook to the Columbia River, the Light-House Board pushed for this lighthouse to be constructed. As a wave-washed rock like N.W. Seal Rock, Ballantyne and the Board initially felt that his experiences at St. George would be very much like there. However, when seeing the damage that these severe storms had wrought at Tillamook, he knew that they had also affected Humboldt Bay and St. George similarly, not to mention that its base was sixty feet lower to the sea—and still under construction.

Congress finally approved sufficient funding at $120,000 in 1887 with even more for the next two seasons, and Alexander Ballantyne looked forward to getting the construction under way. He and his assistants hired the laborers needed for "preparing and laying the stone," along with the "purchase of plant in open market, and for the charter of the necessary vessels on the best terms available." Ballantyne and Payson prepared the bid specifications to hire (lease) the vessels that would haul the finished blocks from the depot to Seal Rock.

Although Ballantyne had heard the reports of what the rains had done at the quarry, he wasn't prepared for what he saw on his inspection. Walking in boots in mud over his ankles, he stared at the sea of gray and brown earthen-mud and rocks that rose above his head at the slope's bottom. Broken sticks of lumber, cables, and cracked parts of what had been a derrick rose from the morass. He knew that underneath all of this debris lay the railroad tracks and a mass of "partly-quarried" stones. The slope above was barren and looked as if a giant had taken a level and cleanly planed down the hill, removing the wood tracks, equipment, cranes, and rock piles that had once been there.

The winter rains had washed down an immense quantity of earth that covered everything, including the main pile of 1,500 tons of dressed rubble. Making the pier solid to ward off the sea, this rock was intended to fill the caisson between its outside granite blocks and cut-reef top. When the men pulled off the project, the rubble had been conveniently left on the hillside for later transfer to the railroad cars. After the torrential rains, the entire mass slid "bodily down" the steep hillside and embedded itself into the soft soil at the base of the steep slope. Unearthing all of this material would take more unanticipated time and expense.

With Captain Payson and his assistants, Ballantyne made his way to the finishing depot. Although the long stonecutters shed, mess hall, and bunkhouse needed repairs from the disuse and rains over the years, these facilities were still habitable. Compared to the quarry, they were in good shape. The two large steam-engine cranes had rusted and the wood mildewed, as had the short, narrow-gauge track that connected them.

Ballantyne looked from the second crane to the dock and must have first thought that a tidal wave had slammed into the wharf. The dock had collapsed into the now-quiet ocean waters with the waves gently lapping into a mass of lumber, sheered-away stubs of pitted pilings, and wood debris. As they inspected the damage closer, the men discovered that the pilings were etched inside and out. Sea worms, or the dreaded teredo, had eaten voraciously into the pilings over time and destroyed them.

One of the nastiest and most common shipworms is the despised teredo. A scourge for sailors and pier builders for centuries, even Columbus had been forced to abandon two ships on his fourth voyage to the Caribbean due to this shipworm infestation. Their only visible evidence are the pinholes left where they enter the wood when young and very small. The damage caused remains largely hidden from view until what's infested simply collapses. Pilings and wooden boats may look sound on the outside, but the insides resemble a termite nest.

The winds, high waves, and ocean had completed the job that the seaworms had started, and the dock had collapsed into itself. The wharf needed to be "practically" rebuilt from the start. The workmen also had to rebuild spar buoys, derricks, and the rigging and plant that deteriorated or was destroyed during the near three years of disuse.

This rebuilding task was one of meeting challenge after challenge. Alexander Ballantyne was a master "taskmaster," however, and he soon had worked out a timetable, assigned men to each repair function, and stayed at the quarry and finishing site to watch over every last detail. With the men working day and night, the reconstruction work took two months to complete. Unfortunately, having to direct their attentions to the repair of those facilities, Payson and Ballantyne were also delayed in their chartering of what would turn out to be three new ships. This resulted in more expense.

As THE CHARTER on the past ships had ended (*La Ninfa* had been outfitted by its owner for a whaling voyage), the expedition was forced to secure a third vessel for its workers' living quarters. Owing to the delays in funding, it was impossible to make long-term arrangements for either *La Ninfa* or the *American Bay*.

On March 29, 1887, Ballantyne chartered the two-hundred-ton schooner *Sparrow* and caused this vessel to be fitted out with water tanks, eating and sleeping quarters, and facilities for fifty men. Another ship, the steamer *Santa Maria*, took on a "large assortment" of tools, ropes, blocks, chain, iron-work, and a powerful steam-winch in San Francisco, steamed for Humboldt Bay, and arrived there on April 7 in two days.

Owing to the continuing bad weather and the deteriorated wharf now being repaired, the ship was delayed for nearly two weeks before sailing for Seal Rock with the moorings and men. After the buoys on board had been anchored in the ocean, the steamer returned to Humboldt and took on larger moorings that couldn't be carried on the first trip. In early May, the *Santa Maria*—with the *Sparrow* in tow—steamed to the rock.

Upon arriving at the site, Ballantyne scanned the reef. It looked as barren and surrealistic as when he had last left it. The flat top of the reef that rose above him with its series of ledges looked like a long-forgotten ancient temple—but with grayed lumber, numerous ones broken and missing, that covered the rocky levels. The storms of water had thrown rocks around the site, gouged at parts where the sticks were missing, and ripped at what had been left behind.

But as he inspected the levels closer, Ballantyne was pleased at the relatively small damage wrought by these storms as opposed to the havoc caused at the quarry. The waves and surf had ripped away portions of the temporary scaffolding that covered the pier foundations and levels. Some of the brass brads that marked the junctions of the various levels were missing, but the blasted contours of the reef were basically as the men had left them. The rough, rocky outlines of each level, upon which the huge granite blocks would be set, were not materially affected due to the rock composition.

His men would need to reset the stones and resurvey the benches to ensure that the pattern was precisely as quarried back on land. These repairs were needed before the contracted ships could haul the large granite blocks from the depot. The seas and disuse also had damaged the equipment left behind. A large blast of sea had cracked the mast of the "big" or main derrick, even though it had been stored forty feet above sea level.

The workmen stared at the power of what had surged into the mast and cracked it so severely. They repaired it with iron bands and then rigged the main derrick along with four smaller ones. After finishing up the repairs to the site, Ballantyne instructed his workers to construct four small-boom derricks at places for setting the blocks, install and connect the hoisting engine and boiler, and build a wharf landing to receive the construction timbers, stone blocks, and materials.

In the meantime, bids had been sought for a vessel to replace the *Whitelaw* to haul the granite blocks from Paysonville to St. George. The District received two bids, one for the services of the *Santa Maria* and the other for the *Alliance*. As the *Alliance* bid was $10,000 under the *Santa Maria*'s owner, the contract was let for its services in mid-April, 1887.

The *Alliance* was delayed in its voyage to the rock when the crew discovered boiler cracks and defects that needed repair. After fixing the problems, bad weather again stormed in and delayed the steamer's voyage. Once she reached the rock with stonemasons and finished blocks in the first week of June, Ballantyne's men then discovered the reason for the low contract price: the ship had not been properly rigged for handling the heavy stones and didn't have the boiler power or carrying capacity to complete the contracted hauling work. When the superintendent heard about the vessel's condition, he ordered his own riggers on board to change the arrangement of masts, spars, and sails so that the heavy stones could be offloaded.

The first large-dimension stone for the foundation levels landed at 10 a.m. on June 7, and this was the first block laid down at the "zero" or widest first level. Workmen set the huge block, which weighed six tons, at 11 a.m. on the next day. Due to the *Alliance*'s problems, the load of blocks was finally unloaded on June 9, but two days later, the men had set everything and were out of materials. They had to then wait for the steamer's return with more blocks. The *Alliance* clearly was not suited for hauling the huge granite blocks, and another vessel had to be hired. Ballantyne reported the facts to Captain Payson, and the District quickly chartered the steamer *Santa Maria* at an additional $7,000 per month "to supplement" the first steamer's services. Today, these would be considered million-dollar decisions.

As the *Santa Maria* still wasn't available for another month, both it and the *Alliance* were chartered (and paid for) until October 8, or the end of the working season. Ballantyne was forced consequently to use three ships for this season, two for supplying the provisions and materials and the *Sparrow* for the living quarters. Owing to the last moment need and shortage of ships, the Service also had to pay nearly double what the going rate was for the *Santa Maria*'s charter.

Given the rebuilding necessitated at the quarry and finishing site, Captain Payson accepted the transfer in 1887 to head up these operations. In one way, the move could be viewed as a demotion, as he moved from being the district engineer and titular superintendent of construction of the entire project to overseeing just one component of this project. To Albert Payson, this wasn't the case. By now, he had been married for four years to a younger woman, whose family was rich, powerful, and very well connected. As seen with General Poe, to move up in the U.S. Army Corps required numerous transfers, positions, and responsibilities in different parts of the country. With Payson's growing connections to the San Francisco Bay area and Northern California, he undoubtedly turned down transfers that would have moved him outside of this area, and, in fact, when he retired, he was still in Northern California.

Clearly, Payson, to his credit, was committed to the successful completion of this lighthouse. As seen in the floral lighthouse given as a wedding present, he took his job seriously and pledged himself to this project and Alexander Ballantyne. The job of quarrying and detailing was all important. The construction was now where the huge stone blocks needed to be finished and laid. From this point on, a continued supply of well-hewed, quality granite block, stone rubble, and flagstone for the huge pier—plus bricks, block, and stonework for the tall tower—were crucial in bringing the long construction process to a successful conclusion.

Captain A. H. Payson had been the district engineer and superintendent of construction from 1883 to 1887. When he transferred to Humboldt Bay, north of San Francisco, to oversee those operations, Ballantyne succeeded him as superintendent of construction (which he already was in fact) and remained with that title until the lighthouse was finally completed. One year later, Major W. H. Heuer was promoted to the position of district engineer.

With ships chartered and blocks moving, the construction speeded up. The complexity in the site stonework is seen in the block processing. When one set of laborers unearthed and lifted a large boulder by pulleys, another group lowered it to the processing facility at the quarry by the sled and windlass cable. Once there, quarrymen attempted to work the stone into a rough block. When that was complete, a wood derrick lifted the blocks onto a railroad car.

The train engineer drove the locomotive with the cars to the wharf and a waiting barge for the trip to the Humboldt Bay peninsula. A steamer captain took over from there, and his vessel towed the scow to the finishing site, where steam derricks lifted the blocks onto handcars. Once inside the finishing shed, the expert stoneworkers shaped, fitted, and polished the blocks. The steam-derrick operators at the rebuilt wharf loaded the four- to seven-ton blocks onto the waiting transfer vessel, in this case the *Alliance*—soon to be replaced by the *Santa Maria*.

The ship steamed in one day to North West Seal Rock and anchored off the reef. When a loading dock was built, steamers could unload there by derrick. This was dangerous and risky work because the vessel had to be maneuvered close to the reef. Ballantyne wrote that the rigging problems with the *Alliance* first had to be solved, before "she could be hauled into the rock to discharge her cargo." The ocean-going vessels usually anchored to large moorings, both on the rock and at sea. (Depending on the conditions, a smaller lighter or the aerial tramway at times would shuttle smaller blocks to the site.) A large, steam-driven derrick next lifted the heavy granite block by a hook attached to the netting around the block; it deposited the stone at a preassigned place. From there, one of the smaller booms lifted the stone into its position, where other workmen ensured that it precisely fitted into its spot.

Each step involved typically a different worker or crew. Men transferred back and forth as to what they did, but the tasks were quite different. Accidents occurred and men were injured, sometimes to where they were taken quietly off the project and replaced. What is amazing is that these steps were carried out so far without a deadly misstep. This was tough, hard work under challenging conditions.

Whether on the reef or at the quarry, the sun was hot during the summer months, but when the overcast skies and storms rolled in, the working conditions were chilling, cold, and difficult. This was physical work, day-in, day-out, for days at a time without rest. Muscles were sore, headaches common, and colds easy to spread. When shoes wore out and spares weren't available, the workmen walked around with their toes sticking out until new boots came in.

The men didn't have the chance to head home after work, pop open a beer, and prop their feet onto the sofa to watch television. Supermarkets weren't around nor were drug stores and modern hospitals. Newspapers weren't close by, and families with their warmth and companionship were miles and states away.

They were instead sleeping inside the quarry barracks on land or the cramped quarters of a rocking ship moored off a seething reef. Food was dependent on transporting the meat, vegetables, bread, coffee, and staples on time. Ice was used to cool and preserve; wood stoves and fires to cook; wood bunks to sleep on; and with card games, debates, arguments, and fights for relaxation. Restful sleep was left for when the work year came to a merciful end, and each year, new workers came on board, and the worn-out ones simply didn't return.

The men were paid laborer's wages at ten cents per hour, and unions hadn't come onto the scene. None of the government support programs that Americans take for granted today existed then.

The men worked, not only because they wanted to, but because there was no other alternative. The reef was isolated, newspapers were days old, and there were no dance halls on Saturday night. With their quarters being a moored ship, these men didn't have convenient "R&R." Everyone who was there had a purpose under taskmaster Ballantyne—and if there was no purpose, then he wasn't needed.

Even given these conditions, what stands out is the risk and danger. The men were handling explosives, huge stones, and equipment, as well as building a massive structure on a slippery rock. The equipment was solid, but not close to today's safety standards. One mistake and a serious injury occurred. To Ballantyne's credit, no one had been killed yet, but, then again, the continued laying down of the tons of heavy blocks hadn't started.

When men slipped off the rock, their fellow workers had to quickly throw them a rope and tow them in. The sea was cold, and even during the summer, men could die from hypothermia just by being in those waters for an hour or two. Moreover, the storms and gales were a constant risk with the seething seas that tossed ships and men around.

ONE WEEK AFTER the first foundation block was secured into place, the *Alliance* steamed to the reef on June 15 with her second load and anchored next to the small wharf, as her crew moored the boat to the nearby buoys. Until the larger wharf was built, anchoring dangerously close to the reef or hiring smaller lighters brought the heavy blocks sufficiently close for the large derrick to be used. The large steam crane belched loudly as it lifted the heavy blocks inside their netting onto the reef. The ocean was calm and the currents manageable that day, and workers continued their hard work in off-loading the vessel as fast as they could.

Owing to the problems with the steamer's layout, even with the changes made to her initial rigging, the unloading took more time than it normally should have. The next day, the winds picked up and dark, gray clouds boiled at the horizon. Ballantyne quickly noticed the building storm, and its sudden appearance made him especially watchful. The skies turned gray and the blackness moved toward St. George.

Within short hours, the surf built up to where the transfer of the granite blocks and materials from the pitching vessel became difficult. Ballantyne quickly gave the signal to stop the unloading and waved the captain to head to the storm moorings anchored farther away. The captain ordered the vessel's steam built up and with smoke pouring from its stack, the ship slowly backed away from the unloading point.

The winds picked up from the northwest and the surges crashed higher against the rock. The superintendent knew that this storm would soon be a ripping gale. He told his assistants, including John Olson, to spread the word that it was time "to pack it up for the day," as this storm was going to be a "good one." The rock's most dangerous section was its northern, excavated part, and the ocean's sprays continually drenched the men, who had to quickly leave when those high waves rose.

With the order given, every man knew what to do, and the ocean sounded harsher with hissing swells exploding loudly against the rock's sides. Those working with tools quickly fastened their equipment to nearby ring-bolts; others weatherized the materials and supplies. Hustling up the trail that snaked around the excavated levels, workmen made their way to the top where the aerial-transit "cage" awaited, its supporting wire-rope attached to a large ring that was bolted deep into the reef's highest point. To the men, the enclosure looked like a bird cage under construction, as only a few ropes slightly longer than a man's height connected the top iron-ring to the lower standing plate.

Six men crowded hastily into the open-roped structure, while those on the outside grabbed ropes with spread-eagled arms. The workers in the middle also reached for nearby lines. When the brake was released, the group swished down the cable over the ocean on their high downhill run to the *Sparrow*.

While the first group of laborers headed down to the schooner on that cold late afternoon, the remaining workers wrapped heavy canvas around blocks of stone, lumber, kegs, and equipment, then tied them quickly down to more ring-bolts set into the rocks. Once their duties were finished, men hustled up to the high point.

By the time they arrived, the tram was back, having completed its round-trip. This group quickly jumped on board and the enclosure hurtled away. Although gravity and the transit line's steep decline carried the cage swiftly down to the schooner, the donkey engine had to pull it back up. The men had connected a long cable from the ship to the rock and then looped it around a pulley and back to the donkey or steam engine. As the engine thumped with its rhythmic sounds, the motor turned a cylinder that wound the cable back and brought the apparatus up.

The tram's wire-rope passed through the *Sparrow*'s masts to a spar buoy moored on its outer side. When the ship rocked and incoming waves approached, the crewmen adjusted the cable to take the slack out of the rope as best they could. As the cage approached the ship, a designated worker grabbed the hand-brake to slow and then stop its descent.

With a complete trip taking five to six minutes, a half-hour elapsed before all of the workers were off. Meanwhile, a large rogue wave crashed against the rock, and its rooster spray flew over the top, splattering the last workers who waited patiently—some anxiously—for the trip back. The swells surged around the rock with a hissing sound, and the small figurine of the moored schooner below rocked from the swells.

Ballantyne was usually one of the last off North West Seal Rock.

Once the command was given, the brake was released and the crowded men headed down. These trips were a breathtaking ride. The cage gained speed in slaloming down stories above the ocean; it raced down with the men to the rising ocean swells, the schooner looming bigger in their sights.

Although those below tried to time when a set of large waves would surge under the schooner to take the slack out of the cable, these swells were rolling past faster than anyone thought. A large roller then rose to seemingly engulf the men inside the cage, as the apparatus slid faster down the bellying rope. Staring ahead, the lead workman saw the wave smack into the cable close to the vessel. The cage angled deeper toward the upcoming wave, and in seconds the two collided with the chilling saltwater crashing into the lower part of the enclosure. The collision jerked the cage's momentum and the men flew forward, while the tram spun around and ocean foam sprayed everywhere.

The cage somehow continued toward the awaiting ship, although slower and rocking with its thoroughly drenched human cargo. When the hand brake was applied full strength, the tram came to a squeaking stop between two masts. Exiting was normally easy, but with the ship's rolling and plunging, the men found it difficult to step onto the heaving platform. Once this was done, they joined the workers who now were congregating in the mess hall. At other times, the laborers would stand about on the deck, relaxing and breathing in the non-dusty, fresher air; this wasn't an option now, and the smell of the sea and salt air was pungent and striking.

The men normally cleaned up before their meals, but on this occasion, the bouncing ship discouraged most from worrying about such matters. Some, however, washed their hands and splashed water on their faces. Since fresh water was now scarce and used only for drinking, the men washed up with saltwater, which didn't work well and left a residue. The small bathroom quarters contained urinals and wood toilets that led to a holding tank; an overhead container with water splashed down when the men wanted their weekly shower.

Inside the lower compartment used as a mess hall, the workers grabbed porcelain plates stacked inside small, fenced-in compartments built against the wall and lined up in front of a cauldron of cooked stew, hard bread, and coffee. They grabbed their utensils and sat down at their particular spot at the table, sometimes nodding to a companion, and started wolfing down their food—at least those who had grown their sea legs, since the schooner was tossing so badly. Many of the men were used to storms on board ships, but this was one of the first times they were experiencing one inside the *Sparrow*.

The light inside the dining room faded, and the grays outside the portholes became darker; a young crewman lit the oil lamps with their lingering, upward drift of smoke. The gale wind's moaning outside seemed to whip over the entire ship, and the vessel's movements shifted people abruptly with their bodies and heads snapping back or to one side. Some gave up trying to eat and slowly walked away, swaying with the ship's motion.

Although the schooner skidded or thudded with each massive wave, most of the large furniture already was secured and didn't shift into a dangerous slide. Tables and benches were screwed into the deck and cabinets to the bulkheads. The bunks and a few compactums (a cabinet that folded down with a small sink inside) were also attached to the floor and walls.

As soon as the first men finished eating, the usual thick haze of smoke from lit cigarettes and cigars filled the room. Exhausted men leaned silently back against the hard-backed benches, talked about work or home to a nearby friend, or stared out at the closed port window as another dark roller surged by. Other workers who hadn't finished their dinner had already left or stayed in their bunks, fully clothed, as the roller-coaster ride of the ship—even if moored to several buoys—took its toll. In storms such as this, it wasn't rare for an anchored or moored vessel to move in the direction of the storm's winds and currents. Nor was it uncommon for nauseous men to run pell-mell to the head or try to hit a bucket.

The thunderous waves smacked against the ship, sounding cracking-like hits against the hull that shook the nerves of some and caught the notice of all. People were stumbling, items of unprotected crockery breaking, and doors creaking. Harsh noises emanated from the deck and toilets. A few men ignored their surroundings and produced a deck of cards, while some continued discussing some topic only important to them. After a while, most of the men had filed out and made the uneasy trip through the hallways to their bunks or the head.

Ballantyne and his assistants spent time in the bunkroom talking with their men. He had the ability to make people feel comfortable and was unquestionably their leader. Ballantyne listened to their complaints, sorrows, desires, and dreams. Whether alone or in front of others milling around at the time, he ironed out their problems. This time, he and his lieutenants asked, "How's work today?", or "Get that derrick problem worked out?" As men flopped onto their bunks, he eventually headed to his quarters.

The tight sleeping quarters were not designed for holding thirty or more men. Two- and three-tiered bunks were set around the room with a few wooden chairs, desk, and closets. Most of the men dressed from their trunks, as the closets were small, few, and couldn't be locked. Despite everything being screwed down into the floorboards and walls, the winds and waves were tossing and mixing toilet items, heavy combs, and loose clothing on the wet floor. Getting needed sleep proved difficult.

Seawater trickled over the floor, which quickly became large puddles, and these puddles joined others. The cold saltwater leaked through the overhead decks and drained from cracks in the wood timbers. The ocean water became an inch or two deep, as it swished back and forth with the vessel's pounding.

Although oil lamps burned inside the quarters, their narrow light created a surrealistic appearance. The ship's movements, shadows of men and furniture, and those few walking around brought about a general unsettling feeling. The stale smoke of cigarettes and lamps mingled with the sharp scent of sweat and some anxiety.

Unable to sleep, men stared outside the portholes at the *Alliance*. They could just make out its outline from the lamps that were burning inside its pilothouse and the quarters toward its stern. Although the ship was now moored to three large buoys, the men could tell by the movements of the lights that the huge waves were bouncing the vessel around. Now and then a light disappeared into the blackness, and then another appeared later in a different section.

The seas raged into the night. As the *Sparrow* creaked and cracked sharply, the wind whistled outside with spray and foam smacking against the portholes and ocean crashing onto the overhead deck with a force that sounded below. The sea continued dribbling inside, and this felt cold on bare feet.

Watching through the porthole, one worker pulled back and mumbled that the ship was moving. He told the man next to him to take a closer look. Another stared through an adjacent porthole. There was no question that the *Alliance* was swinging closer. A powerful storm had the strength to push vessels away, their anchors and mooring weights dragging along the bottom. Cables could snap and buoys cracked apart. The only question was how soon it would take for these gale winds to drive a ship against the rocks or how far.

Realizing the seriousness of the situation, an assistant stumbled down the shifting hallway and sloshing seawater to report to Ballantyne. The superintendent then walked back and stared outside the same porthole. He stepped back in an appraising manner, and the men also could see the once small lights—but now larger—marking part of the ship's outline. The *Alliance* was moving toward their ship. After Ballantyne looked once more through the window, he turned around and walked silently away.

He talked briefly with the captain, and both men knew that cutting the schooner from its mooring lines could make a bad problem into a deadly situation. With these forceful winds and huge waves, there was no way of predicting where the *Sparrow* would wind up, but more than likely it would wreck on either the California coast or the sharp rocks one hundred yards away. Ballantyne walked determinedly back to the crews' quarters and told the men to get up, dress warmly, and put on their rain gear and life jackets. He left an assistant below, more than likely John Olson, to be sure that everyone quickly got ready and were on the stairway that led to the deck.

After slowly opening the door with two others behind him, Ballantyne took a step onto the deck. He was nearly blown backward by a wind gust, while sprays of foam stung his face. Wiping the saltwater from his eyes, he looked at the fast-closing lights. The *Alliance* was now a hundred yards away and coming directly toward the ship. Behind him were the rocks of the reef.

He ordered the men behind to get the rest of the crew on the stairway. Once they were there, he yelled to them over the whistling winds that they needed to get on the deck in case they had to abandon the ship. Groups of men timed their movements to coincide when a swell had passed. They made their way to riggings, railings, and anything on which they could hold for dear life. The footing was slippery, the air cold, and the roar of the winds and ocean nearly deafening.

The *Alliance* had now cut the distance in half to the moored ship; Ballantyne would have to give the command to lower the lifeboats from the davits. A wrong decision would have fatal consequences. If he waited too long, the surfboats couldn't be dropped in time with the steamer bearing down on them. If the lifeboats were dropped too soon, he might lose them with some men in a raging sea with the *Alliance* still around.

Although the large ship was close enough that its outline was just visible, it was moving very slowly and more to one side. The steamer began to show more lights and appeared to be turning. It was as if someone were behind the wheel and steering the large vessel away, but that couldn't be the case, because control in this situation is nonexistent. Yet, the *Alliance* turned near broadside in front of the astonished wind-whipped, surf-washed men. The moorings were apparently holding, but the question was how long?

The vessel's lights appeared broadside, and then began to slowly disappear from the port to starboard side. After several minutes slowly went by, Ballantyne motioned for his men to go below, and he soon joined them. During the night, the steamer seemed to move back toward them, but then again circled away. Although most went back to their bunks, no one could sleep. Those on watch kept a wary eye at both the raging ocean and the out-of-control steamer.

When the darkness of night finally gave way to different shades of gray visibility, the *Alliance* was closer to the *Sparrow* than it was when first moored, but it wasn't threatening the smaller schooner. That early morning, spray flew over both ships, and the decks were deserted but for a few. Whipped by the winds, the whole ocean was wrapped in sheets of foam. The schooner still pitched, as wave crests surged over the gunnels, scattering in drenching sprays over the deck.

White surges and currents of ocean encircled the reef. The blocks set in place at the "zero" level of the foundation were covered by the swirling foam. The men watched incredulously as a stories-high swell crashed against the north side of St. George. Part of the wave cascaded entirely over the western portion, while a taller rooster-tail surged over the other. The violent seas completely covered the reef and the work completed to date.

Forced down below, men drank coffee, smoked cigarettes, or took catnaps. Later, one of the men who had first spotted the *Alliance*'s movements walked on to the deck to see what had happened. When searching where he had first seen the steamer, the workman discovered only whitecaps and gray ocean. The *Alliance* was nowhere to be seen.

The wet and shivering man raced down and told the first man he came upon about the missing vessel. He learned that the ship had steamed away for the safety of Crescent City's harbor. With conditions as they were, Ballantyne had ordered the *Alliance* to leave and return when the weather was better and men could unload the ship. The gale winds and towering waves had severed all except for one of the steamer's mooring lines. That one cable had kept the large ship from crashing into the wood schooner and throwing everyone into the ocean for a certain death. As the *Brother Jonathan* showed years before, most people that June died with their life jackets on and within a few hours from hypothermia, if the crashing waves didn't drown them first.

Owing to the unexpected typhoon, the *Alliance* nearly followed the *La Ninfa*'s performance four years before, but almost taking another ship with it. The steamer anchored in Crescent City Bay and stayed there for four days before the weather sufficiently calmed. It finally steamed back to the rock and discharged the rest of its load on June 22—one week after she had first arrived.

When the waves surged onto the reef, the powerful thrusts tore blocks from their set places, including one 3½ ton dimension stone from its place that was thirty feet above sea level. The ocean pummeled the huge block to the bench (or foundation level) above where it broke into pieces. Workers had previously set the large granite block in mortar cement for twelve hours, but driven away by the high waves, they hadn't been able to set the pinning dowels inside it.

The *Santa Maria* next carried four hundred barrels of cement to the Humboldt Bay depot and soon left with her first cargo of granite blocks and material bound for St. George. During this time, the quarrymen at Mud River also moved stone blocks onto the steamers. Some men spent time in "stripping and clearing" the quarry to allow future mining, while one stonecutter prepared dimension stones with unfinished joints, just in case damage occurred to some while in transit or on site. Ballantyne had been trying to consider every possible contingency.

During the last four months of that 1887 work season, the men at Mud River quarried 5,200 cubic feet of rubble backing; moved nearly 10,000 cubic feet of rubble to the stoneyard, including what had been excavated in previous years; and shipped 3,600 cubic feet of rubble backing and 2,300 cubic feet of dimension stone (or gran-ite block) to St. George.

Despite the bad weather experienced, when Ballantyne closed down the job site on October 3, 1887, his men had built the light-house pier to twenty-two feet high, being eight courses of stone that were eighteen feet high over the initial foundation level of four feet. The first nine levels of blocks for the elliptical caisson pier had been set with some stones at the base weighing as much as six tons. This structure would not only hold the engine room, coal room, and cis-tern, but it would be the base for the lighthouse tower. A high pier was needed so that the light would be a safe distance above the sea, as well as bringing its focal point to where the beam could be seen twenty miles away.

This progress was noteworthy, especially since Ballantyne cited the 1887 construction season for its "prevalence of strong northwest winds, the whole summer being a succession of heavy gales, making construction difficult and dangerous." Every time the seas threat-ened, workmen had to cable quickly back to the mother ship over the aerial tramway—and sometimes on a daily basis.

Needing to repair work damaged by storms, the delays from bad weather, and high ship-chartering expenses, the costs of building St. George escalated. The lack of funding certainty also increased these costs. When appropriations were approved at the last minute, preparations needed to be made "with the utmost haste and the unfortunate scarcity of vessels." This problem was compounded by the development of Southern California (even then) and its voracious appetite for lumber shipped from Northern California and the Pacific Northwest, which cut down ship availability even more. These higher costs caused the total cost of the work to "materially exceed" estimates with the questions now being by how much and whether the challenging undertaking could be completed.

CHAPTER 7

Vintage Years

With the continuation of solid funding, the 1888 construction season utilized the chartered services of the wrecker *Whitelaw* again and the steamer *Del Norte* for the project's continuing supply requirements. As the *Del Norte* wasn't immediately available, the *Whitelaw* was pressed into service until the steamer could arrive. Owing to bad headwinds and high waves, the *Del Norte* was delayed as usual in the spring passage from San Francisco.

With men, anchoring chains, rigging, tools, and lumber from Humboldt Bay to finally start building the landing and living quarters on the rock, the expedition sailed on the steamer on April 26 for the reef. Owing to the stormy seas that nearly drowned two workers and a later gale four and a half years earlier, Ballantyne still limited the work season for the five months from May to September so that his workers could avoid the more dangerous months. Being able to start operations on time in the spring, however, was not always possible due to the same storm conditions.

As with the northernmost parts of California, the weather off Point St. George was brutal and more severe than what was even experienced south of San Francisco and into Southern California.

During the winter months, the storms brought more than four times the amount of rain experienced on average by the rest of the country. Its temperatures during the construction summer months were lower than the average across the United States. In fact, the average low temperature here during summer nights was fifty degrees and even lower.

When the winds rose or fogs settled in, these factors created more wind-chill problems, especially when being six miles out at sea. Even during the summer, workers couldn't swim in the ocean for any length of time—the winds and water are that cold.

As the demolition and initial caisson work had been completed, this work season called for constructing the worker quarters and completing the massive pier. With the merciful end of the blasting and its shrapnel rains of large rocks—which would have destroyed any structures built on the reef—it was time to build those quarters. The large pier now rising also gave some protection against the bad northwest side where the storms rolled in from the ocean.

Leasing ships at $4,000 per month (nearly $1 million per year today) was an expensive part of the ever-escalating budget, and building permanent housing would save on this expense. With the men temporarily sleeping at higher levels on the reef, Ballantyne didn't need to use his aerial tramway except in the case of serious storm surges. This would free up more time for working, as the downtime in moving men off and on N.W. Seal Rock on a routine basis would be eliminated.

Although no strong storms this time stood in the expedition's way, a fog had settled over the reef when Superintendent Ballantyne and his crew anchored off the rock. These mists swayed like a gentle tide, while the waves washed gently onto the surrounding rocks. Despite this serene setting, the fog locked away the warming sun and the nearby ocean undercurrents were always treacherous.

After landing on the reef, Ballantyne and a handful of men looked through the thick, misty haze to assess what had happened since they had left. As the group cautiously took its first steps, the men heard eerie flapping and scraping sounds. Several weird shapes seemed to rise quickly out of the gloom like ghosts in a haunted house. Backing away with the silhouettes moving toward them, they heard startling loud "honks."

One of the men yelled a warning. The group scampered away and up the reef from the bounding shapes. As the loud honking continued, the men watched as a number of seals and sea lions materialized from the fog in pursuit. When one big male rushed at the men, a workman grabbed a large rock and threw it at the enraged defender. The stone bounced in front of the animal, skipped onto a flipper, and caused the sea lion to bellow.

Another man scurried around and threw several rocks—one quickly after another—at the leader that was now mere feet away. Struck on the body and face, the raging sea lion stopped and turned to one side. The remainder of the sea lions and seals froze as more stones came hurtling at them. Every man grabbed whatever could be thrown and hurled it at the group. The leader turned and flippered back into his group. As rocks, sticks, broken hammers, and other tools rained down on the small army of seals, they finally gave up and grudgingly backed away, leaving the reef once more for the workers. As before, the seals would soon leave the reef and find another, less-inhabited spot to call their home.

Walking around the construction area, Ballantyne took stock of the site. Once more, the winter storms had caused damage that needed to be repaired before construction could begin. A few heavy granite blocks at the last constructed level were now leaning at weird angles. Cables and pulleys on the lifting cranes were missing or strewn about. Small rocks, seaweed, rusting tools, and debris littered the lower portions of the reef. The thunderous waves again had forced the necessity of more work. Ballantyne gave the orders to repair the derricks as the first priority, as once the cranes were in working order, his gang could move heavy equipment, blocks, materials, and supplies quickly onto the reef.

The workers camped in tents around the slowly built pier, and the cook prepared their meals over a campfire. At the same time, everyone watched for the signs of the angry sea, when they would be forced to make a hasty exit on the aerial-cable back to the *Whitelaw*. Showers and shaving were nonexistent, and living under these conditions was still cold and foreboding. Working long hours outside and into the night is hard enough without adding cooking and camping out.

With favorable weather gracing the expedition this time, the laborers soon finished the wharf, erected the derricks and large hoisting engine, and reset the moorings. The completion of the quarters to accommodate fifty men was next, and Ballantyne assigned as many of his workers as he could to this project.

Alexander directed his crews to construct the building on the "protected" side of the lighthouse where the tower was to be constructed and to the south. Built with huge support beams, the men erected the wood outline of the massive, near-three-story wood structure against the large caisson, and the foundation for the quarters started on top of a concrete loading dock. Large V-shaped beams underpinned parts of the building that weren't constructed on solid rock. (Concrete would later be poured in large sections to fill and support this space.) The men's quarters would be windowless and sealed as tight as possible against the elements.

The men constructed the building with two-foot thick beams, anchored the foundation into rock and concrete with iron pins, and tied the structure together with large bolts. Ballantyne had the roof constructed particularly strong with internal bracing, as a nearby towering derrick would later lift and store heavy equipment, supplies, and even stone blocks on its top. Given that the building had a projected use over and above being the quarters, its design was nearly as creative as the lighthouse that was being built at the same time.

The structure was completed in mere months, and Ballantyne and his men celebrated when the task was finally complete. There was no need to take stories high, terrifying rides over the raging sea with five others in a four-foot-wide cage—ones that could plow into icy cold seas when a large wave swelled. Workmen could take turns working their shifts and have a close, protective shelter for when the dark, gray storms carried sheets of cold rain or the gales howled with stinging saltwater and suffocating ocean swells.

When the steamer *Del Norte* arrived with it first cargo of building materials and stone blocks one month after construction started, the restart of the masonry work also began. Now the *Del Norte* supplied everything needed on a continuing basis. The men were now quartered on the reef and the *Whitelaw*'s services were no longer required. The vessel steamed back to its San Francisco base.

With decent weather and workers on the reef twenty-four hours each day, seven days a week, work progressed quickly and efficiently. Fifty-two men now labored on the rock and there was no room to spare. Ballantyne had to always keep an ever-alert eye on where his men were and who was doing what.

While this beehive of activity continued, stiff-legged derricks on the rock hauled up crushing weights of stone blocks and men labored nearby setting others into place. The workmen set holding pins, worked granite blocks into place, cemented stones, and constructed floor levels. They swung the stones into position and smoothed in the masonry as fast as the derricks could swing more blocks up. As the Light-House Board's report for that period stated:

The quarries are crowded with all the men who can be worked, and the stone-cutters at the yard are dressing the rock as fast as it reaches them. The chartered steamer runs night and day as her services are required, and the workmen on the pier work on Sundays when there is any stone on hand ready for setting. The weather has thus far been very favorable and work has progressed rapidly.

At that time, Ballantyne estimated—and as the 1888 Report presented—that the total estimated cost to complete the structure would be $721,000. He told the district engineer that the building expenses were now running $30,000 each month. As the total cost at the time for the construction from the start in 1883 through June 30, 1888, was $348,000, Ballantyne's assessment, control, and feel for the project's cost would later prove to be uncannily accurate.

The busy men completed the thirteenth level of blocks and masonry for the caisson pier during the 1888 working season, which consisted of placing "five more courses of masonry with the proper backing." The end of September soon came and Ballantyne didn't want to chance any further problems with men and equipment from high seas, so he ended the season's work and made his report to the Twelfth District and, in turn, the U.S. Light-House Board. With his superiors noting the rapid pace of construction and better economic times, Congress set the appropriation for the 1889 season at a high $200,000—and, again, this amount for one year at St. George could have constructed ten "normal" land lighthouses.

THE OWNER of the steamer *Del Norte* was again the low bidder for the 1889 construction services, and Ballantyne chartered this vessel at $5,000 per month to ferry his men, supplies, and equipment. The vessel sailed from San Francisco on April 11 to Humboldt Bay, where dockworkers loaded the ship with the requisite materials and provisions and the workers boarded the vessel. Six days later, the *Del Norte* arrived off North West Seal Rock.

The men again needed to spend time in rebuilding what the

ocean storms—mild as they were—had damaged during the winter season. The surging waves and howling winds always disturbed the site, and this time during the six-month interval had badly damaged the heavy timber structure used as the workmen's quarters. The workers repaired moorings, rigged derricks, and began setting stone on the fourteenth level by April 30. Ballantyne pushed his men to repair the quarters, as well, with a force of "about fifty men, being the utmost which could be employed profitably"—any more on that small spit would have made supervision and control difficult.

The weather this season was "more severe than in 1888, but rather an improvement over 1887." The severity of these conditions not only slowed work down, but the men had to cope with their fears of high swells suddenly rearing over the reef. The wet sprays constantly dashing over the pier's top made it difficult for the masonry to set, because the showers of ocean washed the mortar away from the stone beds and cracks before it could harden.

One day in May, everyone took notice of the darkening skies, higher waves, and increasing winds; even when an occasional patch of overhead blue opened up, the angry billowing clouds quickly swallowed it. When Alexander Ballantyne felt the first splattering of cold salt spray against his cheeks from a crashing wave, he scanned the reef to see how his workers reacted. They were now somewhat used to this, and the men gave quick furtive glances at the ocean and then at Ballantyne. Seeing no reaction from the superintendent, they went back to their work. Ballantyne walked in his usual confident pace to the worker quarters, hands in his pockets, and entered the building. He strolled into the make-shift kitchen and told the cooks to prepare the evening meal a bit earlier than usual. He felt there was something about this "blow" that would come sooner and be meaner.

The winds and crashing seas began to pick up, and Alexander noticed that the last inserted rock had masonry pushed out from its

sides. He yelled at the nearby workers to remove the excess and protect the concrete seals by anchoring tarps around the cracks, then
bracing them with beams and heavy rocks. One particular wave crashed
loudly against the reef, and its dark, streaked saltwater and white
spray cascaded underneath the worker's quarters. He shouted out to
those still working, "Time to quit," and told them to relax and enjoy
their time off as this day was over. Under better conditions, the men
would have certainly worked until midnight or later.

All of the door openings were closed after Ballantyne—the last
one in—strolled inside. The light of the oil lamps illuminated the
building's stark, rough-hewed timbers, beams, and wood interiors.
After the men had eaten their meal of fried meat, beans, hard bread,
and coffee, some headed to their upstairs bunks or took out a deck
of playing cards. Others joked in small groups or talked about the
work they had completed. Lit with fiery matches, the tips of cigarettes and cigars glowed inside the shadowy confines. The stale air
from the captured burning whale-oil, cigars, and men's sweat had a
sharp smell, and the haze made it difficult to see clearly.

Ballantyne stayed at his desk to one side and talked to a few of
his confidants about the next day's work. John Olson had been
working closely with the superintendent, and his ability to translate
orders to the men brought him to the leader's side. Although John E.
Lind had just started in 1887 on the rock, his steadiness and "quick
read" abilities also brought him to Ballantyne's attention. Men could
come to Alexander and talk to him alone or with others, because
his men trusted him and his advice.

The large building thudded occasionally from the crashing surf
outside and shook from the howling winds. Despite the smells and
smoke, the flickering light from the burning lamps stayed on,
because darkness did not sit well with some. Ballantyne and his
trusted men walked among the others telling jokes, asking about
their work, and telling them that this one would soon blow over.

Alexander was the unquestioned leader of these tough, hard-bitten, grizzled laborers. These men weren't college-educated "Dandies" with trim beards, a three-piece suit, gold watch, shined shoes, and a bowler hat—but instead unwashed, sunburned, crude-speaking, at times angry immigrants, who could only find this type of excruciating, lonely, dangerous work to earn their living.

Ballantyne was like a "house mother" to his workmen, and he heard the men's arguments and insecurities. From feeling down and homesick to loneliness and fear, Alexander listened to their concerns, mediated their differences, and motivated them to keep going. This man was tough, sharp, organized, and charismatic, but with enough compassion to understand his men and have them want to work even harder on this project. He had to be this way; otherwise over years with these types of men, his body would have washed up later on the rocks.

His experiences on Tillamook had forged him with experience in dealing with the even more difficult conditions on North West Seal Rock. Ballantyne had had similar problems with the warring sea lions there. Rain, fog, wind, and wet powder delayed the drilling and blasting at Terrible Tilly, as Ballantyne had also experienced here.

His daily journals on Tillamook Rock indicated his ability to succinctly decide what was important: "Nov. 1, 1879. Very light wind from NE. I commence to build storehouse on NE side of the rock, and a level bench about 35 feet above the level of the sea; some of the men at work putting in ring-bolts."

Then: "Nov. 11. A heavy gale blew from the SSW; increased toward night, and reached its greatest fury about 12 p.m. A heavy sea washed out about 1200 pounds. I resolved not to build any quarters on the south side." What stands out is that Ballantyne and his workers had just endured a bad storm and he decides rationally where he wouldn't build a structure. He doesn't describe terror or failure.

Three weeks later, his journal read: "Dec. 2. A gale blowing from

SW; heavy rain. I caught 200 gallons of fresh water in the morning. Toward night the spray begins to break over the rock." Another strong storm rears its ugly head, and he sees this as an opportunity to catch fresh rainwater.

As to St. George Reef Lighthouse on this May night in 1889, no one could sleep or relax. The deep resonating slams of huge swells shook the entire structure from its walls to the ceiling. Seawater seeped in through roof and window cracks and then drained in rivulets of ocean that ran across the floor. As time trickled agonizingly slow into the early morning, the pounding and shaking from the outside intensified. The deep-resonating thuds of raging seas slamming against the rock kept everyone awake. A surprising silence then pervaded inside, and the walls next started to vibrate from the outside. A massive explosion of sounds suddenly surrounded the men, as one man screamed, "It's here. We'll all drown!"

The rushing sounds, vibrations, and sea spurting inside from every crack gave no doubt that a huge wave had engulfed the entire structure. The seething sounds of a great surf withdrawing from the reef sounded from all sides, followed by another strange silence. A huge roar as if locomotives were exploding past them filled the air, and a giant mass of saltwater blasted in through two side doors. Men watched in horror for split seconds as the ugly waters surged toward them. The rushing violent sea was like a five-foot tsunami, sweeping inside and washing men, bunks, bedding, clothing, and furniture in one swirling mess against the large building's far side. The ocean blew out that doorway and carried several of the workmen—some dumbfounded, others petrified—into the darkness of rocks, while the waters rushed around the reef as if a swollen, salty river had burst its banks.

The men outside held to rock handholds, and the ocean circled down in swirls to the sea. Another large wave washed in, but luckily this one didn't take any workers along in its swirling rush back. Even though the solid quarters were set against the concrete foundation and pier toward the high end of the reef, these rollers had smashed through the entire building.

Ballantyne's strong shouts that the worst was over and to get back inside became a rallying call. As men staggered back, Olson and Lind started their count. Time passed as the workers came in, one by one. They were lucky this time.

With the news that all were accounted for, the doors were shut and barricades of beds and broken wood held against them. The sounds of frantic nailing and slamming of hammers against wood quickly came, as men secured beams and lumber against the doors. A spare oil lamp was lit, and the superintendent under its flickering light continued to assure his lieutenants and men.

Ballantyne made the following note about this inundation in his journal: "The men's quarters, although strongly built, was smashed in during a gale about two o'clock one morning in May." He was impressive with his lack of fear and downplaying of events that ordinary people would find terrifying. Although some decided that "enough's enough" and didn't return the next year, most did—if their body wasn't too beaten up.

Eight years before when building Tillamook Rock, Ballantyne had experienced a "terrific tornado" in early January 1880 that caused the winds and waves to rise mightily. Although the storms drenched his workmen through their rain gear and soaked them to their skins, they continued working until they couldn't keep their footing in the face of that southwest gale. Ballantyne finally gave the order to stop working, and the men retreated back to their wood-and-canvas shack. He then ordered more ring bolts hammered into the rock with additional ropes lashed around the shed.

While the men were in their bunks, the storm began reaching its "terrible heights" on January 6. Ballantyne's log read:

Jan. 6. Storm becoming more violent; men called from work to lash everything securely. At 6 p.m. the storm had increased to a hurricane, and spray and pieces of rock are thrown over the top of the rock. At 12 p.m., the hurricane has become more violent and heavy spray and large pieces of rock are thrown over top of the rock. I call up men to brace roof of quarter with drills, etc.

Jan. 7 at 2 a.m., the hurricane has reached its height; a heavy sea broke over the rock; our quarters withstood it, but the roof of the blacksmith shop was destroyed; darkness too intense to see storehouse. At 4 a.m. I attempted to descend to storehouse to see what damage had been done, but found it impossible to retain my hold. At daybreak, we found that the storehouse had been destroyed, and nearly all the provisions, the water tank, two spars, and a traveler-line were all washed off. The government stores, ropes, blocks, etc. were saved.

His notations again understated what had happened, as most of his written observations did. One of the men said later that Ballantyne's courageous leadership was the saving grace because his coolness had averted a panic. Frightened by the shrieking winds, ocean spray, and rocks raining against their tent, the workers milled around him, as they readied to run from the structure. Fearful that the tent wouldn't withstand the winds and rocks, the mob of men decided to make a run for the better-built, supply house—even though it was at the lower thirty-foot level.

Ballantyne coolly, but firmly, told his men to stay put during the ferocious storm. He calmed his workers and kept them inside, knowing that their canvas tent was secured to the rock and its location higher than the storeroom. The following morning, they discovered that anyone who had ventured out to that storeroom—later totally destroyed—would have drowned. This experience led him to construct a stronger building at St. George, which protected the men in a similar typhoon, but on a rock that was one-half Tillamook's height and without its mass.

The towering waves crested at other times onto Seal Rock, necessitating continuing, extensive repairs. Although "very strongly constructed and braced almost like a ship," the heavy seas washed over and damaged the structure several times, although fortunately no one was seriously injured during those times. The constant exploding surf also caused problems with the masonry. Even though the pier walls continued to rise stories above sea level, the spray from large waves crashed over the structure's top level, making it impossible for hours on end before more concrete masonry could be applied and blocks set into place. As the 1889 Light-House Board Report stated:

> The walls are now sixty-one feet above sea level and yet the spray dashes over the top of the pier to such an extent that it is frequently impossible, for hours at a time, to lay masonry, as the spray would wash the cement mortar off the beds before the stones could be set. It is hoped that next season's work will complete the station.

By October, the around-the-clock work had nearly completed the caisson with its hundreds of interlocking huge granite blocks. The walls of the carnivorous boiler room, coal room, and storerooms inside the caisson were constructed and arched over, including cementing in place most of the stone flagging for the pier's flat top. Superintendent Ballantyne's men secured planks over the opening to make the roof weather tight.

This engineering marvel resulted in a massive five-story pier built around a strong knob of the reef. Although the walls were high, the amount of space inside wasn't, as part of the reef was cemented inside the pier to anchor the lighthouse against the horrid storms.

The men constructed a concrete boat landing with a derrick at the base of the caisson, along with their living quarters. An iron stairway led up the side of the base to its one large entrance door close to its top. This door opened into what would be the engine room with its furnaces and generators, including the equipment necessary to power the steam-driven fog horns. The fog whistles would protrude from the caisson top or catch deck, and this huge base also contained a large supply room stocked with provisions, equipment, and tools.

When finally complete, this oval pier of stone and concrete was near fifty feet high and ninety feet in diameter. Each outside level of the pier was some $2^1/_2$ feet high with one-foot-thick stone flagging laid on the caisson's top. Workers cut a drop of three inches into the stone on the catch deck from the center to the gutters on the outer rim, and this acted as a watershed from which rainwater drained through a four-inch pipe to the cistern at the pier's base.

Because the pyramid-type leveling had an outside and an inside wall, Ballantyne had the excavated square rubble stones placed behind the caisson's interior walls against the stonework. Filling the space between the foundation blocks inserted into the rock and the inside walls of the interior rooms, this design brought about a solid pier. The outside cylindrical granite blocks set the exteriors of these rooms. At the same time, the workers used concrete to build the pier's roof arches and supports underneath the tower floors.

The caisson's first floor contained the engine room, storage, and a stairwell that led to the second floor, all built over the cistern with its capacity to hold 77,000 gallons of water. This first floor was located toward the top of the caisson, and the pier's sides wrapped around the rock pinnacle—blasted into a square top with stepped terraces down, on which the heavy pier stones had been laid.

Constructed in spurts over a seven-year period, the workmen built the caisson with 1,339 granite blocks, and some of the blocks weighed six tons. They fit the blocks together with no more than the required ³/16-inch gap and set the squared blocks in place with metal dowels, cement, and small stones shoved into the crevices. Due to Ballantyne's procedures, none of the huge finished blocks were chipped, and when the last stone was slipped into place, the joints on each side of that block were ³/16 inch thick.

As the pier was now "very substantially" completed, Ballantyne instructed his workers to erect planking to securely cover the pier and protect it from the elements. On top of this huge concrete pier, the plans called for constructing a seven-story lighthouse tower, which with the lantern and lens room on top, its light would shine 146 feet above MHW (mean high water). The pier and lighthouse tower would be one structure, and this massive monument would be the tallest lighthouse on the U.S. West Coast.

However, this work would have to wait until the next season. The men for the first time could safely store their heavy equipment, lumber, concrete, and supplies inside the caisson. Afterward, Alexander Ballantyne and his workmen closed down the site, boarded the steamer, and sailed back to San Francisco. Another work season had ended, and once more the rock was silent, but for the barks of the seals, cries of the seagulls, and crashing surf.

CHAPTER 8

The Medieval Tower

Although "severe rainstorms" had again set back the quarrying schedule, a determined effort had finally dug and roughed out all of the stone needed to complete the lighthouse tower. The stonework was sent to the yard to be shaped and polished, and this work continued at Paysonville during the last construction year. When the last of the stonework was complete by the end of June 1890, all of the workmen were discharged. The quarry and finishing site was abandoned, and a watchman placed in charge of the yard.

No additional work on N.W. Seal Rock was started in 1890, however, as the agreed appropriations weren't made in enough time. Because the final appropriation came in September 1890, no work could be started for that season. In essence, these moneys went for the next fiscal year. The amount allocated was $81,000, which sum set the total funding at $721,000 for constructing the lighthouse and as per Ballantyne's much earlier estimate. During the downtime, the district engineer's office prepared the specifications for the ironwork for the interior staircase, railings, and fittings. Ballantyne was preoccupied during this time to ensure that he could finish the project for this amount in his last year of funded operations. This was also the intent of that "pick-up" final appropriation.

Early that following year, bids were received for the supply steamer's services. The owner of the steam-schooner *Sunol* offered the lowest contract price to ferry and supply what was needed at the rate of $4,000 per month. Captain Robert Waldvig, formerly the captain of the *Del Norte*, skippered the steamer.

The vessel left San Francisco on April 10, 1891, and arrived in Humboldt Bay one day later on what Ballantyne wrote was an "uneventful journey." The steamer left one week later with a cargo of moorings, derricks, lumber, rope, tackle, and equipment. The ship also carried sand, stone, cement, fresh water, and the full complement of fifty workers. Although normally a one-day trip, owing to "very bad weather" this one took four days as the *Sunol* waited in Humboldt Bay due to heavy seas at the entrance bar, and then ran into more bad conditions once in the ocean. The steamer finally moored by Seal Rock in the evening.

Landing on the reef in darkness, the men walked gingerly up to the monstrous caisson that towered over them, moisture dripping down from its sides. Their oil lamps cast shadowy lights on the walls of the living quarters built two years before. As Ballantyne and his group climbed onto the cement foundation of the structure, they saw that parts of it sagged in the middle. Holes large enough for a man to walk through now spotted the first and second stories. Several of the large structural timbers had cracked and inside walls collapsed. Large rocks lay scattered inside and around the building.

For over two years, storms had crashed over the structure and hurled huge stones into it. Seaweed, debris, pebbles, rocks, and an occasional angry sea lion lay around the pier and wood quarters. Again, they would have to repair what the ocean wouldn't allow. Ballantyne's report stated succinctly: "The workmen's quarters were found to have been utterly destroyed by the waves and had to be rebuilt."

Despite what had been left anchored in place before, no mooring buoys for the ships were in sight. The crew later recovered two of them by dragging grappling hooks from the *Sunol*'s stern. They repaired the ones found and replaced the two mooring that had been lost.

After working on the mother ship's anchors and buoys, Ballantyne's men again had to scurry around the rock like so many ants to repair the damage inflicted by the huge waves since their last operation. Working around the clock day-in, day-out, the workmen lived around their quarters during the rebuilding. The weather during this April and the early part of May was noticeably rainy over other seasons, "with strong southerly winds and heavy seas most of the time."

Some workers lived inside tents on the boat-landing side of the reef, a difficult incline, rocky and hard. Others slept inside the part of the living quarters that hadn't sustained structural damage. The interior of the caisson provided additional shelter. When the clouds didn't pour out rain, the cooks prepared meals over fires and shuttled in provisions over the aerial tramway. However, the torrential rains made working, living, and sleeping difficult, not to mention the winds. The gales blew so violently that these conditions prevented the *Sunol* from even approaching at times to land what was needed. When able to move toward the wharf, the boat rocked violently back and forth, whether trying to offload its material to a smaller lighter or even by derrick.

One day, the winds blasted in from the north, and the waves cracked against the reef. The encroachment was high enough to where the workers soon left for the safety of the *Sunol*. The winds suddenly gusted to gale force, and the workers turned at the sounds of a high-pitched cry from one of the men. They watched in awe as two of their workers sailed off the pier wall into its insides. The wind had blasted them from the outer walls. These workers weren't seriously injured, but they sustained numerous, painful bruises and cuts.

Ballantyne was a leader as well as an excellent taskmaster. When the weather was the worst, he was out there with his men lending a hand. When the surf was most menacing, he was one of the last to leave. Everyone worked with his purpose in mind: complete the project. By May 1 they were able to reconstruct their living quarters and rig the big derrick used to haul the heavy stones onto the pier. They also began to replace and set more stone flagging on the pier's top.

When the weather changed for the good, the progress of the work sped up. From mid-May to October, the weather turned out to be "very mild and favorable for working." The workers built a blacksmith shop on the caisson deck's top. This wooden high-pitched structure sheltered the blacksmith, his crew, fires, and anvils used to repair hammers, tools, and machinery. The men would build there the wrought-iron railings, fittings, and metalwork. With its high stack pouring out smoke, operating derrick, and noisy pulleys, the shop was another beehive of activity.

On May 13, the men set the first stone for the lighthouse. The crews worked at a variety of tasks, from applying the mortar and operating the steam derrick in hauling up the stone blocks to setting them in place and cleaning up the debris. Others were building scaffolding, repairing tools, cooking, cleaning, chipping, and hauling. The sounds of cracking hammers, sawing wood, slamming stones, sputtering steam engines, yelling men, and surging sea filled the air around the caisson and the reef.

Tragedy struck, however, later in June. A rigger was holding on to the tag line to the big derrick's boom, or the rope designed to prevent dangerous swings or spins of supplies. Although the weather wasn't stormy or raining, the winds had picked up. The steam engine was clanking, the surf fairly quiet, and the workers were going busily about their tasks.

A strong gust of wind came and swung the netted materials away from the attending man. He was thinking about some other matter, as most did when they were doing an easy task, such as holding on to a guide line. Not paying attention to what was happening, the worker was unaware of the consequences, when the net swung away and the rope tightened in his hand.

The man stood unconcerned at the pier's top, while the line pulled taut and swung away. He didn't let go of the rope. The tightened line jerked him off balance, and the worker lost his footing on the edge of the caisson wall. He fell to his death, smashing into the rocks below. This unfortunate lesson drove home the point that despite the safeguards and record to date, death or serious injury could happen in the blink of an eye, no matter what someone was doing.

By the end of June, the base of the tower was complete. The workers had built its interior brick lining to thirty feet above the beginning level, nearly to the window sills off the third story. Day and night, ships shuttled in stonework, as men worked around the clock with the derricks to offload, move, position, and set the tower's stonework. There was no room for men to do anything except stay at their position and continually do their job. Laborers ate and slept in shifts, as everyone focused on the task at hand: finish the tower. Given the dry, but foggy weather that they now were blessed with, every hour counted and Ballantyne's men knew it.

Covering the period from July 1, 1891, to June 30, 1892, the Light-House Board's Annual Report for 1892 stated:

> The length of time fog prevailed throughout this entire district from August to December, 1891, is without precedent. The season was unusually mild, with little or none of the strong trade winds, which usually blows every day from noon till sunset during the summer months. Hence, the fogs hung along the coast line with a peculiar tenacity.

As the tower rose, the station appeared to be a medieval fortress under construction with its derricks, scaffolding, elevator tower, and structures rising above the caisson. Scaffolding with hatch-marked timber supports soared stories high, and men milled about at every level as they set stone blocks with mortar. A square tower of wood reached upward by the worker's quarters. With pulleys housed inside

and steam-driven winches below, this became the elevator for hauling up the stone and cement to where the men worked. When the
tower's top floor and lantern room above were built, this structure
towered over them and the ocean.

When the hardworking men finally had set the last stone in
place on August 23, 1891, thus completing the tower structure, they
had finished the entire stone frame with its brick lining for the
seven-story tower in little over three months. Their efforts continued
in erecting the cast-iron lantern and lens rooms that were on top of
the stone tower. Ballantyne's men spent the next two months in September and October removing the scaffolding around the tower,
erecting railings and ironwork, completing the concrete arches inside
the tower, laying concrete floors, and building the structure on the
pier top that would house the donkey engine. They finished the
lantern and lens room facilities.

The men completed the lighthouse's interior with livable quarters, including kitchen, bunks, workstations, storage facilities, and
communication facilities. They plastered rooms inside the tower,
painted, varnished, and installed the fixtures. Workers constructed the
twelve-inch-diameter, steam-powered fog whistles on the top of
the seven-story caisson, and the deck was finished so it could function
as a small catch basin to collect rainwater for the cistern. Inside the
mammoth engine room deep within the bowels of the caisson, the
coal-burning furnaces and steam boilers were installed, connected,
and tested.

There is no accurate account of the number of men working on
the reef at this time, but it was well in excess of fifty. What was done
in these short months was a record. But for the one unfortunate
fatality, the men in meeting the challenge to finish the tower in that
year had incurred cuts, bruises, burns, and broken bones, including
serious injury where they were shipped to the mainland for medical
care. However, no one else had died during this time.

Stored in huge interior caverns, coal fueled the furnaces for years, replaced later by fuel oil. This equipment provided the steam to operate the fog signal; in later years, they produced electricity for the lighthouse and its lantern. At first, an oil lamp inside the Fresnel lens produced the light, and a large glass chimney carried the smoke up and through a ball-shaped opening in the lantern-house roof. Heavy weights dropped through deep channels down the tower, which rotated the lens in creating the flashing light. Later, lamps and equipment powered by electricity lit up the horizon.

To finish the construction work with such a Herculean effort, Ballantyne and his workmen labored to October 29—further into the bad storm season than ever before. Then the weather shifted against them and this storm was immense. Instead of having to race for the aerial tramway, the workers now could seek safety inside the lighthouse. This time, however, the winds howled and the surf rose as they never had seen before.

The men watched from the rock as huge waves rose toward them. The horrid surges "shook the rock and its tower to its very base." By now the crews had enough of these dangers from the sea, especially as they watched the savage ocean rise stories above where they once worked. With flat rocks and stubble filling the caisson's walls to the cut rock—but for the cistern and upper levels for the engine room—the station was "one with the rock." The lighthouse stood up to the pounding.

The gale stormed over the station for one week before it subsided sufficiently for the men to leave. As the superintendent reported concisely:

All work was finished by the end of October, but we were unable to get the men from the rock until November 8, owing to the heavy seas. This completed the work with the exception of the lens, which had not arrived from Europe.

Ballantyne appointed three of the workmen to stay on as keepers, including John Olson, and all of the tools and rigging were put
aboard the steamer. All of the moorings were lifted, the men boarded,
and the steamer sailed back to San Francisco. The tools and equipment were stored in Yerba Buena Island again, and "the men and
steamer discharged November 18, 1891."

Even though the lens wasn't installed, the loud foghorns began
wailing on December 1, 1891, and it was crucial for them to be operational. The five-month period from August to December 1891 was
without precedence, as due to the lack of winds, the fog hung along
the coastline with the described "peculiar tenacity." Every fog signal
in the Twelfth District operated greater numbers of hours than
during the previous year—and these sound warnings were important.

Paysonville was left idle. (It stayed that way for decades, but was
activated during World War II as a seaplane base.) The workers took
their paychecks and disappeared. Both on land and at the reef, the
construction activities were quiet, but the whistle foghorn now
shrilled its piercing warnings.

ALTHOUGH THE CONSTRUCTION WORK was finished, another year
passed before the "first-order" lens arrived from France. The lenses
were handmade and shipped unassembled no matter where destined. This intricate system involved projecting light from one source
through a numbers of lenses that were set at the focal point of the
light. The design caused all of the light rays that were emitted to
bend parallel to the horizon, thus sending much more light out
to sea.

Concentric rings of glass prisms were lined above and below a
center-drum section that bent the light in the center into a narrow
beam. The prisms above bent the light down, while those below
bent the light up, and all converged into a solid prism of light that
flashed out concentrically. This bull's-eye design was shaped like a

magnifying glass and produced a more powerful concentrated beam. While an open flame lost nearly 97 percent of its light and a flame with reflectors lost 83 percent, the Fresnel lens retained all but 17 percent of its light. Due to this outstanding efficiency, the light from a Fresnel lens shone brightly twenty miles or more out to the horizon.

Early Fresnel lenses used an oil lantern that burned constantly from dusk until dawn with no flashing or blinking. As more light-houses came into existence, the need to clearly identify each one also came about, and this problem was solved by creating a specific pattern of flashes per minute for each station, which became known as a lighthouse's "characteristic."

A lighthouse's lights were white, red, green, or a combination of the three colors. As the lens revolved, the light sent off a specific pattern of flashes and colors distinct for each lighthouse. When a mariner saw a particular light characteristic, he then knew exactly the point of land his ship was passing.

The Fresnel lenses were divided into different classes or "orders" based upon the distance of the flame to the lens. The "first order" Fresnel lens was the largest lens constructed, and it was made up of hundreds of glass prisms. The lenses decreased in size through a second-order, third-order, fourth-order, and on down. The light intensity and range decreased as the lens size decreased. For example, the first-order lens was nearly eight feet high and six feet in diameter, while the third-order lens was some three feet high and $2^1/2$ feet in diameter. The sixth-order lens was $1^1/2$ feet high and one foot in diameter. Given its location out at sea, the lens chosen for this light-house was the largest one that was available.

The Fresnel lens destined for St. George arrived in San Francisco in July 1892 by ship from France around Cape Horn, and a tender transported it that August to the station where the first-order lens was assembled and installed. It contained hundreds of hand-cut prisms and bull's-eyes. The lens had twelve sides, each with a bull's-eye lens. When including the height of its supporting pedestal below and the housing at top, the light rose sixteen feet high with its six-foot diameter. This was an impressive sight, and its cost alone was $15,000—or about the expense to build a much smaller land light-house with a sixth-order lens.

Although the light was not destined to be operational until mid-October 1892, Ballantyne had learned from Tillamook about the extra precautions for shipping that were needed to be taken before a light became operational. While his crew was constructing Tillamook Light, Ballantyne on several occasions ordered his men to toss "cartridges of exploding powder" into the sea to warn ships to stay away from the rocks. When constructing St. George, he posted one man every twenty-four hours with the sole responsibility to watch out for shipping.

At Tillamook, Ballantyne wrote into his log diary:

April 29, 1880. Dense fog in the morning. A steamer was heard to whistle very close to south of rock. A small blast was fired to signal her off, and she stood to northward. At eight o'clock she seemed to be close inshore, and a giant powder cartridge was thrown over [exploded], after which she stood out.

By January 2, 1881, Tillamook was nearly complete, but the light wasn't ready to be turned on. District Engineer and Superintendent Wheeler was on the rock, as the time was close for the light to be lit. During the late afternoon that day, another storm blew in and by nightfall a strong wind was blowing from the south. A few hours after darkness, Wheeler and others thought they heard loud voices and the creaking of a ship's rigging.

When other men agreed that a vessel of some sort must be off the reef, Wheeler ordered a large bonfire to be built—which in that stormy darkness could have only broken the darkness for a few hundred feet at best. Another worker claimed that he heard a dog barking. The men made out the barest outline of a large sailing ship off the horizon, about an eighth of a mile away. As the ship sailed easterly, her lights were barely seen. The vessel then seemed to turn away and disappeared into the darkness.

The men wondered about that strange vessel during the night. When daylight came, they had their answer. Across the bay on the Tillamook Headlands lay the remains of a large ship that had splintered against the rocky cliff. This was the wreck of the 1,300-ton British bark, *Lupatia*, from Hiogo, Japan, and bound for the Columbia River. The ship had missed Tillamook Rock, but instead it had crashed directly onto the rocky shore. The captain became confused and took his course in the fog and darkness with no landmarks to guide him. All sixteen crewmembers died and only the ship's dog survived. The wreck of the *Lupatia* dampened the spirits of the men and any forthcoming elaborate lighting ceremonies.

The workers felt that they were partially to blame anyway. One said:

If we had only believed our ears. Shouted! Made some kind of noise! Exploded a stick or two of dynamite! We might have warned them off. It was tough, looking at that dead ship day after day and realizing that we perhaps could have saved it. From that hour on, finishing the tower to get the light lit and the fog horn going was more than just a job.

Three weeks later on January 21, 1881, the first-order Fresnel lens at Tillamook beamed out over the ocean for the first time. Ballantyne remembered this when he posted three men to watch over St. George and work the foghorn, even though its light hadn't yet been installed.

WHEN ST. GEORGE REEF LIGHTHOUSE was finally lit on October 20, 1892, its characteristic light flashed alternately red and white with fifteen-second intervals between flashes and was visible for eighteen miles. The light illuminated the entire horizon, according to some, and the *Del Norte Record* reported that "It can be seen from Lover's Rock or Pebble Beach (to the south of the city), and no doubt if the weather is fine, many will take the trip up the coast to see it." As described then, the "gray stone, square pyramidal tower on a pier" dominated the seascape.

When fog rolled in and diminished the light, the fog whistle screamed away. The whistle was easily heard on land, including south of Crescent City. Each thirty-second cycle of the foghorn had a first blast that lasted two seconds, a silence for three, and then followed by a second blast of two seconds, with an ensuing silence for twenty-three seconds. Originally powered by coal-fueled steam engines, over time the energy source turned to oil and then diesel-fuel-powered generators. (In 1931, the signal changed to an air siren, and, five years later, to a diaphone horn powered by compressed air.)

In 1892, the hoisting engine for lifting supplies broke down. Since the engine had been used extensively and hard during the long construction period, its condition and old age meant that a complete new system needed to replace it. A double-drum engine and boiler was installed in its place on the pier's top, and a small structure built over the equipment to protect the machinery from the savage winds and sea. In September, the foghorn was temporarily discontinued when water needed to build up steam ran out, but by the end of the month, more rainfall meant a replenished supply, and the signal was again back in operation.

The exact cost to construct St. George Lighthouse before installing the Fresnel lens was $704,633. The construction period took over ten years and made this project the most expensive and dangerous lighthouse built in the United States. Once the lens was purchased and installed along the new double-drum engine and boiler, the total expense to construct the station came to $752,000, or more than double the initial estimate.

From the time the land was first reserved, seven U.S. presidents and their administrations were involved. The lighthouse is a fifteen-story structure from its caisson "zero" level to its lens ball-roof, and its focal plane (the light's height above the water) shines 146 feet above mean high water. The tower is square with a slight taper toward the top and a spiral staircase is encased inside. A metal hoist derrick with a boom rises with the tower and is connected to it. Extending from the pier's base on the southeast side is a concrete boat landing, and a metal stairway descends to the landing from a door high up on the pier.

The caisson's first-floor level holds a huge engine room, storage facilities, and a stairwell to the second floor, all built over the enormous cistern. This inside area is located toward the top of the caisson, as the pier's sides wrapped around the rock pinnacle, and also holds huge openings for the furnaces and fuel storage. A large skylight was cut into the caisson deck with stories-high cast-iron pillars and steel beams built to support the deck structure. The metal staircase from the boat dock led up the outside walls to large doors that opened into the engine room.

The boiler and now laundry room was on the second level, at the tower base, with the huge caisson acting as the foundation. The third floor in the tower contained the galley, while the sleeping and living quarters were built on the fourth and fifth levels. A later radio room and beds for land-based workmen were constructed on what's called the sixth level, while the lantern room was on the seventh level and led to the lens.

Rough stone laid in courses of graduated sizes comprise the tower. A cylindrical glass and metal cage with a ball-vent and conical metal roof housed the first-order Fresnel lens at the lighthouse's very top. Stone corbels support a projecting cornice below, and protecting railings sweep around its observation deck and the lens room.

Brick held by a layer of mortar line the tower's insides, and the floors of the keeper's quarters were made of seasoned Humboldt pine. Three coats of sand-finished plaster were used in finishing the walls. Port Orford cedar with redwood paneling comprised the inside doors and wainscoting, while other trim was made of redwood. The outside doors and windows were constructed of oak. A single, large window is at the tower base, while double windows are on the third through fifth levels at the north and south tower sides; triple window openings are on the sixth level; single windows line the floors of the stair tower, which juts out in a semicircle from the main, square tower.

Even today, the craftmanship is imposing. The stone and brick walls were recessed inward from the window casements, and the durability and exquisiteness of the "pointing" or mortar joints between stone blocks still stand out. Ballantyne used a "special" mixture so unique that modern experts have difficulty determining its composition. The circular stone stairwell and steps look as if computerized laser beams precisely cut them for their fit, and the brickwork lining with its pointing is as unique. The lighthouse looks like a fortress, because it was built that way: the stonecutting techniques, tools used, and workmanship were taken from those olden times. The station has different "looks" owing to the craftmanship and approach used for the caisson, outside tower, and inside stairwell. The workers even constructed a complete entrance room to the tower—with roof and corners—in stone blocks that still fit together perfectly.

The St. George and Tillamook Rock Lighthouses are the two wave-swept stations built on the Pacific Coast, with very few of this type existing in the country. The square stone tower with its semicircular stairwell on St. George is also considered by experts to be an unusual design. Its $750,000-plus total cost of construction was an incredible amount of money then for a nineteenth-century lighthouse. This sum was double that of the Minot's Ledge Lighthouse in Massachusetts and almost five times as much as the one built on Tillamook Rock.

The construction used more than 175,260 cubic feet of granite, 14,307 tons of stone, 1,439 tons of sand, 335 tons of brick, and 272 tons of gravel, all of which ships had to transport to the reef and haul onto the site in some of the worst weather imaginable. The construction cost ended up $100,000 more than what it took to build the base and erect the Statue of Liberty that was in construction at the same time.

Nearly one-half the cost of building this lighthouse was in the labor expenses on the rock, stoneyard, and stone quarry. Another one-fifth was in "transportation," or the cost of chartering the steamers that plied back and forth in getting materials and men to the rock and housing them. Ten percent was in the cost of building materials and equipment, while another ten percent was due to the cost of building the moorings and their constant replacement.

To construct the same structure under today's conditions—if one could obtain the numerous government permits, settle the litigation, and obtain the necessary approved environmental reports—would be in the hundreds of millions of dollars and could approach one billion. To gain an idea of how costs multiplied over the years, a factory worker earning $1 a day in the 1880s would be earning today at least $200 per day (with benefits). A $1,000 automobile in 1939 would cost upward of $35,000 now.

TWO DISTRICT ENGINEERS oversaw the building of this lighthouse: Captain A. H. Payson from 1883 to 1887, and Major W. H. Heuer from 1888 on. Ballantyne succeeded Payson as the titular superintendent of construction in 1887 and remained in that capacity until 1892. When the construction was complete and awaiting only the Fresnel lens installation, Alexander Ballantyne tendered his resignation that June to the Light-House Board. Three weeks later, the captain of engineers for the Board in Washington, D.C., accepted his resignation and wrote:

The Board also desires that in accepting Mr. Ballantyne's resignation, you [Major W. H. Heuer, the Army Corps Engineer
for the Twelfth District in San Francisco] express to him, on
behalf of the Board, its appreciation of his services during
the construction of this station [St. George], and of the
exceedingly satisfactory way in which he carried out his share
of the work.

Months later in January 1893, the captain of engineers sent a
letter directly to Ballantyne confirming that he was now employed as
a superintendent of construction with the Light-House Board at
$200 per month ($2,400 annually), or well in excess of $100,000
per year now. This was a definite promotion, as Alexander joined
two other men—one in New York City and the other in Washington,
D.C.—as regional superintendents with Ballantyne based in San
Francisco. He was "detailed for duty wherever his services are
required," in essence becoming the West Coast roaming lighthouse
construction consultant. He reported to Major Heuer in this regard.

Having taken over from Captain Payson as district engineer,
William H. Heuer was born in Missouri in 1843, a West Point grad-
uate, and in the early 1880s became the engineer for the Seventh
and Eighth Coastal Districts (Florida and the Gulf Coast). He accepted
a transfer to the Twelfth District in 1887, worked on St. George with
Ballantyne, and continued in that capacity until the mid-1890s. He
then transferred away, but came back to San Francisco in 1897 in
charge of the "fortifications and other government work." He reached
the grade of colonel of engineers in 1904 and retired three years
later. Twelve years after his "retirement," Colonel Heuer was in charge
of the Twelfth District's rivers and harbors. Heuer was a lifelong
bachelor, and his life was quite different from that of Captain Payson,
who married well and turned down reassignments so that he could
center there on his social and political life.

Meanwhile, Alexander Ballantyne continued with his special project consulting for the Light-House Board. Five years later in 1897, he transferred back to the Twelfth District as its "Superintendent of Construction," where he continued for several years. In 1903, Alexander Ballantyne was listed as the new "District Engineer" and many workers followed his position with titles such as mason, brick mason, bricklayer, foreman carpenter, carpenter, painter, and on. Given the sizable construction and renovation of lighthouses then under way on the West Coast, he was the second-in-command of a very large organization.

His projects ranged the coastline. For example, Ballantyne in 1903 journeyed south to Los Angeles as part of a specially selected party to appraise a tract of land at Point Dume that was north of the city. The federal government had brought condemnation proceedings against the owner to secure enough acreage at Point Dume to build a lighthouse. Under special authority of the U.S. Attorney General, a federal district attorney had then appointed these members to the appraising committee.

Alexander Ballantyne continued working for the Twelfth District for a few more years before retiring. He had worked in supervisory capacities in building lighthouses on the U.S. West Coast for more than a quarter century. Owing to his oversight and courage, only one man lost his life in the construction of both Tillamook and the great, dangerous lighthouse at St. George.

As expected, this station was one of the least sought-after assignments in the service. Potential wickies had already heard what duty would be like on Dragon Rocks. It had earned its reputation.

PART III

SURVIVING THE ROCK

CHAPTER 9

The First Wickies

The Commissioner of Lighthouses believed that only St. George Reef and Tillamook Rock were so difficult to operate that they required a crew of five lighthouse keepers. Four wickies were on duty with one keeper ashore on leave and available to replace an injured man. Owing to the hazards of this duty, families were not allowed to live on site, and a keeper's family (if a wickie had one) lived on St. George Point or in nearby Crescent City. The only way to land on or leave St. George Lighthouse was by a derrick and its sixty-foot-long boom. With a hook, lighthouse personnel hoisted the small lighters (supply launches) onto the rock. The sea could be rising or falling as much as fifteen feet during this operation—or a sneaker wave could rise and jeopardize the transfer. Gales could suddenly storm in and isolate the rock from land so that men couldn't be brought off, and food, supplies, and water could be exhausted. Before motorized launches, keepers had to sail or row through those treacherous waters. The uniform assessment from the very beginning was that duty on this rock was "one of hardship."

When St. George's lamp was finally lit in October 1892, most of the lighthouse staff—including head keeper John Olson and assistant keeper John E. Lind—had been part of the work crew that built the station. Olson started his lighthouse duty on November 1, 1891, with two other construction workers, when Ballantyne and his men sailed off after completing the structure. Due to delays in receiving the huge but magnificent first-class Fresnel lens, the station blasted out only its fog whistle for nearly one year until the lens was installed.

By staying on, John Olson became the first appointed head keeper at St. George. For those cold months and stormy winter weather, he and his crew kept a careful watch for approaching ships, maintained the foghorns, repaired problems, and acted as the caretakers. Once the station's lens was operational, their duties became more complex. The crew needed to keep the windows and lamp room free from the salt spray and smoke from the oil lamp that created the light that the Fresnel lens amplified. With its delicate system of large counterweights and bearings, the machinery that revolved the light needed to be kept in good order. The complex-for-the-time arrangement of furnaces, steam generators, and fog siren had to be continually maintained so that these important warning sounds always pierced the thick fogs. As always, windstorms and bad weather roared in. The *Del Norte Record* in Crescent City reported:

> John Olson, Chief Lighthouse Keeper at the North West Seal Rock, came down from there in a twelve-foot boat belonging to the station. A *Record* reporter who interviewed him learned that during the heavy storm of the last week in December [1893], the ocean as seen from the lighthouse was a magnificent sight. The waves were running high, with the sea white with foam, and as they struck the rock, the spray would come flying over the roof of the building in sheets. [This would have been the shed on the pier's catch deck.]

The uniform assessment was that this rock's tough duty "tries and proves a man." These wickies considered any other station duty on land to be "sissy" duty as they involved less risk and hardships.

As bottled water had not yet been invented, nor pumping fresh water into stainless steel storage vats, the men drank the contaminated rain runoff from the catch deck when the kegs of water couldn't be delivered. When long storms hit, fresh food could become nonexistent. Owing to the limited water supply, the weekly bath or shower could just as easily disappear. Refrigerators, televisions, radios, electric toasters, and other modern conveniences didn't exist. Men washed their clothes—when they did—by hand in vats or in the sea. Medical help was limited to the kits and rough instruments around or when a launch ventured out. When tools or equipment broke down, the men forged what was needed in the blacksmith shop. Their duties were continual and lasted for three to six months in the first years without a break.

Their responsibilities were generally the same as with all lighthouses of this period. Pursuant to the regulations, at daybreak a wickie walked up the stories of spiral staircase to the lighthouse room. After inspecting the light, lens, and equipment for possible repairs, he stopped the descending motor weights of the clockwork, wound up the cable, and disengaged the gear wheel that allowed the weights to run down. The keeper extinguished the light, wiped down the chimney, removed the lamp from the Fresnel lens, and placed it on a service stand. The keeper then dusted everything with a feather duster, wiped the lens and lamp inside and out with a soft linen cloth, and then washed off any parts spotted with oil with a little "spirits of wine" (alcohol). As part of this cleaning, he passed a small bottle brush through the interior air tube that circulated the oil to the light. If required, the wickie cleaned the lens with whiting (pulverized chalk) or polishing rouge.

Needing to keep the apparatus completely dust-free, the keeper wiped down the pedestal and lantern-wall interior, then swept the staircase and closed the curtains around the lamp room to protect it from the hot sun. Finally, he draped the protective covering, if one was available, over the Fresnel lens.

Once all of this was done, the wickie took the oil lamp away and weighed it to calculate the amount of oil consumed during the night, which he then duly noted in the log. The keeper placed any unused oil into a container reserved for the "leavings." Once the lamp was cleaned, the keeper trimmed or replaced the wick, set it inside the fuel apparatus, and readied it for the upcoming night. With the lamp ready to go, a spare lamp was placed nearby for replacement if problems arose.

Following the daybreak routine was critical, as the worst failure of any keeper was for the lamp to not be ready for lighting or go out for some reason during the night. In England, such a failure pursuant to its rules was immediate dismissal and automatic forfeiture of any pension earned to date. In the United States, the failure was also cause for termination. These penalties and knowing that the lives of mariners depended on the warning light was why keepers went to such extraordinary lengths during horrible storms to "keep the light."

An hour before sunset, the keeper walked again up the long staircase and started the process to start the warning light. Given everything being in order, the wickie removed the curtains, folded them, and placed them inside the service closet. If needed, he hoisted up the lantern to the full height of its pedestal. If the oil had congealed during the day due to cold weather, the keeper needed to heat the oil (if lard) and place the hot liquid immediately inside the lamp before he lit it. After lighting the lamp, the wickie geared the cogwheels, withdrew the bolt of the main wheel, and removed the pin that held the motor weight, allowing the weight to drop and the gears to rotate the apparatus. If the station had a stationary light and not revolving, these steps weren't necessary.

During the night, the keeper on duty had to inspect the flame at least once, more if a storm threatened the light. If the wick became charred, the watch would replace the old lamp with the spare unit, which presumably had been cleaned and filled with oil. Once the new lamp was placed inside the Fresnel lens, the keeper had to trim, fuel, and ready the old one as a spare—just in case.

Whether it was day or night, when storms, fogs, and inclement weather rolled in, the stations needed to boom out their sound warnings. As inclement weather limited the range of the warning lights, these fog devices were a crucial component of a lighthouse's navigation and safety warnings. In the early days, keepers fired cannons, banged on metal pans, sounded bells, and employed other devices. At the same time they were responsible for the light's function. As foghorns were developed and installed, the wickies needed to watch the coal or wood supply, fire up the boilers, repair the machinery, and keep the horns operable and able to bellow their warnings.

The foghorns at each lighthouse carried a different characteristic or signal, as did the lights, so lost mariners in a dense fog could approximate their ship's position just by hearing these sounds. The large foghorns used at immense stations such as St. George required not only constant vigilance, but consumed vast amounts of coal and water in firing up the boilers and creating the steam that blew the whistles or horns. In an average year, the twelve-inch steam whistles at St. George burned from thirty to forty tons of coal.

As for the lamps, kerosene fueled the light at St. George for twenty years until an incandescent oil-vapor light finally replaced the "earth oil" or kerosene wick. Years then passed before electric-producing generators were installed. Keeping adequate supplies on hand of kerosene, water, and coal to keep the horns blowing and lamps burning was a constant responsibility. Because ships were the only way of resupplying a wave-washed lighthouse, storms could keep the necessary supply vessels away for weeks at a time.

Like other lighthouses in treacherous waters, the lucky fishermen and sailors caught in windstorms with swamped or overturned boats ended up half-dead on the rocks. The keepers revived these men and fed them until the storms abated so they could return to land. Dead men also mysteriously washed up on the rocks, and the keepers usually had no idea at the time what had happened to these people. The currents off North West Seal Rock were very tricky. Owing to the bottom's contours and different currents sweeping north and south into the area, the undercurrents and ocean's flows could switch at a moment, trapping the unwary against waves a distance away, then sweeping a small fishing boat and its crew into Dragon Rocks.

The cold conditions, treacherous waters, constant moisture, and risky isolation from even relief crews brought death and serious ill-nesses over a short time period to several keepers at St. George. Nearly one year after the station's lamp burned for the first time, first assistant keeper William Erikson and the station's eighteen-foot surfboat were lost in a gale. Knowing how bad conditions could be in these seas, Erikson headed away by himself in the small craft, but the stormy conditions quickly turned to the worse. Somewhere between the lighthouse and Crescent City Harbor, heavy winds and seas swept over the keeper and his craft with both disappearing for-ever. In the estate proceeding, John Lind attended the hearing to tell about the storm circumstances and apparently testify that Erikson's death was not a suicide. Six months after that tragic event, George Goldsmith, who was the other assistant, abruptly resigned.

The Light-House Board's Annual Report for 1894 stated matter-of-factly:

> In January last a new standard 18-foot boat was supplied. This was made necessary by the loss of the first assistant keeper on October 17, 1893, together with the standard boat then at the station. No vestige of man or boat has been discovered. A set of boat davits were put up on a wharf at Crescent City to enable the light-keepers to secure their boat while they are on shore.

Close calls and injuries continued over the following years. While attempting to hoist another boat from the water in April 1901, assistant keeper Gottfried Olsen broke his leg and was transferred to shore duty. After becoming seriously ill on the rock, assistant keeper Julius Charter died in Crescent City in November 1902. At the end of April 1903, lighthouse keeper Charles Steiner also became seriously ill and had to leave the station.

Among the eighty men who served between 1891 and 1930, thirty-six resigned and twenty-seven transferred to other stations. Additionally, two men died, another three became seriously ill or injured, and eight others were noted as having just "left" or were dismissed. Many of those who resigned, left, or were dismissed did so in a matter of months. Some quit or "resigned"—as noted in the registry—after several weeks, including one hardy soul who showed up on October 16 and resigned on November 21. At best, the average tenure lasted between three and six months.

CALIFORNIA'S REDWOOD COAST reaches from the Golden Gate of San Francisco to the Oregon border. It is wild, rugged, lonely, and dangerous, just as the Oregon coast is as it sweeps from there to the Columbia River and Washington. Mariners had to watch out for the heaviest fog on the Pacific Coast with the possibility of gales shrieking with gusts greater then one hundred miles per hour, white-flecked monster waves higher than ten stories, and terrible conditions that could last days and even weeks. The coastline then offered relatively few safe harbors during storms. Powerful, sometimes impossible-to-pass surf ringed the ports, and the offshore rocks were hidden like mines laid during a war. Rocky islets, reefs hidden by high tide, and powerful currents combined to make this a dangerous coastline.

St. George joined numbers of other lighthouses that dotted the California, Oregon, and Washington coast. The maritime industry thrived during these times, especially as trade up and down the West Coast to British Columbia depended primarily on ships. Railroads had not been constructed in the same spidery-web ways as on the East Coast, and the West Coast was virgin territory as contrasted from the eastern half of the United States.

Lighthouses were placed to dot the coasts for every twenty miles as a navigational aid for ships, as well as providing warning and life-saving functions. They also were important in watching over the inland lakes of the United States. (The website of lighthousefriends. com contains pictures, descriptions, and a brief history of many of the lighthouses that graced the United States, including both coasts, the Midwest, and from Texas to Florida.)

On the West Coast, a few lighthouses are descriptive of the different locations and circumstances that brought about their distinct construction and operation. The Farallon Islands, for example, off Northern California came from the word Los Farallones (or "small, pointed isles"), which the Spaniards gave when they discovered these rocky, barren islands located twenty-five miles west of San Francisco. The largest and tallest of the islands is Southeast Farallon, which rises to 358 feet, and the Twelfth District constructed the Farallon Islands Lighthouse at that island's top.

During the early 1800s, Russian and Aleut seal hunters established a camp on Farallon where they harvested hundreds of thousands of seals for the meat and fur. The salted sea lion meat was destined to supply the Russian fort, Fort Ross, to the north. These hunters lived in wood huts covered with sea lion skins and burned animal fat to cook with and keep warm. When scurvy broke out in the encampment, the men became too weak to hunt, but they were able to survive by eating the eggs of the seabirds.

By the 1840s, the continued slaughter of the seals had reduced their population so greatly that the expedition camp closed down its operations and the hunters left the islands. When the California Gold Rush began in 1848, the ensuing heavy ship traffic made the Farallons a bad risk, as these fogbound, unmarked islands menaced the clipper ships and paddlewheelers who anchored nearby before sailing into San Francisco Bay when weather permitted.

During this time, chicken eggs were rare, and any fresh food commanded prices nearly as high as the gold that was being so passionately sought. A dozen eggs of the murre, a small seabird, reportedly tasted "quite like chicken eggs" and could bring over one dollar each—when a day's wages were less than that. During the egg-laying season from May to July, the competition for the valuable eggs on the Farallon Islands became fierce. Two men died in a shoot-out between rivals in 1863 that became known as the Egg War. Lighthouse keepers even moonlighted as egg pickers to earn the additional money, and the government was finally forced later to control these rogue operations. It declared itself sole owner of the island and made egg collecting illegal.

Owing to the narrowness of southeast Farallon's summit, a tower could only be built on top of the peak, and the Board caused the keeper's quarters to be constructed on a large plateau on the island's eastern side. After the workers completed the tower, however, the design proved to be too small to house the first-order Fresnel lens, so the men reclimbed the summit, tore down the first tower, and built a larger one. Hauling the building supplies up the crumbling slopes proved again to be difficult. After the laborers conducted a sit-down strike, the construction company finally relented and delivered one seasick mule to help pack the supplies up the steep slope. Once completed, the lighthouse's light began shining in December 1855.

When a ship foundered three years later on the island during a dense fog while the light was on, the need for building a fog signal was underscored. The supervisor knew about a large blowhole on the island, so he ordered his workmen to build a chimney over the blowhole with a whistle on top. The only problem was that the blanketing fogs didn't always roll in when the surf was high enough to activate this foghorn. A shrieking gale later created a storm surge so strong that it blew the chimney off its foundation and sandblasted the buildings with small pieces of granite. In the early 1880s, the Light-House Board authorized a more conventional foghorn to be built.

Over time, keepers and their families came and left Farallon.

The Coast Guard families who were stationed there, however, had the same medical problems as anyone else. In non-serious cases, physicians gave advice over the lighthouse's short-wave radio. In serious cases, a patrol boat motored over to bring the patient to San Francisco or a helicopter shuttled a doctor there. When the transportation costs of attending to pregnancy problems and childhood diseases became too high, the Coast Guard decided in 1962 that the Farallons would no longer be a family station. Ten years later, the station became unmanned when the light, fog signal, and beacon functions became automated. (For this and other interesting lighthouses, see the discussion at lighthousefriends.com, other websites, and the books listed in the bibliography.)

To the north, Cape Mendocino is the westernmost point in California, as well as one of the highest sites ever built in the United States. Located one-third up the redwood coast from San Francisco to Crescent City, the area is known for the large rocks that protrude from the shallow waters along this stretch of coastline, including Blunt's Reef located three miles from the cape.

With materials and supplies landed to one side of Cape Mendocino and hauled up the steep slope, workmen began building the station. The workers in one year built a forty-three-foot tower, a two-story brick dwelling, a carpenter shop, and a barn on a cliff that was 422 feet above sea level. When the original light at Point Loma, California, was moved, Cape Mendocino became the highest lighthouse in the United States. The iron, sixteen-sided, pyramidal tower was bolted to a concrete pad, and the first-order Fresnel lens in December 1868 began sending out its characteristic signal of one white flash every thirty seconds.

Living on this wind-exposed cliff could be difficult, especially when gales broke windows and earthquakes rattled the station to cause significant structural damage. Heavy rains during the winter season washed away parts of the land and cliff. In just over forty years, the keeper's quarters had to be completely rebuilt three times. During the 1870s, earthquakes also struck three times, one requiring the residence to be razed and rebuilt, another that split the ground fifteen feet from the tower, and a third that battered the station.

Owing to its remoteness from roads and cities, a lighthouse tender needed to bring in supplies. In 1881, the tender *Manzanita* moored offshore, more than likely off the beach to the south of the cape, and inspector Charles J. McDougal boarded a boat for shore. McDougal was the inspector then of the Twelfth Lighthouse District in San Francisco. As the boat tried to run through the surf, the large breakers became unmanageable and capsized the small surfboat, tossing everyone into the frothy waters. Weighed down by the payroll of gold coins for the keepers that he had strapped around his waist, McDougal unfortunately drowned with two other men. Owing to the intercession of McDougal's friends, his wife, Kate, was appointed to be the keeper at Mare Island in the Oakland Bay area. (This story is told more fully in chapter 11, "Keepers in Skirts.")

It wasn't until 1905 that the Board stationed the *Blunt's Reef Lightship* offshore to more clearly mark that deadly reef hazard. Some ten years later, the passenger steamer *Bear* ran aground nearby in another heavy fog that had lasted for two days. When the ship's surfboats tried to bring the passengers to shore through the heavy surf, the small boats capsized and five people drowned. Seeing this tragic state of affair, those remaining aboard the stricken ship decided to take the remaining lifeboats and rowed out to sea to the lightship. One hundred and fifty survivors managed to squeeze onto that vessel until they could safely head to shore. To lessen the chances of this type of disaster happening there again, the Twelfth District later installed a radio beacon on the lightship.

The Light-House Board then ordered the construction of new dwellings three years later at different site locations on the grounds of Cape Mendocino Lighthouse, including separate residences for the head keeper and his two assistants. However, the reefs off that coast continued to prove deadly. In 1921, the liner *Alaska* struck Blunt's Reef and forty-two lives were lost. When the crew arrived to the north from the Humboldt Bay Lifeboat Station, they only found the mast of the *Alaska* sticking above the ocean.

The commanding views of this location proved advantageous. Five years later, one wickie noticed that a passing steam schooner was on fire. Using the station's telephone, he sent out an urgent call for assistance. When a rescue vessel finally arrived by the smoking vessel, the men discovered that the fumes from the smoldering fires had overcome the crew. The keeper's alertness had saved the crew's lives.

After World War II, the Coast Guard started its overall movement toward automation. It deactivated the Cape Mendocino Lighthouse in 1951, and workers installed a reflecting light beacon on top of a steel pole, 515 feet above the surf. The abandoned lighthouse slowly rusted away until the Cape Mendocino Lighthouse Preservation Society saved the tower by relocating it by helicopter to a place twenty-five miles to the south. The lighthouse has been restored, painted, fitted with glass, and is on display at Mal Coombs Park in Shelter Cove, California.

SURROUNDED BY RUGGED MOUNTAINS and dense forests, Crescent City was an isolated town in the nineteenth century. Never a populated area, its citizenry was some one thousand hardy people in the late 1800s. Located basically midway between San Francisco and Portland, its crescent-shaped bay and safe harbor was ideally suited as a re-coaling, shipment, and passenger stopover for the vessels that steamed up and down the West Coast. With the city's incorporation in 1854, its residents immediately urged their politicians to flex their muscles and get them a lighthouse. One year later, Congress appropriated $15,000 to build that station.

The site selected was Battery Point, a rocklike islet that was part of the city and accessible when the tide was out. Battery Point Hill is two hundred yards from shore at the westerly end of the bay, and it gained its name from the cannons mounted on the point from the ship *America* that previously burned in the harbor.

During high tide, the rock becomes an island and is only reachable by boat. Located close to land, the point is conveniently reached during low tide by a leisure walk. During the station's construction, wagons easily brought the necessary materials, supplies, and workmen to the construction site, although improvements needed to be made to the trail.

The men excavated a cellar and laid a stone foundation. In less than one year, the workers constructed the station in the preferred design: a Cape Cod cottage for the quarters with a short tower that rose from its middle. The 1½ story residence was built of brick, while the fifty-foot high tower (including the height of the quarters) was constructed of stone, and the walls were two feet thick. The tower had white walls, a red roof, green shutters, and a black lantern room. The iron lantern room held a small, fourth-order Fresnel lens, and its light was seventy-seven feet above sea level and visible for fourteen miles.

The light became operational on December 10, 1856, and on that day Battery Point (or Crescent City) Lighthouse became the ninth California lighthouse in existence. The first permanent lighthouse keeper was Theophilus (Theo) Magruder, who was appointed in late 1856 and ran this station for three years.

Several years later, Joseph A. Lord, the senior messenger for the Wells Fargo Company, boarded the sidewheeler *Brother Jonathan* in San Francisco on July 28, 1865. Two days later, Mr. Lord left the ship early that Sunday morning to visit with his family. He had met his wife, Mary Magruder, in Crescent City, and the young Mrs. Lord had come here to visit her foster parents, who had once run the lighthouse.

The stopover gave Lord a chance to visit with his family for a few precious hours before the ship would next leave. A last-minute replacement on the steamer, he was also guarding a sizable amount of gold for his company on that voyage. The messenger then boarded the *Brother Jonathan*, and it steamed away, short hours later fatally crashing on Dragon Rocks. Nearly everyone on board died, including Joseph A. Lord. Waiting at the wharf, his widow received the news of her husband's death before anyone else. After tenderly embracing her husband that early morning, she learned mere hours later of her great loss.

Five other keepers tended to the lighthouse after Magruder's tenure until the mid-1870s, when John H. Jeffrey became the keeper. Jeffrey was appointed keeper of the light in 1875, when the lighthouse's future was uncertain. He and his wife Nellie served for forty years at the station, and for part of that time, Nellie was employed as the first assistant keeper, as both raised their four children.

During their tenure, extreme dry and rainy years occurred for long periods. When the city endured a drought, the keepers actually had to contract for fresh water to be delivered. During the wintertimes at the harbor's mouth, strong storms could arise, although not as bad as at St. George. During the worst ones, waves crashed onto the lighthouse site and even washed over the top of the light with foamy white water. During one of the worst ones, the gale winds sheered the chimney from the kitchen roof, as one breaker washed down the opening, smashed into the stove, and set the room on fire. The next wave that swept over the house poured down the same hole and put the fire out.

When John Jeffrey's long term ended, John E. Lind in 1915 became the head keeper at Battery Point Lighthouse, where he and his wife, Theresa, viewed this position as "heaven." After spending five years from 1887 to 1892 in helping to build St. George, Lind stayed as an assistant keeper, starting his duty one month before its light first beamed out into the ocean.

Spending nine more years as a wickie on that wave-crested rock—called by the U.S. Lighthouse Service as "the most dangerous construction work ever undertaken"—he waited for a transfer to better duty on another Northern California lighthouse. (When the term "Service" or "U.S. Lighthouse Service" is used, this refers to after 1910, when Congress abolished the U.S. Light-House Board and created the Bureau of Lighthouses—better known as the U.S. Lighthouse Service.) During this time, Lind endured some of the most difficult years anyone could have. In 1901, he finally left and transferred to the beautiful Pigeon Point Lighthouse in San Mateo, California (near San Francisco), and eventually became head keeper.

Fourteen years later, after nine years at Pigeon Point and another tour of duty, he succeeded the Jeffreys in 1915 at Battery Point Lighthouse. He was within rowing distance of where he had first started his lighthouse career on North West Seal Rock. As opposed to his earlier tour, his family could live with him and walk to land during low tide. Fresh food, water, coal, and equipment were easily supplied, and his children were able to attend the local schools.

At larger stations on land, the keeper and assistant keepers lived in duplex dwellings that could house a dozen or more children. These lighthouses were self-contained tiny communities that raised their own livestock, chickens, sheep, and hogs; they tended their own gardens, traded for necessities, and repaired their own equipment. The Light-House Service supplied their equipment needs, medical supplies, and usually a circulating library, in addition to paying them a salary.

Not every land-based station had these amenities. Some lighthouses on remote points were more isolated than others. For their children to attend school, these wickies needed to board their kids in faraway towns, with or without their spouses, or work a job swap with another keeper. Where the terrain was especially rough, the Service also had to bring supplies to these stations by tender or lighter.

Depending on the sand or soil, some locations were easier than others in being self-sufficient. The rocky coasts off New England, Maine, and California were not always suitable, even when the people imported soil, because storms quickly washed this away;

however, some were rich, if not in the ability to grow vegetables, but with seals, seabirds, and their eggs, such as the Farallon Islands. Battery Point Lighthouse was such a choice location.

Unless he knew that an inspection was imminent, Captain Lind like most keepers didn't wear his lighthouse uniform, wearing instead his vest over a white shirt, trousers, and a gold chain that hung from one pocket to his watch in another. He usually wore a yacht club–like black cap with a lighthouse insignia. Lind kept a diary of his time there, and passages from it can be viewed at the Battery Point Lighthouse Museum at the site. In the 1920s, he noted the two-way radios in use at the time. "I have a new fangled way of talking," Lind said. "He talks, and I talk, and then there's a lot of static. I'd rather send a letter."

His children attended school in Crescent City like everyone else. They walked over the rocks at low tide in the morning, and Lind rowed over during high tides in the afternoon and brought them back. If a storm's choppy water delayed their return, the kids stayed at the McNamara's, relatives of Mrs. Lind.

John Lind liked this duty so much he asked to stay past the mandatory retirement date. In 1928, Lind wrote a letter to Washington, D.C., stating that he wanted to continue on, even though he would soon be seventy years old—the retirement age at that time. The Commissioner of Lighthouses made an exception and agreed to let Lind stay for another two years.

At the same time, his wife's brother, Cliff McBeth, had started his lighthouse career also at St. George. Cliff said later, "I was glad to get off that rock. It was like a prison with its six-foot-thick walls and no place to go. It was a miserable place, just miserable." He watched deep, "green water" swell over the caisson, ninety feet above the ocean's level, and those surges left a lasting impression. On his free time, he fished and once caught the "biggest ling cod you ever saw."

One time, Cliff and another mate took the launch from the reef to Crescent City to buy fresh food and supplies. On the way back to

St. George, they ran into growing ocean swells and rocked into the pickup point. The men at the top lowered the hook, and as it came down, another large roller surged under the boat. The launch dropped quickly as the wave passed, the hook missed, and Cliff's companion pitched into the cold sea. As his friend tried to stay up with the boat, Cliff reached back, grabbed the man's trousers, and hauled the shivering man back into the boat. As the wet wickie clambered on board, another swell bottomed out and they were able to hook the ring for the stories-high transfer.

Cliff managed a transfer when he could to Piedras Blancas Light Station in San Luis Obispo County. Like other land-based stations, the Service had constructed two houses close to one another and behind the lighthouse. One structure was for the assistant keepers, while the head keeper and his family lived in the other. His children, including son Lind, grew up on this station.

The families grew fresh vegetables in a nearby garden, owing to the suitable sandy loam soil. They caught fish to eat such as bullhead sharks and rock cod. Cliff was an excellent carpenter and often helped a local farmer, Ed, two miles down the road. Ed, in turn, returned the favor with fresh slaughtered meat. Once a month, Mrs. Lind drove the family's old Packard fifty miles over a two-lane, bumpy road to San Louis Obispo. She there bought the staples needed, such as flour, salt, pepper, sugar, and a bottle of whiskey for Cliff.

When it came time for the kids to attend high school, the family moved to San Luis Obispo, where Cliff's wife took a job as a stenographer while her boys attended high school—and the family came together on weekends. Once the kids graduated, she moved back to the lighthouse to be with her husband. After a long stay at Piedras Blancas, Cliff and his wife retired to San Luis Obispo.

Meanwhile at Battery Point, various keepers and Coast Guardsmen came and went, but none had stayed as long as Jeffrey and Lind. In 1946, Coast Guardsman Wayne Piland and his family came to the lighthouse. They raised chickens inside a wire fence, and goats roamed to graze on the island, which kept down the growth of the poison oak. Over time, Wayne and his son would be involved in several emergencies that involved the men at St. George Reef Lighthouse.

Although strong storms were generally worse at St. George, the 1950 gales were particularly bad in Crescent City. These surges with their force tore apart a new jetty under construction and washed boats ashore as their anchors dragged behind. The high winds and seas drove barges aground or used them as battering rams against docks, and then the huge waves washed over Battery Point.

The Pilands were inside their quarters behind the heavy-boarded panels that tightly latched over the window openings. When Wayne Piland believed he could safely peek outside at the conditions, he cautiously ventured outside the back door. Although a massive green wave quickly swept in, rose over him, and smashed him down onto his back, he was able to scramble back inside and close the drenched door.

The storm had sufficiently passed by the third day for the Pilands to look outside. Once there, they discovered that the ocean swells had carried small-bottom rocks and seaweed onto the rain gutters on the roof—seventy feet above the ocean's normal level. The seas had cracked the windows in the lantern room, and seasoned mariners could only guess how bad these storms had slammed into St. George Reef Lighthouse, now completely hidden by the wind-blown near-black clouds.

When crossing to the islet from the mainland, visitors had to exercise caution even during low tide. Three Coast Guard officers stayed a little too long during their inspection, despite Piland's warnings for them to leave sooner. Although the short trail appeared dry when they left for the town, in minutes the tide and waves rolled up to their waist. Although the men were thoroughly wet, the only injury they received this time was to their pride.

Another time Wayne and his daughter, Nancy, were walking across

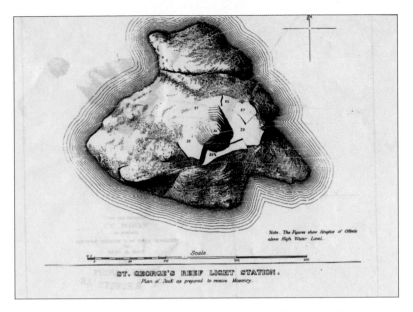

Early topographical map of North West Seal Rock showing the reef's contours and excavated design cut for the caisson. *U.S. National Archives*

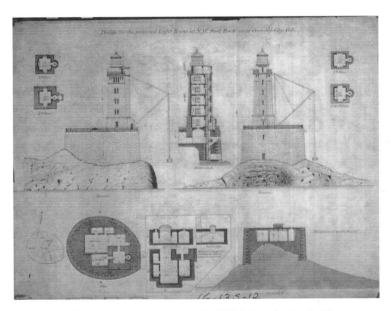

Alexander Ballantyne in 1883 drew up the initial plans for the lighthouse. The final drawings in this picture incorporated nearly all of his design considerations. *U.S. National Archives*

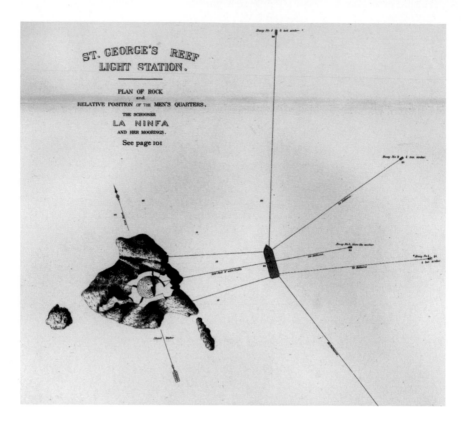

Due to the ocean conditions, *La Ninfa* was moored to at least four mooring buoys. The cable for the transporting "cage" was another anchoring device, which was securely attached to the ship. *U.S. National Archives*

The *Whitelaw* and other steamers towed the quartering schooners to the reef, brought in materials and supplies, and transported workers. *Del Norte County Historical Society*

The five-story caisson takes shape, following the plans to anchor the structure to the reef. The sticklike timbers in the air are the lifting derricks, and those on the ground are replacement poles. *Del Norte County Historical Society*

This rare photograph shows the 1880s St. George construction crew. *U.S. National Archives*

In 1890, the workers had to repair their "temporary" living barracks (structure to the left) and start construction of the lighthouse tower. *Del Norte County Historical Society*

The men also worked hard under difficult conditions in the operations on the slopes of the Mud River quarry. *U.S. National Archives*

The tower is nearing completion. Laborers worked on their assigned tasks at the various levels of the scaffolding; the living quarters are at the lower left. *U.S. National Archives*

La Ninfa operated as the interim quarters for the construction crew and later was used in the whaling and sealing trade. *San Francisco Maritime National Historical Park*

When its captain became confused in a dense fog, the 360-foot-long steamer *Queen Christina* ran aground off Point St. George and became a total loss. *San Francisco Maritime National Historical Park*

Landing and leaving were always risky at this wave-washed lighthouse. *Del Norte County Historical Society*

St. George Lighthouse was six times more expensive, took years longer, and was more remote than Tillamook Rock Lighthouse. It was also built on a reef one-half the height. *U.S. Lighthouse Society Collection*

Owing to Ballantyne's ingenuity and tenacity, Tillamook Rock Lighthouse withstood the poundings of wind and sea long after its construction. *U.S. Coast Guard Service (courtesy USCG's Historian's Office)*

Lighthouses located closer to shore and in usually gentle waters can take a variety of forms other than the typical more expensive base and high tower. The lighthouses shown are American Shoals (Florida) with its spidery legs, New London Ledge (Connecticut) with enclosing walls, and Five Fingers (Alaska) on jutting land. *Lighthousefriends.com*

The lighthouses shown on this page are the cylindrical "sparkplug" Orient Point (New York), icy Spectacle Reef (Michigan), and iron-legged Thomas Point Shoal (Maryland). *Lighthousefriends.com*

Working on a lighthouse—and St. George in particular—with hardened men was not for the weak of heart. *U.S. Lighthouse Society Collection (five-man crew)*; *Del Norte County Historical Society (St. George keeper)*

The long boom was a favorite lookout point. *John Gibbons Collection*

Like other wickies and Coast Guardsmen, John Gibbons never shirked from undertaking maintenance, inspection, and painting duties. He is the mate shown leaning toward the left. *John Gibbons Collection*

Fifty years later, Gibby stands by the lighthouse's Fresnel lens that he once maintained *(above)*, but which is now on display at the Del Norte County Historical Museum. *Lorraine Gibbons*

Air compressors replaced the steam-engine-driven foghorns, and all of this equipment was housed inside the huge engine room. *U.S. Lighthouse Society Collection*

Steam-powered, one-foot-diameter trainlike whistles were originally used as fog signals. The second one was a backup in case of malfunction. *U.S. Lighthouse Society Collection*

After the Coast Guard assumed control, the air-powered foghorns were changed in favor of the two-tone diaphone horn. *U.S. Coast Guard Service*

The first-order Fresnel lens used in the tower was the largest of its type, nearly eight feet high and six feet in diameter by itself. Its pedestal added another seven feet. *Del Norte County Historical Society*

Moments before the 1951 tragedy, the crew prepares to depart. As the launch lowers, Petty Officer Beckett sits on the inboard side and talks with Walker, who is fastening his life jacket. These two men and Costello (at the helm) died minutes after this picture was taken. The other two men, Mulcahy and Vandenberg, survived. The last picture shows the boat just before the rogue wave slammed into it.
U.S. Coast Guard Service

Regardless of the
technique, landing
supplies and transferring
men was always
dangerous. *Del Norte
County Historical Society
(top and bottom); U.S.
Lighthouse Society
Collection (man on cable).*

The wave crashing into St. George in this classic photograph reaches eight stories in height. *U.S. Coast Guard Service (courtesy USCG's Historian's Office)*

With the lighthouse in the background, the Coast Guard anchored this forty-two-foot-high, self-contained navigation aid off the stormy reef in 1975. St. George Reef Lighthouse was then abandoned due to its high risk and cost. *U.S. Coast Guard Service (courtesy USCG's Historian's Office)*

Tillamook Rock also experienced huge waves, but it was twice as high as St. George. *U.S. Coast Guard Service (courtesy USCG's Historian's Office)*

During low tide, keepers and their families could walk from Battery Point Lighthouse to the city. *U.S. Coast Guard Service (courtesy USCG's Historian's Office)*

St. George Lighthouse was built where the dragon roared. *U.S. Coast Guard Service (courtesy USCG's Historian's Office)*

the rocky bottom. Although the weather was stormy, the ocean had pulled back and exposed the way. As they were crossing, the ocean suddenly built up and boiled back in. The two raced for the other side, where Wayne pushed his daughter to the safety of a high rock, joined her, and both clung to it as the seas rushed by.

In October 1953, the lighthouse became automated, and the local Del Norte County Historical Society leased the lighthouse from the Coast Guard, as its curators maintained the premises while living on-site. Roxy and Peggy Coons were the curators at the lighthouse eleven years later when a great tsunami crashed into the city.

Peggy awoke around midnight and noted an extreme high tide rising in the harbor. She awoke her husband and together they watched as the powerful waves pummeled Crescent City, killing eleven people, injuring scores, and destroying thirty city blocks. Owing to the lighthouse being on high ground, the station received no damage, although the highest, fourth wave was twenty-five feet high and crashed 2½ miles inland. (Their description of the destruction wrought on that city, and the story of that tsunami, is written in another book by this author, *The Raging Sea*.)

The station is open to visitors during low tide. The fourth-order Fresnel lens from the lighthouse is on display, along with historic photos and other memorabilia connected with it. Tours include walking through the lighthouse residence, viewing the rooms where original furniture still stands, and climbing to the tower. For more information on the Del Norte County Historical Society and the Battery Point Lighthouse see www.delnortehistory.org/lighthouse/ and delnortehistory.org.

ON THE COAST HIGHWAY from Crescent City to Tillamook Rock lie more lighthouses to visit, including the Washington coast. One that stands out on the way to Tillamook is Yaquina Head Lighthouse, located just north of the town of Newport on the Oregon coast. Located on a high cliff, this station was difficult to build.

Construction began in the fall of 1871, but it was often delayed due to the inclement Oregon winter. The materials had to be shipped by sea, then unloaded at a landing site located seventy feet down and two-thirds of a mile away. As the seas rose unmercifully, two small boats and their cargoes were lost when they overturned in the surf, as well as a larger vessel that waves damaged when it entered the bay.

Manufactured in Oregon but shipped eventually from San Francisco, 370,000 bricks were used in the double-walled construction of the tall tower. This design provided not only insulation from the cold and heat, but it also allowed air to circulate and dry out the continued dampness. Owing to problems in shipping the Fresnel lens from Staten Island, New York (parts of the lantern were somehow lost in transit), nearly two years passed before the lighthouse finally shone in August 1873, although a foghorn was not installed.

The station included a two-family, two-story dwelling, and later a second keeper's dwelling. Yaquina Head is the tallest lighthouse on the Oregon coast at ninety-three feet, and with the height of the cliff, its light shines 162 feet above the ocean and is visible nineteen miles out to sea. Owing to the tower's exposed position, storms and lightning have damaged the station at times.

When the station eventually became automated, the facilities were turned over to the Bureau of Land Management and now include a visitor's center with vista points to watch the coastal wildlife. Visitors receive an "I Survived the Climb" button at the top after climbing the 114 steps (including the landings) to the light's top. However, its views of the surrounding ocean are striking. For more on this and other lighthouses, see Lighthousefriends.com and other search engine results.

THE ELEMENTS conspired against the wave-washed, isolated stations more than their land brethren, even when the ocean storms didn't rage. During early 1895, the winds whipped up the seas around

St. George Lighthouse, but no rains appeared as the fog-banks continually rolled in. With the need to continuously run the foghorns, most of the cistern's water supply was consumed by the steam boilers, necessitating strict conservation efforts for what little remained.

As the drought continued, the District Light-House Board decided on March 1 to change the fog signal to much longer intervals of silence, thus reducing the expenditure of steam and saving some of the water supply. The foghorn now gave off a five-second blast, which was then followed by a silence of seventy-five seconds. Of course, the men's showers went by the wayside, but these had been weekly at best. Fresh water for consumption was expensive and prohibitively so with respect to the boilers.

The St. George furnaces consumed one ton of coal for every twelve hours of whistle use in generating the steam required to drive the foghorns. When the horns ran continuously over days, even weeks, notwithstanding the water levels, the furnaces consumed ever-increasing amounts of this fuel, which had to be resupplied by boat. When the coal was delivered to the station, the wickies had to move those great quantities into the bunkers inside the caisson. When adequate rains finally fell to fill up the cistern, then the foghorn could be blasted longer and more frequently, but this meant wishing for storms that carried more problems than rain.

When the drought ended, a storm whipped up with mighty waves that surged over the caisson deck (the catch deck) and destroyed the shed built on top of the pier, then used as a blacksmith shop. When the wickies ventured out after the storm, they only found a few twisted parts of the foundation left, as the powerful, high surges had chiseled everything else away. A boat brought workers to the station, who then rebuilt the shop and the protective structure. Other workmen retubed the hoisting boiler, among the continuing repair needs and maintenance.

Although the storms generally rose from the south, the huge swells usually raced in from the north or northwest side, where the galley windows also looked out over the ocean. In a strong storm the keepers watched the green water engulf those windows, which meant that the ocean had totally inundated that side, as opposed to heaving up white, foamy sprays. On the east side, the keepers could see land. To the south of the lighthouse lay South West Seal Rock, Star Rock, and the other islands that stretched toward land. When large waves struck on the north side, it was possible for men to walk around on the southeasterly side, the power of the wave having been interrupted by the tower.

The assistant keeper, Gottfried Olsen, was injured in a "freak" accident in 1901, as the crew tried to hoist the station's launch from the ocean. The boom of the hoisting derrick wasn't long enough to reach beyond a dangerous eddy located off the reef, and its position blinded the operator from seeing waves approach. Two men were needed then, one shouting instructions and the other operating the derrick. When picking up or lowering the crew, the observer had to count the waves rolling into the north side. As these usually came in sets of three, the men waited until the third one passed and then dropped the hook. Typically, the operators had a window of thirty to forty-five seconds in which to operate, but problems occurred when the waves or currents didn't cooperate.

An unseen wave caused turbulent currents in one bad eddy that ripped the hooked launch away and caused the boom to swing wildly. A part of the apparatus struck keeper Gottfried, breaking his leg. A new ninety-foot long boom was built on the derrick in 1902 and attached to the tower. This device greatly improved the ability to remove the launch from the ocean, as the boom now extended beyond one point where the dangerous eddies existed. Two men, however, were still needed to safely run the transfer operation.

Six miles out in the ocean, St. George was so isolated that for years the only visitors were the monthly crew transfers by launch from Crescent City and the quarter-annual visits of the inspectors. When the lighthouse's boat couldn't make shore, no mail or fresh provisions was deliverable for up to two months. Aside from what the crew on passing steamers occasionally threw off in oil cans, magazines and newspapers were old and worn.

Even retrieving the oil can and its contents became an adventure. The crew had to lower its boat into the choppy water, retrieve the containers, and return. The water was always rough at the pickup point and approaching that area was usually difficult. Hooking the boat and being lifted to the catch deck ninety feet above the ocean was always risky, and accidents happened on a frequent basis. And being out in the ocean can be a dangerous venture by itself.

Caught in a southeast gale while attempting to reach Crescent City, head keeper John Olson was held captive for seventeen hours in an open boat. Regardless of Olson's ocean experience, this was a frightening experience. Being in a small launch with twenty-foot waves and a shrieking wind—no matter how strong or tough—is unnerving, and the distance from St. George to Crescent City Harbor was thirteen miles. The high winds and choppy ocean could keep a boat circling for hours without being able to find safety at either place. However, Olson was able to survive.

In 1903, the local newspaper reported that one keeper headed out in the station's boat, only to run into more unexpected winds. Although a gasoline-powered boat had now replaced the station's surfboat (one account called it a "sailboat"), the engine failed during the supply run. The account stated that Olson's assistant spent fifty-six hours (over two full days) aboard the helpless boat "undergoing a perilous experience." This was an understatement. Although the Battery Point Lighthouse keepers at Crescent City kept a continuous vigil for their fellow wickies—and were ready to rescue anyone they spotted—the basic fact was that every trip from St. George was a lonely and potentially risky venture for anyone who tried.

The Light-House Board's report for 1904 gave the news that "a gasoline launch twenty-two feet in length, propelled by a three-and-one-half horsepower engine" was at the station for the trips to Crescent City. Regardless of what was in use, the change from boats with oars to gas-engined launches greatly helped in the movement of crews and supplies.

On October 21, 1907, the rocky coast off the point claimed another victim. The *Queen Christina* was one of the largest freighters on the Pacific coast with a 360-foot length, 48-foot beam, and displaced 4,268 tons. She had sailed from San Francisco with a cargo of wheat and was headed for Portland, Oregon. On that day, she steamed into a blanketing fog off Point St. George. Believing that he was on a course seven miles offshore, Captain George R. Harris of the *Queen Christina* continued on.

With no radar, ship-to-shore radio, or automated navigational devices to communicate with, Harris and his ship continued through the blanketing fog, as he didn't hear the warning foghorn or see any flashing lights. The shocking, rending sounds and trembling of iron plates grating over hard rocks abruptly vibrated throughout the huge vessel. There was no question that the *Queen* was in bad trouble. The ship had run solidly aground and the sea was now surging inside it from the rips through its hull.

The crew first tried to stem the problems by closing the watertight doors and running the pumps, but the freighter began to list strongly to one side as waves crashed over it. The captain and his men realized the vessel was doomed. After giving the order to abandon ship, Harris led his crew from the freighter, and the men safely made their way through a fairly calm ocean in two lifeboats to the nearby point.

Once receiving the news, the steam-schooner *Navarro* quickly left its dock in Crescent City to pull the freighter from the rocks. Men managed to climb on board the ship in the swells over the reef, haul a tow line up, and secure the thick hawser to the vessel. The *Navarro* worked its way out to pull up the slack, and then with thick smoke pouring from its stacks, the steamer tried to pull the *Queen* away. Although the cable held, the *Navarro* was not able to work the freighter from the rocks. Captain Harris then ordered his men to salvage as much as they could. Despite more attempts over time to remove her, the *Queen Christina* stayed pinned onto the reef.

Harris tried to blame the great loss on the St. George keepers, arguing that the foghorn had not sounded before his vessel slammed into the rocks. Since the thick fog would have blocked the station's flashing light, the foghorn would have been the only working warning as to the coast's closeness. Most mariners backed the lighthouse's personnel who said that the horn was always in operation, especially local fishermen who knew that in such a pea-soup, blanketing fog, a ship could be close to the foghorn and still no one on board at times could hear it.

People speculated that the vessel would rip apart in the first winter's heavy storms. Due to her tough construction, however, the *Queen* didn't break apart until two years later in January 1909, when massive winds and seas from a winter gale tore over the ship. The surges ripped down her masts and the superstructure, leaving only a part of the bridge crumpled over, but still visible after the crashing seas passed.

As SHORT-WAVE RADIO, telegraph, and telephone were not invented or able to be installed at St. George for some years, letters delivered by launch constituted the communication between personnel and the Light-House Board. The station's needs ranged from motorized launches, installing stronger winches at Crescent City Harbor for its boat, and replacing equipment to a different arrangement in the hoisting-engine position.

The derrick on the pier's top was located some seven stories from the ocean's surface, and the hoisting engine's position had brought about keeper Olson's broken leg. Its location required one man to call out or signal the operator about the best time to lower the hook, and this reliance on a "spotter" caused risky miscommunications.

A June 15, 1906, letter sent by keeper John Olson to Major

C. H. McKnistry, the engineer of the Twelfth District, stated the problem and recommended that the engine and its housing be relocated on the south side of the derrick mast, so that one man could both "run the engine and see the boat, or, load from the boat under the derrick at the landing." Whether concerning this problem or the need for a new winch at Crescent City Harbor for the station's boat, letters swapped back and forth on these subjects between the lighthouse and San Francisco headquarters. Olson also recommended retubing the steam boilers that drove the hoisting engine and "fog-signal" with a new smoke stack for the caisson (for the fog-signal boilers), along with his continued requests to reposition the hoisting engine.

As an example of the red-tape bureaucracy, two years later in 1908, the discussion by letter still continued. The Twelfth District engineer sent a letter to the "Keeper, St. George Reef Light-Station" asking for more information before making a decision, such as the name of the equipment maker, the identifying numbers of engines, drums, and plant, along with requesting a sketch of the present and proposed location of the hoisting engine. Four days after receiving this request, Olson dutifully sent a three-page letter with blueprints of the engine, the five-story pier, and derrick, along with his rough sketches of the present and proposed locations.

He recommended that one corner of the housing be extended eight feet over the pier, but that the engine and boiler would rest on the caisson. A cast-iron anchor and beam would support the corner over the rocks. The house was to be placed "close-up" against the porch door, with a door cut through the engine house, so that the operator could get out on the south side. The new structure was to be eleven feet by fourteen feet, and a section of the pier railing was to be taken out, boat davits moved, and alterations made.

Olson eventually received his authorization from the Service and the hoisting engine moved. Although this approach and the derrick were later changed, there is no question that Ballantyne built the lighthouse without such interference or delays, whereby it nearly took an act of Congress to move one derrick after he turned the keys over.

Numerous equipment changes were accomplished over time at St. George. To increase the light intensity, an oil-vapor lamp (designed like a Bunsen burner) in 1911 was installed in place of the wick lamp. Two years later, air sirens powered by compressed-air equipment were substituted for the steam-powered fog signal. In later years, the red panels for the light were removed because the color red substantially reduced the candlepower, so that captains at distances saw the white flashes but not the red. In 1936, an air-powered diaphone horn replaced the sirens. After the authorities constructed a breakwater in Crescent City Harbor in the 1930s, the Service leased docking space on a wharf for its launch. Rather than hauling up the station's boat to the lighthouse, it made more sense to keep the launch in the safer confines of Crescent City. This arrangement stood the test of time.

The Fresnel lens meanwhile operated through its hundreds of prisms that focused the light of the kerosene-fueled lamp into a continuously beamed light. As the heavy weight dropped down the tall tower, the series of pulleys turned the gears of a circle of numerous wheels, set at angles, with bearings. Taking the whole night (from sundown to sunup) to drop the tower's length, the weight and pulleys kept the lamp's characteristic flashing, no matter where the observer stood. When the weight hit bottom, the keeper on the watch had to wind the one-hundred-foot long cable back up on the drum, so it would be ready for the next night—or depending on the conditions, that same evening.

Kerosene fueled the lamps until the 1930s, as the weights dropped and the gears ran that turned the light. When electricity came to St. George and other lighthouses, this important development replaced the wick with a lightbulb and the weight with a motor. Whether driven by electricity on land or by batteries and generators on wave-washed rocks, a small, 120-volt motor now could turn the entire series of brass wheels and axles continuously around during the night. Designed nearly a century before, the system of pulleys, wheels, bearings, and axles were so fine-tuned that they could still be used.

THE MOST IMPORTANT RESPONSIBILITY of the wickies was to keep the station's light clear and running from one hour before sunset to one hour after sunrise. When oil wicks were in use, keepers had to shave the wick, make sure sufficient oil was always available, wipe down the lens and windows from smoke, and keep all of the equipment, including the foghorn, in good operating shape. Crews also needed to clean, repaint, and even re-cement where the saltwater corroded metal, fittings, walls, and equipment. They had to remove ice, salt spray, bird droppings, and even dead fish that washed onto the station's shores.

When the light sources changed to kerosene lamps, vapor lamps, or even the electric lightbulb, the lamps and lenses needed continual and complicated maintenance, especially as the technology increased. Foghorns became more complex. Keepers at stations like St. George needed to be knowledgeable on both first-class Fresnel lights and foghorns, as numbers of lighthouses didn't have the large lamps or even foghorns driven by large steam generators.

The responsibilities included cleaning and polishing the lens, cleaning and filling the lamp, dusting the complex driving mechanism, as well as cleaning the walls, floors, and galleries of the lamp room. Every aspect of the station needed continual inspection for damage or erosion; it had to be swept and dusted, cleaned and repaired, and painted. This work involved the landings, windows, doors, tower stairways, derricks, boat docks, or storerooms—and all these functions continued every day, week, and month.

The lens had to be carefully washed every two months and polished at least annually. The crews had different assignments on non-
maintenance responsibilities, ranging from monitoring coal, water,
food, and supply levels to engineering, navigating, cooking, and pur-
chasing. Windows were cleaned and storm damage repaired. Men
had to maintain and repair their station launches, lifting engines,
and facilities.

A continued source of effort was directed to counter the constant
saltwater erosion and salt air corrosion. Keepers continually chipped
away old paint and rust and repainted the spots. "Painting, painting,
and more painting," said one keeper at St. George. In fact, one estimate held that nearly one hundred coats of paint over time were
applied to its engine room.

Men at the same time had to guard against complacency when
the weather conditions were poor, but not apparently dangerous.
Off-hours needed to be filled, and this could be a real challenge.
Some personnel liked having all that free time for themselves, while
others chaffed at having nothing to do except the cleaning, painting, and repairing "something." Being on an isolated, faraway tower
like St. George tested the souls of many and most soon transferred,
resigned, or were fired for having a bad attitude. However, some
keepers stood out as to their longevity.

Fearless, old John Olson spent a long twenty-two years over two
stints at St. George Reef before finally giving in and transferring to a
different lighthouse. In fact, twenty years later in 1911, Olson was
on his second tour of duty there, when Georges Roux first signed on
as an assistant keeper. An ex-French sailor, Roux even spent more
time on St. George than Olson did. These exceptions did exist, but
they were few and far between.

The yearly salary for a lighthouse head keeper on the U.S. West
Coast averaged about $1,000 in the 1890s and basically stayed in that
range for several decades. Assistant keepers received less, and during
this time period the Service paid them between $500 and $650 per

annum. These salaries were viewed by some as being low for the risk, isolation, and hardships. However, given that room and board was provided, during hard economic times people took that employment with its isolated, relative low paying status, saying that, "a job was a job."

The Light-House Service rated lighthouses and set salaries based on these ratings during one period of time. In determining annual salary, it reviewed factors such as the amount of work (a foghorn required considerably more effort), the ability of non-paid people (such as families) to help out, how long operations were needed in that year, and other factors. An easier station, less remote, and with helping family members would have less pay. Consequently, the lowest-paid stations were typically the one-family stations in the Great Lakes where the lighthouses closed during winter months. The highest-paid stations then were St. George Reef Lighthouse, Tillamook Rock, and Mount Desert Island in Maine.

Regardless of the higher salary, duty on St. George was considered by many to be too risky and hard, and the turnover rate was high. A number of them transferred to other stations, but this duty forced out men each year who never went back to a lighthouse. Some of the ex-keepers, however, stayed on land and started up businesses in the area. They established cafés, became fishermen, worked as loggers, or went back to the sea as sailors.

Georges Roux set the record for longevity on St. George Reef, which today is still hard to believe. He came to the reef as an assistant keeper on October 7, 1910, was promoted to second assistant about one year later, and then served seven years until he transferred in 1917 to another lighthouse. When that ten-year stint ended, Roux came back to St. George—one of the very few to do so—and was appointed its head keeper on May 1, 1918. He served in this capacity for twenty years until 1938. Roux was a very self-contained man and obviously liked being at sea on this station.

He was born on December 7, 1877, in La Rochelle, France, and remained single. This status proved quite helpful, since any family would be hard pressed to put up with a husband's duty that lasted as long as six months and where they weren't allowed visitation. In the 1920 census, Georges Roux was listed as a lodger with many others in a Crescent City hotel operated by one Amelia Tongli. He was listed then as "Keeper, U.S. Lighthouse," age forty-two, a single man, year of immigration was 1900, and year of naturalization as 1905.

His crew was also listed in that census and at the same hotel: William W. Mitchell, age sixty-two, born in Pennsylvania, single, and the carpenter; George Cottingham, age forty-three, born in Michigan, married, and listed as a janitor; and Robert Wilson, age fifty, born in New Jersey, single, and designated as the "seaman, U.S. Lighthouse." These men didn't remain long: Mitchell lasted fifteen months at St. George before he resigned, Cottingham transferred two years later, but Robert Wilson stayed 4½ years until his transfer came through.

In the 1930 census, Roux was listed again in the Crescent City, Del Norte County, California, section. Creative spelling made this notice interesting: George "Rouse," age fifty-two, single, and who was the naturalized "light keeper." Listed also were members of his crew: Joseph Marhoffer, forty-nine, single, and born in California; George M. Woods, forty-nine, single, and a South Carolinian; Michael Dolan, forty-eight, single, born in New York; and George W. Petersen, forty-three, single, and born in Illinois. All of these men were listed as being a "light keeper"—and all, except one, in those censuses were single.

This group remained longer under Roux. Marhoffer started his service at St. George in 1913 and lasted nearly two years, when he then transferred; he returned in 1920 and worked another ten years before leaving for the last time. Woods stayed six years before he was "dismissed," and Dolan made it for over ten years. George Petersen started in 1929 and continued for ten years until the U.S. Coast Guard in 1939 took over all lighthouses.

Men left or transferred from St. George for a number of reasons. Many couldn't stand the hardship of no family, no close friends, or the risks of that station. St. George stood in the middle of the ocean with spells of high surf, gale winds, depressing fog, and continuous rain. Even when the sun did shine, on most days men couldn't walk around the tower on the catch deck because the surf's spray from the close waves rained over them. In some cases the only lighthouse job they could find—one with frequent openings—was here. As soon as another position opened and they were accepted, they packed their bags.

For example, Thomas Atkinson became head keeper at Point Cabrillo in California after putting in time at both St. George Reef and the Farallons. John E. Lind spent his time on that wave-crested rock, patiently waiting for transfers to Northern California light-houses. When he came to Battery Point—just miles from St. George— Lind and his family stayed past their retirement. Cliff McBeth managed to get off St. George for the tranquility of Piedras Blancas Light Station. Some keepers died, some became ill, and some Georges Roux types loved this isolated duty, even up to their death. For those few who fell in love with such isolated, hard duty as St. George, a passage from *The Lighthouse Keeper* by Henryk Sienkiewicz puts this into perspective:

> A lighthouse-keeper is no longer young, gloomy by nature and sufficient to himself. When forced to leave his lighthouse among other men, he walks in their midst like a man woken out of a deep sleep. Yet Skawinski was happier than he had ever been in his life before. He rose at daybreak, breakfasted, cleaned the lens of the lantern, and sitting in the balcony

gazed far out to sea; and his eyes could never have their fill of the pictures he saw before him. On the immense background of turquoise blue there was usually a flock of swelling sails, shining so brilliantly in the rays of the sun that he had to close his eyes against the excessive glare.

Sometimes the ships, taking advantage of the eastern equatorial winds, went by in a long line, one behind the other, like a string of gulls or albatrosses. The red buoys pointed out the road rocked on the waves with a light, gentle motion. Every day at midday a huge grayish pennon of smoke appeared among the sails. It was the steamer from New York bringing passengers and cargo to Aspinwall, drawing behind it a long frothing trail of foam.

The U.S. Light-House Board selected one keeper from Tillamook Rock to watch over its exhibit at the 1898 Panama Pacific Exposition in San Francisco. The Board intended this as a reward for the man's long and faithful service at the isolated station. One week after being in the crowds, the wickie, Robert Gerloff, begged to return to his station. He announced, "No more of them noisy, wisecracking crowds for me. I'll live here until I die." When it was time for his retirement, Gerloff pleaded with the Service to let him stay on board the rock as a paying guest—but his request was denied and he had to leave.

Turbulent windstorms in that region continued without warning. The schooner *Mandalay* in October 1918 was steaming from San Francisco when another violent storm overtook it off the redwood coast. Just miles south of Crescent City, a huge wave crashed over the boat washing one man overboard with his two dogs. Five minutes later, the man—complete with the two dogs gripping his trousers tightly by their jaws—was washed back onto the ship by another towering wave. The vessel managed to turn around and make it back to San Francisco, but it ran aground to avoid sinking from the extensive damage already sustained.

A savage storm suddenly rose and struck St. George on December 7, 1923, causing such powerful, mountainous surges to crash over the high pier that the seas tore the donkey-engine from its moorings and destroyed the mechanical hoist. The entire lighthouse shuddered time after time as the large waves washed over it, and the ocean's power broke or badly damaged all of the station's steam pipes, water pipes, and hoisting derrick controls. The head keeper was onshore at the time and couldn't return to the station for two weeks, although he maintained communications through the recently installed radio-telephone.

In 1924, another storm caught the 122-ton steamship *Shark* while crewmen were trying to unload its cargo in Crescent City Harbor; the winds and waves pounded it mercilessly until the vessel broke apart. Six years later, the 301-ton steamer *South Coast* was hauling cedar logs through the fog from Crescent City north to Coos Bay, Oregon. The ocean was smooth with only a hint of wind, and the captain and his eighteen-man crew had little concerns. The vessel never reached its destination. At the small coastal town of Gold Beach, Oregon—forty miles from St. George—the residents reported seeing a "flash at sea, followed by a dull boom." The next day, boat reports of debris sightings came in that included empty lifeboats, cedar logs, and a vessel's pilothouse.

Rescue craft were unable to locate any survivors, but a later inspection of the lifeboats indicated they had been torn from their davits (the arms on a ship that hold a lifeboat and lower it) and the pilothouse pushed off the deck. Seven years later, a survey ship was running depth soundings off Port Orford to the south of Coos Bay, and a diver was sent underwater to investigate why the cable drags had fouled. The diver reported that this snag was the missing ship *South Coast*, and the vessel's location indicated that it had struck a reef while running blind and had capsized.

In 1932, the superintendent of the Lighthouse District, Captain H. W. Rhodes said, "It (St. George Reef Lighthouse) tries and proves men. Show me the man who has put in the required time of service there, and I'll show you a man who is a man—and, what's more, a lighthouse keeper too."

So true. However, a high percentage of keepers did keep leaving, and it was common before the Coast Guard took jurisdiction that men applying for a career in the Lighthouse Service would turn down appointments to St. George and simply terminate their careers.

More important, fellow keepers had to be compatible, a hard task on St. George owing to their isolation and confinement. Since roommates, who only come together for a few hours during week evenings, find it difficult to get along, imagine having to live with someone for weeks or months at a time on a twenty-four-hour, seven-day-a-week basis. Arguments can ensue between the best of friends, let alone living together in cramped quarters with no break from one's routine and depressing weather marooning everyone on a dangerous rock prison in the ocean.

One year before his tenure ended, Georges Roux and his men experienced in 1937 some of the harshest and stormiest weather in the station's history. Since the weather conditions cut off all contact with the mainland for fifty-nine days, no supply tender was able to approach and deliver food to its famished crew, or deliver mail, supplies, and other essentials. There was no contact with the outside world for that time.

Although the crew had worked together with each other for years, they came down with acute cases of "cabin fever." With the winds howling outside and the gray-green waves swelling to crash against the tower, the men were trapped inside those bitterly cold, wet, and imposing walls. If the conditions weren't dangerous enough, fresh water, coffee, fresh food, and tobacco "came into short supply."

The four men under Roux stopped speaking to one another for one month, and to say "good morning" became a personal affront. The irritating tone of men's voices added to the screeching winds, moaning diaphone foghorns, and the tower's shuddering. Individuals ate facing away from one another, avoided the table all together, or ate by themselves. Fist fights broke out and men threatened one another; it was a miracle that no one was murdered or severely injured.

"After the first four weeks," Roux said later, "we were so talked out and thought out that just to say 'Please pass the salt' or 'Lousy day today, ain't it?' became a serious personal affront." He continued:

> It got so bad that we would try to ignore the presence of each other to avoid scraps. This despite our being solid friends for years. Toward the end, when we opened a can of beans or some kind of can and ate it cold, we would face away from each other—not looking, not talking, just so fed up with each other's company that it was almost unbearable.
>
> I've heard of men going stir-crazy in prison, well, that's just what almost happened to us. Funny thing, the moment the weather pressure let up and life in the tower resumed to normal, so did our pressures and we returned to normal, too. We were friends again. Talked our heads off.

After those horrid two months, a supply ship finally ventured out and normal crew exchanges resumed. Meat, vegetables, and warm bread replaced the steady diet of cold cans of beans and soup. The continued, nerve-wracking blasts of the diaphone foghorns came to a merciful stop. Men smiled again, worked together, and played cards on off hours.

Having tensions arise was not uncommon at other stations,

including similar differences, fights, and conflicts. On adjacent Tillamook Rock, one wickie even tried to murder the head keeper by mixing finely ground glass into the man's food. The aggressive assistant who wanted the other's position quickly resigned when confronted with the facts. In the late 1950s at another station, two keepers became jealous of one another's attentions toward the other's wife. In the ensuing altercation, one picked up a hammer and the other grabbed a knife. The knife was faster, resulting in death to the hammer holder.

However, the wind, waves, and currents created more danger than one's fellow workers. One morning in 1939, Captain Georges Roux was at the Hobbs & Wall Wharf in Crescent City Harbor for his return trip to St. George. He had left the rock "several weeks" before on shore leave and was looking forward to coming back. He had had his injection of social interaction, customs, and landlubbers, and the captain was ready for months of being on the rock in total control. Roux had also bought provisions for the station, but as a squall had pushed into the area, he was deciding whether he should head off into the ocean or wait.

The decision was easy. Although the skies were solid gray from the overcast storm clouds, windy, spotty rain, and choppy ocean, he assessed the conditions as being rough but workable. Besides, he wanted to get back to the reef and he had groceries. A dockworker handed the bought supplies to him, and Roux stacked them in the back and pulled a tarp over them. He pulled himself into the launch, and the man on the dock lowered the boat from its davits into the bay waters. Once the motor warmed up, Captain Roux nodded to the man and left the wharf about ten o'clock in the morning bound for St. George.

With the engine noisily chugging behind him, he kept a steady grip on the wheel, as the launch bounced over the growing waves in the harbor. He passed the breakwater and angled to the northwest for his trip to the lighthouse. This trip normally took about an hour in decent weather, and his arrival time should have been about eleven o'clock, despite the growing surf.

Looking continuously up at the skies, Roux knew that the storm clouds gathering over the horizon would soon sweep in, but he felt that the launch would arrive at the station just in time. The patters of rain still fell against his weather-beaten face and streaked against the launch. With his back hand, he adjusted the canvas wrapped around the provisions and continued on.

The boat slammed into higher swells and whitecaps began to grow higher. The wind picked up. Spray flew over the boat as the wind-whipped swells became flecked with foam. He tasted the salt-water swept against his mouth and lips. The launch pitched violently when hitting one particular large swell, and the midmorning air had become chilly.

As Roux pushed through the ocean, he wasn't fearful, because he had done this before on many occasions. Soon he was angling toward the southern portion of the lighthouse where the derrick was ready to pick up the boat. The massive station loomed up and looked like an ancient, English battlement.

The surf had indeed built up and surged against the rocks on the northwest side, spraying upward, and then crashing over and around the rocks toward the boat-lifting area. As he neared the area, the launch seemed to skim over the hissing foam. The waves were lower here, since the station provided a barrier to these types of storms. However, these currents were mean, treacherous, and strong, and Roux had to be watchful of the rollers that could sweep in or back toward him.

The crew had spotted him and readied to lower the hook. The timing had to be perfect, but this would be difficult under the current conditions. He cut the motor and drifted in as the hook quickly descended toward him. The seething rocks of the reef warned him about its proximity, but Roux held to the last moment and then quickly threw the engine into reverse. As the launch seemed to stand still, he stood up to grab the hook and attach it to the lifting lines. A large wave suddenly washed in, lifted the boat up toward the reef, and Roux missed the hook. As the swell surged past, the boat dropped like an elevator, throwing the wizened but lean, tough man against the hard deck. He landed on his chest and head.

Although stunned by the hard blow, Roux pushed himself up. He didn't feel much pain because of the cold winds and chilly water. The captain grabbed for the steering wheel as the boiling currents swept the boat closer to the rock. He could nearly touch it, but the saltwater poured off the reef and created an opposite underwater current.

Without hesitation, he gunned the straining engine. The propeller bit into the water, gave a metallic howl, and the launch worked its way backward. As he tried to maneuver again toward the hook, another surge crashed around the rock and swept the boat to the west side. He crashed again against the boat and felt something snap inside his chest. He felt a shot of pain, but then turned his attentions to the runaway boat, now completely out of control.

A huge thundering resounded from the higher side of the reef, and as he looked up, he watched incredulously as the raging surf pushed over the reef from the opposite, northern side. It crashed over the launch, smashed him down again, and filled the boat halfway with water. The motor coughed and then sputtered, as Roux worked to gain control over the boat. As the engine misfired, he waited, knowing that if it quit, he would be swept against the rocks or rolled over—a fatal result.

He lowered the throttle, and the motor seemed to regain its rhythm. As soon as this happened, Roux applied more power and

the engine thankfully responded. The launch continued back in
reverse at an angle from the rocks. A large wave surged into the caisson from the other side and broke into a rooster-tail of spray that
blew over the reef into the landing area.

As the rolling currents swept him toward land, Roux realized that
he had no choice but to somehow make his way back to the port.
The boiling surf, powerful undercurrents, and wave surges around
the lighthouse had made it impossible to land there.

Working his way through the seething, twenty-foot waves in the
open sea, Roux slid the launch through the troughs and finally
found an opening that allowed him to turn and motor up the back
of a large roller. He surfed down and was heading back to land. The
skies were now dark, the winds howling, the surf crashing, and the
ocean waves menacing.

He opened a water cock to drain out some of the seawater. Holding one hand on the wheel, he used the other to bail. On a wild
roller-coaster ride that would have terrified anyone else, Captain
Roux kept the tiny surfboat headed for shore, as he ran quartering
with the waves. At times this was difficult, since the rollers seemed to
sweep in different directions, but he tried to meet the waves at an
angle, rather than perpendicular, and to stay away from the deep
troughs.

The hissing surges of gray-green water pounded over the launch's
gunnels with their higher crests, filling the boat with cold saltwater
that sloshed back and forth with the boat's pounding. The odds were
strongly against his survival. Another hissing comber washed over
him, causing him to gasp for air and cough up seawater. The soaking-
wet man hunkered down in the boat's middle. He kept his hand on
the launch's throttle, the boat low in the water.

He now knew what had happened to the others, including that
assistant one year after the lighthouse began operations. He couldn't
recall the person's name, but Roux knew conditions like this would

have easily overcome that man and his surfboat. In a battle for his life, Georges kept the launch on its course, shivering from the cold and wincing from the pain that encircled his chest, as the large, white-capped rollers hissed around the tiny boat.

He didn't know how long he had been out there, but Roux kept his wits with the knowledge that if his time was up, the ocean would do its course. As night started to overcome the dark grays, he finally saw the rocky outline of the breakwater. He motored around it and into the protective confines of the harbor, as the waves became somewhat smaller.

One newspaper account reported:

> Captain Roux returned to the harbor, arriving around six o'clock that evening, his boat filled with water, the groceries a total loss, feeling glad to be alive after the worst experience in his long career as keeper of the dangerous light on the tiny speck of rock ten miles offshore.

Unfortunately, the ordeal had taken its toll on the sixty-two-year-old mariner. He was suffering from hypothermia, severe bruising, and more than likely broken ribs and internal injuries. The savage seas had given him a terrible beating. Roux was soon taken to the local hospital in Crescent City. There he died.

His obituary read in part:

> Captain Georges Roux, 62, for nearly thirty years keeper of the Point St. George lighthouse, died suddenly at the Knapp Hospital here early Monday morning following a brief illness. Roux was badly battered a few days previous to his death when he attempted to reach the lighthouse following several weeks' shore leave and it is believed that this experience brought out exhaustion from the effects of which he

never recovered . . . Capt. Roux was able to bear around following his attempt to reach the light, but evidently suffered
injuries which brought on a fatal illness. Cause of his death
was chronic nephritis [an inflammation, usually of the kid-
neys] complicated by terminal pneumonia.

CHAPTER 10

Lighthouse Life

A s with many lighthouses, life on St. George was a mixture of boredom, fear, and awe. It combined both pleasure and pain. The keepers had to maintain and repair the facilities and equipment, day or night, so that from sunset to sunrise the lamp stayed lit, the light shone brilliant, and the foghorn blasted. The work of a keeper was long, continuous, and at hours many would find difficult, if not impossible.

Although St. George personnel received a higher salary than most lighthouse keepers, a constant turnover continued until the last years of Georges Roux. Owing to its isolation, risk, no family or friends, and savage surroundings, this station's pay never seemed to be enough.

When a new recruit came to a lighthouse, the person usually had a rough idea of the work awaiting him. Surrounded by the Pacific Ocean on a wave-washed rock, however, was a different proposition with the landings especially rough for the uninitiated. When boats arrived with new recruits and supplies, the boatswain on the boat deck shouted loud instructions to the launch's coxswain. The boat had to motor in swiftly as the crew quickly secured the boat to the boom's hook. The boom swung the boat upward and then dropped

it onto the boat deck, some twenty feet above the crashing surf—if
the weather was good. In early times, the boom swung the launch
up to the caisson's deck, a seemingly death-defying aerial trip of
seven stories up as the winds blew and boats seesawed with the wind
blasts.

Author Jim Gibbs noted his experiences when first arriving on
Tillamook Rock Lighthouse. Strapped to the boson's chair, the young
Coast Guardsman was being hauled up to the lighthouse. When the
cable suddenly went slack, he found himself dragged through the bitterly cold ocean. Swinging in the air, Gibbs arrived on top looking
like a "wet, bedraggled cat." Similar misfortune awaited those who
came to St. George, but the approach was more dangerous.

Most lighthouses were constructed on land, inside protected
coves, or close to land in safe areas, where families were permitted
with their support, closeness, and warmth. Tillamook and St. George
Reef Lighthouse were the exact opposite, St. George being the worse
of the two. The seething surf and ocean was so close to this reef and
station that becoming drenched by spray was commonplace. No protecting rock walls and height existed, and this lighthouse was five
times farther from land than Tillamook.

North West Seal Rock required strong and thick construction.
Concrete was used on the outside of the pier and tower, for example,
including forming the tower's floor arches and the floors under the
foghorn, landings, steam engine, and derrick base. Ballantyne took
pains to construct the interiors, however, with durable but more
pleasing appearances. Brickwork was laid inside the tower, along
with tongue-and-grove floors in the keeper's quarters; the floor surfaces were polished and varnished, as were the oak doors and
window trim. The cedar inside doors and wall panels initially had a
rich appearance with their redwood trim. The crews had finished the
walls of the keeper's rooms with three coats of "plaster, sand finished." All of the metal work received four coats of paint.

However, due to the constant saltwater and air, everything had to be continually repainted, revarnished, and protected. Different color coats of paints and applied protections over time replaced the new look. Despite the initial attention to details, the rooms were sparsely finished, and a hard, forbidding feeling came into existence. When the crew locked shut the Dutch-door windows on each floor during stormy weather, and the smoky oil lamps left their residues on the walls, this feeling became accentuated.

The first hours at any station were the worst. When a prospective wickie arrived at the rock, the weather could simply make the statement. A blustery, stormy day with waves thundering high over the rocks left an indelible mark; sunshine with blue skies and gentle waves gave another. As the new recruit scanned the lighthouse's insides, the person saw starkness, unfamiliar surroundings, and uncertainty.

The first views of one's room brought the realization that this place wasn't home but more like barracks life in a plastered room built inside a stone tower. Then there were the crewmen who were also assigned to this duty. The first evening meal gave the new assistant keeper the chance to meet his fellow "cellmates," as one crewmember observed. Manners, personalities, likes, and dislikes were quite different among the men.

This wasn't an office job with suits, civility, and clean smells, but around-the-clock living with rough-cut, tough, seamen where water was rationed for weekly showers and shaving regulations not enforced. Some workers hated taking baths until their companions drove them to it. What do you do if a long-standing keeper took a strong dislike to you? There was no place to hide, no new job to look for until your duty ended.

When night came, the crashing sounds of the surf, moaning winds, flashing of the light, ear-splitting shrills of the foghorn, and loneliness would take time to adjust to. Climbing for the first time up a darkened spiral staircase that wound its way to the top created its share of uncertainty, especially when cold winds swirled noisily down the tower. The initiate heard different sounds, groanings, and eerie stories about ghosts and goblins. He saw strange reflections.

Jim Gibbs tells the story about his hearing sounds and thinking about those ghosts during the first nights of his imposed service on Tillamook Rock Lighthouse. The sound of a footstep in his room one dark night jolted him wide-eyed and awake. The wickie knew that one man was on watch at the time, while everyone else was presumably in their bed. He heard another step. Then something seemed to brush his face, followed by a light touch to his throat.

Gibbs imagined that someone was holding a knife near his throat. He leaped to turn on the light switch and stumbled over something. Scrambling over to the switch, he flipped it on. In the light, he stared at a "mammoth goose" that was waddling around the room. Blinded by the lighthouse lamp, the large bird had crashed through his open porthole and broke a wing in the process. Gibbs took the goose to a sheltered, rocky spot and carefully put it down on the ground. But by the following morning, the wounded bird had disappeared.

Each new person always received the worst shifts and jobs. The long duty at night, storm watch, and repairing near inaccessible places were usually assigned to the lowest man on the totem pole. This included the most risky jobs of painting the boom or parts of the station that were stories above the rock. On St. George, Tillamook, and most other lighthouses, one of the unwritten laws was also that the newest man aboard was the cook, and it didn't make any difference whether he knew how. The new recruit needed to learn—no excuses—and he had that job until a "newer" man came on board. Depending on the particular crew, this time period could take months, if not a year or two.

When fog draped its heavy shroud over an area, the lighthouse's foghorn didn't stop blasting until the dark mists dissipated—and that could take days. Every thirty seconds or so, the shrill sounds ruptured the air until the blessed event of a lifting fog mercifully occurred. The first fog signal employed at St. George was a steam-driven whistle similar to those found on a train or a tug. However, it took more than one hour to build up a sufficient amount of steam. When air compressors were installed, the men simply started the foghorn by pushing a button.

As these horns blasted, keepers over time could permanently lose part or most of their hearing. These deep moans, shrill whistles, and sharp howls were heard continuously until the foggy conditions changed. Wickies changed their way of talking when the horn sounded and would only talk during the intervals of silence. After the foghorn stopped, the keepers and their families often found themselves still talking in that same strange staccato language.

DAYS AND WEEKS PASSED, as the new keeper tried to become accustomed to isolated lighthouse living. The long foggy periods were the hardest, especially in the beginning with no radios, telephones, or land communications. An important rule was to leave people alone in their rooms—one had to have privacy somewhere.

Another learned lesson was to do what you liked when not sleeping or on duty. Men tried many types of activities, ranging from painting, horseplaying with the others, and writing letters to reading books, and later, listening to the radio. Some took longer shifts in trying to pass the time. For those who couldn't adjust, this duty was equivalent to jail time where the cage was a wash-spit of rock and a forbidding tower.

The facilities weren't always the best. Gibbs related the Tillamook Rock story of having to use an open, overhanging privy where the surf crashed ninety feet below and the winds whistled out of control.

Using a commode takes a lot of faith when someone looks down a toilet, sees the crashing ocean below, and feels the winds blasting up.

Whales, seals, sharks, seabirds, and all types of sea life were abundant at lighthouses. Great California gray whales annually made their trek from the Bering Sea to Mexico's west coast, and they and the playful stragglers that didn't keep up with the migration were seen around the West Coast stations. These whales were up to fifty feet in length and wickies estimated that they weighed more than one ton for each foot.

The abundance and variety of the marine life was a definite plus. However, there was a flip side to this enjoyment. Dead bodies of fish and drowned animals washed onto shore or against the rocks, as birds dashed against the lighthouse during the night and their broken bodies were discovered in the morning. Since the station windows were inches thick, the birds were always the loser.

The Light-House Board even noted in its 1900 report an actual attack by flocks of geese, brants, and ducks on Hog Island Light in Virginia. Shortly after twilight one day that year, hundreds of the birds began slamming against the lantern panes and tower. Before long, one large goose circled high in the sky, then soared down to burst through a glass pane, and shattered a lens panel from its collision. Other large birds followed their kamikaze leader, even though the keepers were now firing shots into the air to frighten the birds away. Nothing worked. When the wickies ran out of ammunition, they grabbed a chair, mop, bucket, or anything handy to swing at the incoming, dive-bombing flights.

Sixty-eight bodies of different birds lay crumpled on the tower by morning, and more splattered bodies lay around the deck and inside the lantern room. Near miraculously, the light wasn't extinguished, but the wickies had to clean up and construct a wire mesh around the broken lantern windows. Two nights later, the birds came back with another assault against the light. The men knocked 150 birds to the ground, but this time the attacks succeeded in darkening the lamp. When the light was extinguished, the flocks of birds withdrew and didn't return. The wickies repaired the damage to the lens, light, and lamp room, and the lighthouse's operations began once more. The birds never appeared again in such numbers.

In 1927, numbers of ducks and drakes slammed into Maine's Saddleback Ridge Light Station one February night. The birds seemed to steer away from the lamp light, only to hit the black adjacent structure, seemingly blinded or distracted by the flashing light—and this was the experience at most lighthouses. The keeper later picked up 124 seabirds in mounds around the tower and most were dead. Such bird collisions were more apt to happen at new light stations, and the numbers decreased as the years passed and the surviving birds became wiser. To prevent damage to the lantern room glass, the Service erected iron screens during periods of heavy bird migration. The attacks on Hog Island and Saddleback, however, still remain somewhat of a mystery.

Lighthouses were, of course, a naturalist's paradise. Not only did numerous bird species, fish, and marine life exist, but land-based wickies also wrote about their deer, bear, raccoon, possum, and other animals. Wolves howled around northern Midwest lighthouses and in Alaska. Bears knocked over trash cans and searched for food, once they discovered that a human diner was now open. Rattlesnakes abounded around West Coast lighthouses, while cottonmouths hung around in the South.

At Matagorda Lighthouse in Texas, one keeper wrote in his logbook in 1929 about his fear of the snakes that slithered around the station. Poisonous ones appeared during high tides and storm surges, as numbers of rattlesnakes and water moccasins sought refuge in the structure. He requested that antivenin be kept at the Texas lighthouses in case of snake bite. The authorities granted his request.

Jim Gibbs related the story on Tillamook Rock about the masses of stinging jellyfish that turned up off its rocky spit, until the seagulls and terns flew over and began feasting on them. New birds arrived and fought with the fat birds over the jellyfish and usually won. Since swimming off these and other rocks was prohibited—although someone would try it on very calm days and grab a rope back onto the reef—the mosquitoes, gnats, and flying insects were bothersome.

Because storms cracked booms, threw boulders and stones against lighthouses, and the saltwater corroded metal and ate away at structures, maintenance and repairs were also a continuing responsibility—or headache, depending on one's view. Much of the earlier equipment was made of brass, which required constant polishing. As salt air quickly worked its way even through paint, stations required constant painting. Storms not only broke lighthouse windows, but the wind-driven, sand pitted lamp-room windows that needed to be replaced at towering heights, so the warning light could penetrate the glass.

Any conflict between crew members over time could become a bad problem, whether this was a challenge to fight, duel with knives or guns, or not talking with one another for weeks on end. "Familiarity breeds contempt," especially when people live in small quarters. Minor differences over how one talked or even liked their food could become major issues. One long-told tale related how the keepers of an Alaskan lighthouse differed over whether they liked their potatoes fried or mashed. This ended with the three estranged keepers not talking to one another for six long months, each standing watch and cooking his meals in absolute silence.

Another problem was that not everyone cooked well, and this made getting along more of a problem. The stories abounded about men who hated another's cooking and picked up the burned chicken, stuck vegetables, or pudding-like gravy and hurled it at the running cook. If someone was a bad cook, then he tried to exchange that duty with another man and instead washed the dishes. The problem was when he couldn't.

Women were understandably not allowed on St. George and Tillamook Rock, as the months together with no outlet and quick-rising sexual tensions would create more havoc, not to mention the risks to young children. Families lived together on other stations, but the duty on these wave-washed rocks was too perilous. Pets such as cats and dogs couldn't survive at these places. On other stations, the men had dogs, cats, horses, mules, and even deer and exotic birds as pets. Here, keepers had to wait until after their tour of duty. As one wickie on St. George observed, "Cats, dogs, and other pets here just didn't seem to last very long."

Since families were welcome at most other lighthouses, the stories about these experiences were passed along. At a Lake Superior lighthouse, one Malone had helped build the lighthouse and then applied for the position of keeper. The inspector told Malone that he wanted a married man for that position. A bachelor at the time, the man immediately headed to the mainland, found a bride, and quickly married. New inspectors were assigned to this district about every two years, so the married Malones adopted the custom of having and naming a new child for each inspector. Their plan broke down, however, when three different inspectors came, one after another, due to the Spanish-American War. The Malones raised twelve children in all at the Isle Royal Lighthouse on an isolated station at the northern part of the lake. This was the record for wickie kids, until one keeper at Great Duck Island on the Maine coast had seventeen children, all of whom were "well reared, mostly at this one station."

Lightkeeper James Corgan wrote the following into his 1875 log of Manitou Island Light Station in Lake Superior:

July 15. Principal Keeper started at 8:00 P.M. in the station boat with wife for Copper Harbor (distant 14 miles), in anticipation of an increase soon arriving. When one-and-one-half-miles east of Horseshoe Harbor, Mrs. Corgan gave birth to a rollicking boy; all things lovely, had everything comfortable aboard. Sea was a dead calm.

The boy grew up to become a state prison warden.

At many other lighthouses such as adjacent Battery Point, families tended vegetable gardens for both food and relaxation. Fishing and clamming were nearly year-round. At some locations, such as California's Point Sur, workers moved gardening soil by buckets to the top of the 250-foot-high mountain. The next problem, however, was that the lighthouse gardeners had to fight off the birds, gophers, and bad weather in order to grow anything. Although the West Coast usually enjoyed a long growing season, this didn't matter at places such as St. George with its tough weather conditions, salty moisture, lack of freshwater, and no soil.

What everyone takes for granted on the mainland, however, were problems at an isolated lighthouse. Receiving mail, fresh food, and potable water at remote locations created major problems when lousy ocean conditions set in for a time. On one station on an island off Washington, the only regular means of communication was by the Indian mail carrier's canoe. The mailman made the seventeen-mile trip twice a week, including taking passengers to the station. One longtime carrier had three of his canoes smashed when trying to land in the surf, and at times he had to throw the mail sack from his bobbing canoe to the wickie who stood on a nearby rock.

Dried hardtack, biscuits, canned goods, and even war rations could be stored for a time—although their quality left much to be desired—but potable water was another matter. Before tenders anchored offshore to pump freshwater into holding tanks, drinkable water also came from collecting roof runoffs and storing this in a cistern. As at St. George, this process could be problematic, if not downright hazardous with bacteria-infected water. Strong doses of chlorine had to be added, which didn't do much for the taste. Droughts were always an issue, not to mention that salt from the ocean, dirt, bird droppings, and even part of the roof often found their way into the water. Crews had to keep an eye on the storm clouds, and then race to soap down before the downpour occurred. What they did about the potable water is another question.

Storing tasty fresh food was also a thorny issue, no matter where one was stationed or the conditions. Keepers, however, tried to rig storage chests for meat, milk, and other perishables, and then lower the contraptions by a rope into the ocean. The risks for this approach included raging storms, hungry seals, and bad ropes. Storage during the winter was easier than in the summer, but, on the other hand, getting fresh food to isolated locations was more difficult when the winter storms of sleet, winds, and waves were at their worst.

Being warm and dry usually doesn't concern most people—unless you're on a lighthouse. During stormy times in the winter, duty on wave-swept towers was shaking cold, damp, and quite uncomfortable. Living in a cold tower was akin, as one said, to "being in a dungeon," and the keepers had to walk around with ropes tied around them to lessen the danger of a gale blast sweeping them off the stories-high tower or pier.

When summer came to the lighthouses, the visitors and tourists praised the beautiful flowers, glistening ocean, and beauty of the towers. Working inside the lamp room, however, could be an oven-hot, sweat-box experience due to the continued hot sun and oil lamp. No temperature-controlled furnace or air conditioners were in service during those early days, and years would pass before they were introduced.

Not every lighthouse keeper looked forward to the summertime visitors. To stop being pestered by summer tourists on land-locked stations who wanted tours, keepers invented all sorts of excuses. Since visitors couldn't go unescorted up tower stairwells, one keeper became tired of walking up and down the tower so many times each day. He finally painted his steps bright green and hung up a "Fresh Paint" sign.

For years after the U.S. Light-House Board was formed in 1852, the appointment to a lighthouse required having good connections in the local and state government, along with being a member of the party then in power. With the advent of Civil Service and its examinations, this appointment process became less notorious; however, being connected would always be an asset.

THE RESPONSIBILITIES OF LIGHTHOUSE KEEPERS for a good light and workable foghorn meant that someone was daily tending the lamp and lens, cleaning the windows from the smoke and saltwater, wiping down the foghorn, and keeping all of the equipment in fine, working shape. People needed to clean away the daily bird droppings, salt spray, ice buildup, and the smoky film from the oil lamps. Depending on the facility, light stations were staffed therefore with between one and five keepers. One was the head keeper while the others were assistants and in descending order of rank and time.

Whether the light source used an oil lamp, oil vapor lamp, or electric bulb (much later), the lamps needed constant servicing—not to mention the foghorns. Driven by large steam furnaces or generators, some foghorns were complex assemblages of machinery. Those lighthouses with no fog signal or just a bell to ring needed but one or two attendants. The type and size of the Fresnel lens—whether a huge first-class lens or a much smaller fifth-class lens—was also a factor. St. George and Tillamook required the full complement.

The Lighthouse Service manual established the various responsibilities and the primary person who would do them. Where stations had two or more keepers, the Board divided the work into two "departments." The person in charge of the "first" department was responsible for cleaning and polishing the lens, cleaning and filling the lamp, dusting the apparatus and its framework, trimming the wicks, and doing everything so that the lamp was ready by ten o'clock that morning for its evening lighting. This work was usually reserved for an assistant or head keeper.

The wickie given the responsibility of the "second" department cleaned the utensils (trimming wicks, supplying oil, tools, etc.) used in the lantern and watch room; cleaned the walls, floors, and galleries of the lantern room; and swept and dusted the tower stairway, landing, doors, windows, window recesses, and passageways. Keeping the tower and quarters painted was important not only for preserving the stonework, metalwork, and wood, but also in keeping a lighthouse's distinct colors.

The written instructions set down precisely every procedure, even to mandating that keepers wore linen aprons when cleaning the lens to avoid scratches. The detailed criteria regulated everything from how to whitewash stucco to how to keep a good light and what to inspect. The employees were highly regimented, and the Service strongly emphasized cleanliness with the rules leaving little leeway. However, whether someone followed these regulations was another thing altogether. And from families to individuals, men and women bartered, exchanged, and transferred duties back and forth.

Cleaning windows at your residence isn't a risky problem, unless you're doing this on a lighthouse tower and holding to it in heavy winds. To reach the highest lantern-room windows, the wickie needed to stand on the gallery railing or onto a small window—not an easy job, especially when the footing was slick from rain or ice. Even though handgrips were installed along the vertical window frames to prevent keepers from losing their foothold during storms, deadly mishaps still too frequently occurred.

At St. Augustine Lighthouse in Florida, one man fell to his death when he constructed a scaffold to paint the tower; while on the equipment, he made one misstep and hurtled six stories to his death. His wife became the keeper for the next four years. An assistant at Cape Disappointment Lighthouse, on the Washington side of the

Columbia River mouth, came close to meeting his Maker. Although a storm raged along the coastline, the scheduled maintenance had to continue. As soon as the man stepped onto the wind-and-rain-lashed gallery, the door behind him slammed shut and he was locked out, fifty feet above the rocks. He spotted a lightning-rod cable that ran down the tower, grabbed it, and inched himself over the railing to start down. A wind gust blew the man perpendicular to the tower, and then slammed him down against its wall. Although the keeper lost his grip, he managed to land on the lower gallery, found an open door, and pushed himself safely in.

Formal inspections of lighthouses began in the 1850s. These visits were intended to keep the keepers' attention during the year on properly maintaining their stations. The manual called for unannounced reviews, and the wickies were instructed to be in uniform when any inspector arrived. The Light-House Board later prescribed the correct uniform attire: sharp, deep-blue (stated to be "dark indigo"), long-sleeve coat with gleaming brass buttons, railroad-looking conductor's hat with glistening rim, similar dark indigo trousers, and shined shoes. The Board reimbursed each keeper a set amount as a clothes allowance, but any later damage was at that person's expense.

The Board's written policy was that the keepers and their assistants were to wear their uniform at all times at their station, except they could remove their coat and wear the service-prescribed linen apron when cleaning. The regulations stated that the men could wear a "brown-working" suit when working outside the tower's interior.

The coat was to be double-breasted with five large regulation buttons on each side. The vest called for was single-breasted without a collar (in later years, a rolled one was prescribed) and cut to show six inches of shirt. These regulations were very detailed. For example:

The coat will be the length of the extended arm and hand and will be provided with two inside breast pockets and two hip pockets, the latter to have flaps that can be worn in or outside. Each sleeve will have two small buttons on the cuff seam.

The cap was made of the same dark blue cloth. Over time, a gold-thread design indicated whether the person was a keeper in charge of the light station or the first, second, third, or fourth assistant. Small gold stripes were worn vertically on the left sleeve to show each five years of service. In the 1910s, the Service developed flags and efficiency pins to be worn. It didn't prescribe a comparable uniform for the women or family members who weren't appointed as keepers.

Despite these instructions and formalities, there is little doubt that unless there was a formal or public occasion, most wickies usually only wore the prescribed uniform for the inspector's visit. Painting, cleaning, repairing, and other work duties were easier when not in uniform, especially when you had to pay for its replacement. Realizing this state of affairs, some inspectors would sound the tender's whistle as they approached the lighthouse. This warning gave sufficient time for the men to clean up and put on their uniforms.

When on a wave-washed rock, spotting the inspectors was also easy, as they would be on any tender that approached the lighthouse. If on a land station, the families asked their neighbors to alert them when one was approaching. For example, the keepers asked their friends to signal, drape a white bedsheet from a top balcony or window, or otherwise alert them with some agreed sign. Further, the stations had some idea when an inspection was coming up and would then be especially on guard.

As the Lighthouse Service continued to regiment operations, the paperwork requirements increased even more. Keepers were obligated to submit monthly reports about the station's operating condition, including fog-signal use, personnel absences, repairs, and expenditures for supplies. The keepers kept receipts and records for supply deliveries, shipwreck reports, damage to station and property, use of lamp oil, and any unusual occurrences. The wickies were required to keep a log with at least one line written each day, a daily-expenditure book, and a general-account or ledger. The daily log almost always described the day's weather, as this was the critical factor in the operations, along with any inspection visits, work going on, and deliveries of important equipment. Although there were no early requirements that employees knew how to swim (which accounted for a number of accidental drownings), the paperwork requirements meant that a wickie had to know how to read and write. Although these regulations were designed to minimize theft, neglect, and misuse, the actual control depended on how vigilant the inspector and district was.

THE REAL DANGER was that much of the time spent on a lighthouse was safe and secure, even when the weather was inclement. Men became used to arriving and leaving the lighthouse, whether it was in a sling or inside a launch hoisted up by derrick. Keepers became accustomed to their daily routines. Then disaster would strike unexpectedly or they would be called into action. As one wickie said, "This could be weeks of being comfortable or bored, punctuated by an hour of pure terror."

A young man slipped unexpectedly over a cliff two miles from the Heceta Head Light Station in Oregon and fell eighty feet to the rocks below. A passerby alerted the attendants at the lighthouse about the accident, who at the time were cozy and comfortable inside their quarters. With only a lantern and flashlights to guide them, the two wickies and two others risked their lives to inch their way through the darkness for 1,500 feet over a narrow trail that was between eight and twelve inches wide. One slip and the person would fall over three hundred feet down to the crashing surf and craggy rocks below.

When their path stopped above the injured youth, the men dropped a line down to the rocky craig. The wind meanwhile blew so strongly that it seemed to be whistling. One by one, the keepers rapelled down to the victim and discovered that he had a compound fracture of the leg. After setting the leg, the men lashed the youth to a board, and those above hauled the young man up. The wickies climbed back up with the aid of the rope and brought the injured kid back to safety.

One unnamed keeper was acknowledged for the following:

> Back in 1914, he ran a line through the surf to a drifting lightship; two years later, he rescued a man from drowning; three years after that, he towed a disabled steamer to safe anchorage; a year more, and he helped float a grounded transport; three more years, and he helped a disabled tug-boat and dredge from a highly dangerous harbor position; a year later he rescued, at dead of night in rough sea, two fisher-men who were physically exhausted and without provisions; and a few years ago he rescued the entire crew of a Coast-Guard patrol boat.

At Tillamook, on October 21, 1934, keeper Henry Jenkins fell asleep during a storm. Unexpectedly awakened, he found himself awash in his room's closet with a mouth full of saltwater. Incredibly high waves had risen and crashed over the lighthouse, cascading down to the men's sleeping levels and bursting waist deep into their rooms. Making his way through the seawater to the gallery area, Jenkins discovered that the surges inside had blasted the heavy iron stove from its bolted foundation.

By ten in the morning, the mountainous seas continued crushing down on the station and hurling large rocks onto its roof, as Jenkins heard the rocks slamming against the concrete-and-iron top. Head keeper William Hill shouted for everyone to run to the lantern room and bolt the emergency storm panels to protect the light. Before they could race up there, however, the entire tower shuddered as a twenty-five-ton piece of Tillamook Rock crashed into the sea, followed by the shattering sounds of a sixty-pound boulder crashing through the lantern-room's glass windows.

Tons of water, broken glass, rocks, dead fish, and seaweed surged down the tower, flooding the living quarters downstairs and forcing the men to climb to the steel roof supports to keep their heads above water. The giant wave had totally engulfed Tillamook Light Station with its tower 133 feet above the sea. It had been entirely under water. The surge passed, but the men knew that another one would follow; the structure shuddered and groaned.

In rising waist-deep water, the men fought their way to the tower's stairway and struggled up to the lantern room. They found thirteen window panels destroyed, along with an inoperative lamp and lens. Submerging men at times to their necks in the rushes of water, the surging seas carried rock fragments, glass, and even small fish into the tower, and flying glass shards badly cut one assistant's hands.

That night and into the following day, the four men worked to cover the open panels and rig an emergency light. On the second night, a feeble but steady light was finally generated. The U.S. Lighthouse Service still knew nothing about the distressed situation at Tillamook. Keeper Jenkins was an amateur radio operator, however, and jerry-rigged a transmitter. He contacted another radio operator in Morse code, who in turn called the district headquarters, which immediately dispatched the tender *Manzanita* to the rock. It wasn't until five days later, however, that the seas abated enough for the tender to transfer fresh food, water, and personnel for the station's aid.

Hurricanes swept over the East Coast and from Florida to Texas, just as nor'westers howled through the Pacific. The New England and eastern states have witnessed numbers of these killers, and one of the worst occurred on September 21, 1938. The New England Hurricane of 1938 killed hundreds, left thousands homeless, and devastated wide swaths of primarily Long Island, Rhode Island, and New Hampshire.

Nearly every lighthouse in the region sustained extensive damage, with some stations experiencing tragic loss of life. A bus approached a narrow spit by Narragansett Bay, Rhode Island, with seven children that included two of the station keeper, Carl Chellis, who operated the Beavertail Lighthouse. A wall of ocean crashed over the cove and smacked into the bus. As the vehicle flooded with saltwater, the driver opened the door to let the children out. Scared and shouting for help, the kids climbed onto its roof. Another storm surge swept in and hurled the bus with the screaming children into the raging ocean. Only the driver and the son of Carl Chellis survived. When learning that his daughter had died at the scene, Chellis ran over and in anguish began kicking in the bus windows, one by one.

On that morning, the winds and seas overcame the Whale Rock Lighthouse off Rhode Island, killing the keeper and leaving nothing left but the stubs of brick and a concrete caisson. Five people lost their lives—including the keeper's wife and son—at Prudence Island Lighthouse further inside the bay. The list of destroyed lighthouses was staggering: Castlehill (tower devastated), Palmers Island (station-dwelling destroyed and keeper's wife drowned), Woodhole Great Harbor (destroyed), Whale Rock (lighthouse devastated), Prudence Island (dwelling and fogbell tower gone), Tarpaulin Cove (fogbell tower gone), and others.

The Bolivar Lighthouse guarded the entrance to Galveston, Texas, when the terrible Galveston hurricane of 1900 roared into the Gulf and inundated the entire city with savage ocean surges. The keeper, Harry C. Claiborne, had purchased a month's supply of food before the 120-mile-per-hour winds and huge seas roared in. Terrified residents sought refuge in the tall, black tower, which was built on land with large metal plates held together by large bolts the size of doorknobs. The keeper and his wife welcomed each one, and Mrs. Claiborne fed the people with bread and boiled beans.

Before the storm ended, 124 people had taken refuge inside the tower, two standing on each step of the spiral staircase that led to the lamp room. The person on the bottom step was in cold, chest-deep saltwater. As the gale winds buffeted the tower, the keeper stood watch for the entire time inside the lantern room. The tower's movements forced Claiborne to hold on to wall handholds, but the lighthouse withstood the assaults from the sea.

Located on the ocean with its violent disposition, lighthouses faced more than stormy seas, erosion, and howling winds. Earthquakes destroyed lighthouses—and also created tsunamis. Two lighthouses stood on Unimak Island in the Aleutians off Alaska. Owing to the island's isolation and difficulty of supply, the Service and later U.S. Coast Guard once again allowed only men to serve there, including Scotch Cap Lighthouse that faced the Pacific Ocean. Scotch Cap was built on a concrete pad halfway up a cliff, and the tower light was ninety-two feet above the ocean with the structure constructed of strong, reinforced-concrete walls.

On April 1, 1946, a sharp earthquake erupted in the early morning, which even shook the lighthouse located miles away. A second, much severer shock occurred one-half hour later around 2:00 a.m. At approximately 2:15, a man on watch in a radio-direction station on the bluff above heard a strange sound, as if "a hundred airplanes were approaching." The log at the radar station read, "Terrific roaring from the ocean heard, followed almost immediately by terrific sea."

The crew at the summit top scrambled out into the darkness and listened to the ocean thrashing below. They yelled down but there was no response. When the sun rose the next day, the men found only the concrete pad remaining with a few twisted beams where the lighthouse had once been. The over one-hundred-foot-high tsunami had smashed the lighthouse to pieces and killed five men. Searchers discovered later only the small parts of two bodies on an adjacent hill.

Other risks were present, from Mississippi floods to Midwestern tornadoes. During cold winter nights—especially for eastern and midwestern stations—the snow, sleet, and ice could be as formidable. At Great Lakes locations, the stations closed down each winter due to the ice that clogged shipping lanes and engulfed the towers. Snow and sleet storms bedeviled shipping and stations on both sides of the coast, especially to the north.

The wickies at Sharps Island Lighthouse in Chesapeake Bay experienced unexpected dangers in 1881 when the neighboring ice flows began to break up. This station consisted of a round house built upon a screwpile structure with iron-spindle legs that anchored into the mud. As massive piles of ice moved out from a nearby river, the huge blocks sailed against the lighthouse. They rammed its iron legs, and after the first collisions, the keepers knew that another strong hit would knock the tower from its perch.

A sharp collision against the structure then knocked the house completely off its legs. The residence angled away to one side, slid into the ocean, sank into the mud for a moment, then resurfaced, floating like a boat. The floating house with the trapped wickies drifted for hours before finally grounding on land five miles south of its initial location, and the relieved men could finally scramble safely back onto firm land. Later retrieving their valuable equipment and tools, the Light-House Board gave commendations to the men for surviving and saving what they could. One year later, a new cast-iron caisson and tower was constructed.

A wintry gale blasted in and lashed the Lake Erie area in the late 1920s for three days. Sheets of frozen sea and spray totally encrusted the Ashtabula Lighthouse, which was on the lake and located one-half mile off the shoreline. The crusts of ice soon locked the two keepers inside a tomb of frozen spray. Trapped inside for two days, the men eventually thawed their lighthouse door open, but then had to tunnel through five feet of ice to reach freedom.

Fires also erupted. In December 1909, a steam tug was towing a

four-masted schooner by Norfolk, Virginia, when rough seas caused
the towline to snap. The schooner shot out of control around the
entrance to Hampton Roads and rammed into the Thimble Shoal
Lighthouse, knocking over a coal-burning stove. The force of the
impact scattered hot-burning coals over the station floor and started
fires. When the conflagration reached several stored oil cans and oily
rags, the structure erupted into flames, and the two keepers were
lucky to escape in the station's boat. The tug's crew rescued the two
men, but in an hour, the fires consumed the entire lighthouse, leaving only its iron legs sticking up from the sea. A new cast-iron lighthouse was erected five years later.

From Execution Rocks Lighthouse in New York to Makapu Point
in Hawaii, fires broke out in more stations. Whether from a lightning bolt or a lit match, any spark could prove fatal with the flam-
mable fuels used in the lamps. At Makapu Point in 1925, a keeper
was filling the alcohol lighter that was used to start a vapor lamp.
When some of the alcohol dripped onto the floor, the assistant for
some inexplicable reason lit a match to take a closer look. The ensuing flash fire and explosion killed the man.

Despite these calamitous times, numbers see the isolation of a
lighthouse as the ideal retreat from the everyday pressures of life—
and various wickies were attracted to this. However, as one keeper
said, "The trouble with our lives is that we have too much time to
think." Entertainment devices such as television, CD and DVD play-
ers, and laptops were decades away, and isolation and monotonous
routine lead some people to think strange things.

One keeper at the isolated Cape Sarichef Light Station in Alaska
became insane when he thought the ghosts of the Aleut hunters
killed by Russians were surrounding him. The wife of a Cape Disappointment keeper committed suicide by leaping from a cliff. At
Washington's Cape Flattery, a despondent crewmember jumped into
the sea but was saved. Men at St. George were forcibly restrained
from committing suicide when they couldn't handle the stress.

Although keepers and their families faced boredom and isolation, the self-sufficient life and "being their own boss" offset much of this. Many of the keepers who remained long-term employees developed a strong love of serving on their light station and being by themselves.

IN 1910, Congress abolished the U.S. Light-House Board, which had been created in 1852, and created the Bureau of Lighthouses (better known as the U.S. Lighthouse Service) under the control of the Department of Commerce. The Service's nine-person board was a definite advantage over the fifth auditor, and the federal government also wanted to create civilian control over the previous Board's military dependency.

The districts in the Bureau of Lighthouses basically remained the same geographically as before—including that for the Twelfth District—although they were renumbered. All of California's lighthouses were in the Twelfth District, but after the reorganization, the area was called the Eighteenth District. George R. Putnam, a civilian who went with Perry to Greenland in 1896, was selected to head up the new Bureau. During his twenty-five years as the head, the number of lighthouse stations, buoys, and light ships grew rapidly. By 1924, the United States had the largest lighthouse service in the world with nearly 17,000 of these warning and navigational devices in place.

The civilian Life-Saving Service merged in 1915 with the Revenue Cutter Service to create the modern U.S. Coast Guard. Under federal legislation enacted in 1939, the Coast Guard assumed control of the Bureau of Lighthouses, and enlisted Coast Guardsmen took over the lighthouses from the keepers as they retired. President Roosevelt wrapped the Lighthouse Service into the Coast Guard and its operations for budgetary reasons and because the Service had become too unmanageable. Bureau employees had the choice of becoming a Coast Guardsman with a position (a Head Keeper became a Chief Boatswains Mate), retiring, or staying on as a civilian employee and continuing to wear their Lighthouse Service uniforms. About one-half of the keepers chose to stay as civilians. Regardless of which alternative they decided on, they were under the jurisdiction of the Coast Guard.

In addition to the numerous regulations that existed on what wickies were to do, the Coast Guard continued the prohibitions as to what they couldn't. Keeping a station in good order was always important, and inspectors would "write up" the custodians for imperfections. If bad enough, a second offense meant dismissal. The Light-House Board warned one Point Loma Lighthouse keeper in the 1890s about the inspector's unsatisfactory findings and that a second violation would mean dismissal. When the inspector reported months later about the continued existence of the problems, the Board immediately fired the man, even though he had twenty years of service.

Being absent or sleeping on duty was another prohibition. If an inspector or officer came across someone doing this, the penalty was swiftly applied. If the violation was severe enough, the Board fired the man or the Coast Guard court-martialed him. However, it was known that young Coast Guardsmen—if close to land—rowed from their station and clandestinely met their girlfriends. After their romance rendezvous, perhaps including a few glasses of wine or a couple of beers, the happy men rowed back to their outpost.

Although the rules of the Service and followed by the Coast Guard were very specific, being your own boss can tempt anyone. Another rule outlawed drinking or intoxication on duty, and most keepers followed this. However, it's the exceptions that are the Devil and can become the rule. For example, on Christmas and New Year's Eve, exceptions were made. This was for starters, unless the head keeper despised any drinking or an inspector walked in.

Given the toughness of this work, isolation, stress from foghorns, and risky duty, alcohol was certainly used by some. Old-timer keepers who ran a station could get away with a lot more than the new "rookie." And they did. Although drunkenness was a strong cause for dismissal, one story by author Ralph Shanks is about the wickie that loved to carouse in San Francisco bars. He motored sober across the bay to drink, got into barroom fights, and then sped back drunk across the bay in his boat to the lighthouse. When his conduct caused people to start complaining, including a boat or two that the keeper nearly clipped, the district supervisor transferred the man to another tower far away from temptation.

During the Prohibition, various station keepers collaborated with the rum-runners when they were bringing illegal booze into the country. It also was fairly easy to set up equipment and distill alcoholic liquids at isolated lighthouse locations—and this happened on St. George Reef as discussed in a later chapter.

Keepers were also forbidden to "engage in any business which can interfere with their presence at their stations, or with the proper and timely performance of their lighthouse duties." Dating from the mid-1800s to when the Coast Guard assumed control, the relatively low salaries forced some keepers—or at least as they rationalized—to take a second job to make ends meet. Wickies typically moon lighted as fishermen, ferrymen, and boat pilots, as this was close to their profession. While on leave, others would substitute-teach, minister, or even work as a carpenter's aid. Back on the lighthouse, the keepers during their free time could write books, collect saleable collections of sea life, and even scheme to start a business with a partner on land.

These jobs were certainly legitimate employment, even if they were against the Board's rules. The keepers interpreted these regulations, however, that they could engage in anything to supplement their meager incomes, provided it didn't interfere with their duties. One lighthouse operator set up a thriving "summer colony" for tourists until the Light-House Board cracked down on that use of its facilities.

One wickie stands out above the rest with his "entrepreneurship." Tobias Cook was a Boston lighthouse keeper, who set up a cigar-manufacturing facility on Little Brewster Island in the 1840s. Mr. Cook transported young women out to the island to make the products, which he then brought back to sell in Boston as imported cigars. He paid the workers, however, substandard wages and they lived under unsanitary conditions. When people discovered the extent of his operations, the authorities shut down his business and forced him to resign.

THE OLD-TIMERS on St. George pointed to the savage waters and typhoon winds that stranded them and their crews, their continued hard work to keep the lamp lit and foghorn going, regardless of conditions, and the isolation. As most were single men, they knew that on other tours of duty, they could head to a local bar fairly easily, unwind, and find women to talk with and hold. This wasn't a possibility for weeks on end when ordered to report to this station.

The cold winds, ocean spray, and moisture seeping inside during winter made living difficult, and those wind-chill conditions could freeze both bones and soul. The continued maintenance responsibilities from these year-round conditions caused crews over their tours to paint rooms and walls, again and again; scrape plaster and re-cement the same areas, over and over; and work at the same rusty problems on the equipment.

The keepers couldn't count on scheduled departures or leaves, and personnel could spend days and weeks waiting to get to shore. Wickies had to pack and get ready, then wait for the weather to clear. Once they were off the rock, they started thinking when they would have to come back—and hence the high turnover greater than at other stations.

One seafaring man observed:

Lighthouse life is like living on a lightship: It's boring, you're living in a 100-square-foot room with four other men for a month without any relief. They don't always take showers, bitch about everyone else, and the human politics can be pretty bad. There is a hierarchy based just on how long you've been there as to the worst jobs assigned. You're always painting and maintaining the facilities. The captain can be an ego-maniac where it makes no difference how well you do anything as to his constant criticisms and commands.

After their duties were completed, however, the men also remembered the passing mariners who dropped newspapers and magazines in floating cans for them to read. They recalled the fishermen who yelled up for the latest weather information, or dropped by to chat and give them fresh-caught fish. There was a romance, a love, an affair with lighthouses and the sea. Lighthouses capture those who have seen them and fascinate those who haven't. These structures are this country's version of the great castles of Europe, and there were wickies who felt the same with passion.

The successful rock-living keepers loved the sea, its smell and mysteries, and the life of being on their own with no one around to tell them what to do. They couldn't work a routine, white-collared "citified" job if you told them that was their only choice. The old-time keepers couldn't and didn't want to fit into any life of plowing fields, cutting down timber, or working in a machine shop. They were one with the sea, rarely fearful, and basically indifferent to angry oceans and powerful winds that ordinary people trembled at.

Numbers who stayed on these reefs for years developed hobbies. On Tillamook Rock, one custodian practiced his golf swing with a small ball attached by a long string to a railing. Discovering a secret cove of hidden books, Jim Gibbs headed down to that secluded room and read. He later wrote numerous, well-written books about the sea, ships, and lighthouses.

Others on St. George tried their hands at fishing, collecting marine fauna, or even writing poetry. Some keepers learned to paint, and these passions continued into their retirement. The most popular recreation was reading, and most lighthouses had book collections, including St. George, although its library for years was out of date and limited.

During the Lighthouse Service days, St. George families could live either in their own residences in the city or two small houses maintained on the Battery Point side. However, the long tours away and conditions discouraged families from applying or staying any longer than it took to transfer away.

After World War II, the Coast Guard took over the former navy radio compass station on Point St. George to use as the St. George Reef Shore Quarters, and the men could spend their shore leave with their families in those facilities. The leave launch motored to and from Crescent City from its permanent mooring, and the St. George crew used the short-wave radio at the Battery Point Lighthouse to call the reef and find out whether that day's sea conditions allowed them to return.

Although female keepers weren't appointed to the St. George Reef Lighthouse, they were a continuing presence in U.S. lighthouse history. The risks and extreme conditions present in this calling forced them equally to reach for heights of uncommon courage in order that others could survive.

CHAPTER 11

Keepers in Skirts

W omen lighthouse keepers were far more numerous than is commonly known. Where families were allowed, the wives of keepers always assisted or took over responsibilities and duties. More than 250 female wickies over time either worked alone running a station or were officially appointed as an assistant keeper working with their spouse.

The first woman to serve at an American lighthouse was Hannah Thomas, whose career as keeper at the Massachusetts Gurnet Point Light lasted for ten years from 1776 to 1786. During this time period, she tended to four flat-wick lamps, each having four large wicks. The lamps burned whale oil, which required replenishing them up to three times a night, not to mention the daily wick trimming, cleaning, maintenance, and emergencies—every night and day without relief.

Well-known New York lighthouse keepers prior to the Civil War were Ann Wilbeck (Stuyvesant Light), T. Hudson (Cow Island Light), Miss C. A. Murdock (Round Out), and Mary A. Foster (Old Field Point). Amy Buddington was the keeper at Connecticut's Stratford Point Light in 1853; Margaret Stuart was appointed the wickie at the Bombay Hook Lighthouse in Delaware for twelve years (1850–1862). Then there were Virginia Amelia Dewesse (Old Point

Comfort Light in Virginia for four years), Miss Mitchell (Piney Point Light in Virginia), and Barbara Mabrity (Key West, Florida), to name a few. Abbie Burgess worked at Matinicus Rock Light in Maine (1853–1872) with her father and husband, and then assisted her husband at White Head Light in Maine (1875–1892).

Female lighthouse keepers operated in Maryland (three) during this time period, Mississippi, New Hampshire, Indiana, Massachusetts, Mississippi, and nearly every other state in the Union. At Biloxi Light (Mississippi) in the Gulf of Mexico, Mary Reynolds was the keeper from 1854 to 1866, followed by Maria Younghans for fifty-one years (1867 to 1918); Mrs. Younghans's daughter, Miranda, then ran the light until 1929.

California also had its fair share of women keepers. Albert and Julia Williams came to Santa Barbara in 1856 to take charge of the newly built lighthouse. Mr. Williams tired of these duties, however, and hired a man to take care of the light. His wife then agreed to assume these responsibilities in 1865. After her husband's death seven years later, Julia F. Williams kept the station running until 1905—for a total service of forty years.

Acts of heroism followed these responsibilities, and numbers of women saved the lives of countless men, women, and children. Assistant lighthouse keeper Roberta Boyd was twenty-one years old and in charge of the Spruce Point Lighthouse, near St. Stephen on the Saint Croix River in New Brunswick, Canada, on October 8, 1882. Her father, who was the head keeper, was away at the time. Following the instructions of her father, Roberta had climbed the lighthouse tower's stairs several times during the day and evening to refuel the lamp and check the light apparatus. After her last inspection, she walked back down the staircase to the living room below and talked with her mother. As a storm front had pushed in, it was difficult to hear each other over the roars of the wind and noisy splatters from the rain hitting the roof.

Roberta thought she heard noises emanating from the outside, but she wasn't sure due to the weather conditions. Stepping out the door, she definitely heard cries of terror from the river. Telling her mother to watch the light, she raced down to the boathouse. Boyd pushed the boat away from the dock into the swollen, rain-filled river and rowed in the direction of the cries for help. She soon picked up the outlines of an overturned sailboat and headed her rowboat toward a man who was struggling in the muddy water. Grabbing the man's shoulders, she helped pull him aboard. Seeing another struggling man nearby, she rowed close to the frightened person, grabbed his arm, and used all her strength to yank him into the small wood boat.

The powerful flood by now had carried the rowboat a good distance down from the lighthouse, and the exhausted, shivering men could not be of help. Although she was also quite tired from her efforts, Roberta Boyd rowed against the crosswinds and undulating river for half an hour before she could finally approach the dock. Near exhausted, she fought against the river to bring the rowboat to the upstream side of the dock, tied it when the boat slammed against the pilings, and then helped the men out.

Once inside the warm living room, the two men recovered in a few hours. A grateful Canadian government presented her with a valuable gold watch that honored her achievement. Her neighbors at St. Stephen presented her with a gold chain for the watch. The Canadian Department of Marine and Fisheries gave her a boat with these words engraved on the stern: "Miss Roberta Grace Boyd, grace darling of the Saint Croix, October 8, 1882."

AT CAPE ANN LIGHTS on Thatcher's Island off Gloucester, Massachusetts, Mrs. Maria Bray and her two children were alone on a stormy Christmas Eve. Her husband had left before in the station's dory and apparently had become lost in the blanketing snowstorm of 1864. The winds hurled the snow with terrifying force as flurries built up snow banks and obscured the path between the two 124-foot lighthouse towers. Mrs. Bray made her way to the first tower, located three hundred yards from the second one. She mounted the staircase with her container of oil to fill the lamps that had burned low. Inspecting the equipment, levels, and being satisfied with the light apparatus, Mrs. Bray then checked the moving weights and balances. Although the cold seeped into the tower and was closing down the island, everything otherwise seemed to be in fine operating condition.

When she was back on the ground, Mrs. Bray found it nearly impossible to see anything through the blinding snow flurries. Despite this lack of visibility, she turned her attention to the second tower and walked the one-fifth mile to check on it. She continued her efforts during the night, pushing a path through the snow under hard conditions to tend to the lights and keep them burning. She was successful in her efforts, and her husband was able to return and rejoin her that morning. Thanks to her tending the tower lights, he was safely guided back to his station.

Margaret Novell came from a prominent New Orleans family, and she married a wealthy cotton broker. His business bankruptcy, however, forced the family into working for their living at a lighthouse. She raised chickens in the station yard, kept a Spitz dog outside, and listened to a talking parrot in her kitchen. After Mr. Novell died in a drowning accident in 1891, leaving her with two small children to raise, Margaret carried on his duties as the keeper of the Head of Passes Light in Louisiana. Five years later, the Light-House Board appointed her to be the Head Keeper at the lighthouse at Port Pontchartrain Lake in the same state.

During her long tenure at that station, Mrs. Novell saved people from a sunken yacht, washed-over schooner, foundered sailboats, and even a small plane that crashed into the lake during a windstorm. When the intense hurricanes in that region stormed through, she kept her lighthouse doors open for those folks whose homes were being swept away. During one great storm in 1903, her lighthouse was the only structure left standing on the lower coast, and over two hundred survivors crowded for safety into that station. After the storm finally swept away, Mrs. Novell began raising relief funds and helped the residents find normal lives again. She tended to Pontchartrain for twenty-eight years, and then transferred to take over the operations of West End Light for another eight years.

After her retirement in 1932, Novell reported:

> There isn't anything unusual in a woman keeping a light in her window to guide men-folks home. I just happen to keep a bigger light than most women, because I have got to see that so many men get safely home.

KATHERINE AND JACOB WALKER of Sandy Hook Lighthouse in New Jersey met in 1868, fell in love, and married soon afterward. They lived at Sandy Hook Light until a position opened up at Robbins Reef Light, located between Manhattan and Staten Island on the west side of New York Bay. The couple had two children there, first a boy and then a girl. Katie rowed their children ashore every day to attend school at Staten Island, and they stayed home only when the storms whipped up waves that were too high and dangerous to travel over.

Surrounded by water on all sides, the lighthouse was a conical iron tower that rose forty-six feet above its granite base and looked like layers of cake with its brown-and-white colors. The structure had five large rooms with deep portholes for windows. Captains on incoming ships saw Robbins Reef as one of the first warning lights when they entered the bay.

This lighthouse marked the entrance to the dangerous Kill Van Kull channel, a three-mile-long waterway linking upper New York Bay to Newark Bay. The nearest point of land from this narrow ridge of jagged rocks is Staten Island, which is two and a half miles away, and New York City that is three miles away. At high tide, the ocean completely covers the rocks.

When her husband caught pneumonia some time later, he had

to convalesce at a hospital on Staten Island. For days when her husband was sick in bed at the lighthouse, Katie walked quickly up the stairs to tend to the light and then hurried back down to press her husband's hand and give him liquids to drink. To her, it was a "bitter night" when attendants came and took Jake away to the hospital. They brought the sick man down the iron ladder, which was at the front and the only stairs of her lighthouse home. Katie stayed behind on Robbins Reef Light to watch over its light and the station's operations.

On the tenth day after he had been taken away, a voice called up unexpectedly from the stairs and said, "I'm sorry, Mrs. Walker, but Jake's worse." She knew that her husband had died. Years later, she still wondered if she had made the right decision to stay on the rock and tend the light—but there was no one else who could. The light had to stay on.

The lighthouse department sent a person over to relieve her on the day of her husband's funeral, and this was the only time that she had relief. Katie was born in Germany in 1847. When coming to the United States, the ship captain made a mistake and discharged the passengers on the New Jersey shore instead of docking at New York City. Jacob Walker was the assistant keeper at Sandy Hook Light, and he later met the little immigrant widow and fell in love with her while teaching English to her and other immigrants.

The loneliness of Sandy Hook at first nearly overwhelmed Katie, and she refused to unpack her bags. As she began to grow happier with lighthouse life, she finally unpacked her trunks and accepted the myriads of boats and ships that whistled to them as being her neighbors. However, one time when Jake overstayed his time ashore, she packed her trunks once again. When her husband came back, he just laughed and unpacked them. When he died, she packed her trunks to leave for the last time. Although deeply grieving, she continued watching over the light and lighthouse's operations until someone else could take over.

Katie stared through the lighthouse's porthole and saw her husband's grave on Staten Island Hill. She looked at the burial spot every day, regardless of whether it was snowing, raining, or showing a fine spring day. She finally decided to remain on as the keeper, if the Light-House Board would allow her, keeping in mind her late husband's admonition: "Mind the Light, Katie!"

Some at first objected to her application, noting her small size: four feet, ten inches with a weight that was never more than one hundred pounds. However, the government agreed with her request, and Katie Walker became the keeper of Robbins Reef Light on June 6, 1895. She was the only woman "from Maine to Florida" who was a head keeper in a lighthouse that was surrounded by water.

She tended to the light by herself for five years as she waited for "little Jake" to grow up, and Katie's only help in watching over the station was what her pre-teenage children could give her. She never slept at night, as she needed to watch over the lamp. Every three to five hours she had to place a freshly filled set of kerosene lamps with well-trimmed wicks and a clean glass into operation or else the light went out. The clockwork that drove the rotating lens needed the dropped weight to be rewound or the light stopped flashing. When a sudden fog appeared, Katherine Walker started the engine that operated the warning horn. When the sun rose and the weather was clear, she drew the blinds and slept until it was time to row her children to the mainland for their schooling.

When Jake finally turned eighteen, the Board appointed him as her assistant keeper. From then on, she referred to him as her "assistant" and not as her son. Katie stayed on the lighthouse for seven months at a time before she rowed ashore to Staten Island for one day—even when Jake was on duty. She traveled to New York City for the afternoon, then hurried back to turn the switch on the light when the sunset gun on Governors Island boomed out.

The light had four large lenses, each one foot in diameter that concentrated the light so that it was visible twelve miles out to sea.

Not only did the machinery need to be rewound often with trimmed, filled wick-lamps ready, Katie had other responsibilities. She oversaw the lamp's brass in being cleaned daily and the lenses polished every month. Maintenance, painting, wiping, and cleaning were a constant chore for her and Jake, but she was the one with the responsibility.

During the winter, she scraped the frost off the lamp-room windows so that this wouldn't interfere with the light's intensity. When the fog rolled in, Mrs. Walker started the piercing fog signal, and if it didn't work, she climbed the tower and hammered on a large bell to warn ships away from the deadly rocks.

Over time, she was cited for being responsible in saving over fifty people. When someone was in danger, Katie raced to grab her oars, rowed out to the rescue, and pulled the people on board her boat. A popular fishing place, the Robbins Light area was known for the tidal whirlpools on the reefs' outer fringe of rocks. As fishermen were attracted to the surrounding natural feeding grounds for blackfish and striped bass, sudden squalls swept in that swamped boats and hurled men against rocks. Katie Walker commented about those she saved:

> Generally they joke and laugh about it. I've never made up my mind whether they are courageous or stupid. Maybe they don't know how near they have come to their Maker, or perhaps they know and aren't afraid. But I think that in the adventure they haven't realized how near their souls have been to taking flight from their body.

Twenty years later in 1915 on Christmas morning, she gave her children permission to row ashore and spend some time with their friends for the holiday. Katie remained on the lighthouse to watch over its operations. Although the morning was clear, as soon as the children left, a sudden storm arose and a shrieking gale slammed into the coast by that evening. She started the foghorn, and as the snow changed dramatically into driven, bitterly cold sleet, she heard a loud "snapping," as if the winds had ripped away the chain holding the one remaining rowboat to the dock.

Katie wrapped herself in a coat and ventured outside. The winds blasted against her face and body, nearly whirling her off the landing. The wind-driven sleet came down in sheets and covered her hair, as she said later, "like a hood." Ice, snow, and sleet covered the rocks, and she had to be very careful when walking because one slip meant certain disaster. She slowly felt her way along the icy walls, and then Katie came to the dock and rowboat.

As she had thought, the gale winds had forced one of the chains loose. As she reached for it, a blast of wind attacked the boat and chain, and the loose end of the metal snapped back to hit her in the eye. Although the impact of the chain stung, she grabbed it. Katie quickly secured the boat and started back to the lighthouse.

She couldn't see ahead due to the blinding sleet, and her injured eye was already half shut. Slipping now and then as the gale winds blew hard against her, Katie fought her way to the lighthouse. She made her way to the balcony, but had to be careful because the wind gusts were so strong they nearly blew her off. "Death was waiting for me on the rocks below," she later told reporters.

She sank to her knees to keep the winds from pummeling her off the metal terrace. With agonizingly slow movements, Mrs. Walker worked her way over to the door. She waited until the winds died down momentarily and then quickly reached to open the door. It was frozen closed. She slammed her crouched body against the entry several times until it finally opened slightly. Once it did, she pulled it open and quickly crawled inside. Knowing that her children would not try to return in the dory until conditions were better, she spent Christmas and that night alone in the lighthouse.

Katie Walker was calm and collected when working on the station. However, afraid of the cars, turmoil, and clatter, she disliked

cities and was frightened when visiting New York City. On the lighthouse, she had her freedom, tranquility, and never once had concern or "fear of dust or burglars." Assisted by her son Jacob, Katie
watched over the light at Robbins Reef until her retirement in 1919
at the age of seventy-three. She died eleven years later.

IDA LEWIS is the woman lighthouse keeper credited with the most
number of officially listed rescues and is probably the most famous.
From the age of twelve until her death at age sixty-nine in 1911, she
spent all of her years at Lime Rock Lighthouse on Rhode Island. Her
father became the first keeper of Lime Rock, located on a tiny island
situated one-third mile from Newport. Captain Hosea Lewis had
been there less than four months, however, when he suffered a disabling stroke.

Since the ocean completely surrounded Lime Rock, the only way
to reach the mainland was by boat. As the oldest of four children,
Ida rowed the others to school every weekday and bought needed
supplies from the town. Although the wooden boat was heavy, she
became very skillful with its handling and became an expert swimmer. Despite having to help her mother care for her invalid father
and a seriously ill sister, Ida took over the prime responsibilities for
the lighthouse's operations, including trimming and filling the lamp
during the night, polishing the carbon off the reflectors, and extin-
guishing the light at dawn.

A strong swimmer who could handle a sailboat or a dory, Ida
accomplished her first rescue in 1859 when she dragged four boys
from their capsized yawl into her lifeboat. On another occasion, she
reportedly saved three men whose boat had swamped, while picking
up sheep—and then rescued the sheep as well. She became known
throughout the country for her successful rescue attempts, never hes-
itating to save the lives of others at the risk of her own. With her
standard shawl draped over a brown poplin dress, Ida's profile and

courage stood out as she worked her way through raging ocean waters to extend a life-saving pole or oar.

Newspapers and magazines lauded her fortitude and commitment with lead articles. This fame brought countless visitors to Lime Rock to catch a glimpse of the famous Ida Lewis. Her wheelchair-bound father entertained himself by counting the visitors, which at times numbered one hundred per day and nine thousand for one summer. Admiring fans sent Ida numerous gifts, letters, and even proposals of marriage, some of whom offered to give references as to their good character.

The people of Newport, Rhode Island, declared July 4, 1869, to be "Ida Lewis Day." They presented her with various awards, as well as a brand-new mahogany lifeboat with red velvet cushions, gold braid around the gunwales, and gold-plated oarlocks. After officials made several laudatory speeches about her, it was Ida's turn to speak. The bashful woman asked a friend to give her thanks, climbed into her new boat, and rowed back to Lime Rock, happy to be away from the fanfare and congestion on land. Although Ida was uncomfortable with all of the attention she received, despite her attempts at avoiding publicity, fame continued to follow her.

Her picture adorned the front cover of *Harper's Weekly* in July 1869, where she was pictured as standing with her arms crossed beside a wave-splashed rock in Newport Harbor. President Grant that year also visited her in emphasizing the country's recognition of her feats. Ida escorted him around while showing the lighthouse and its operations, and the president said later that his visit with her was "one of the most interesting events" in his life. When she worried about President Grant getting his feet wet as he stepped on the narrow shore of Lime Rock, he laughingly responded, "To see Ida Lewis, I'd gladly get wet up to my armpits if that was necessary!"

She married Captain William Wilson of Black Rock, Connecticut, in 1870, but they separated after two years. Ida and her mother tended Lime Rock for her father from 1857 until his death in 1872. Although her mother was appointed keeper for seven years, Ida continued to perform the primary duties. By a special act of Congress in 1879, Ida Lewis became the keeper of the light with her own salary at $500 a year. The U.S. Life Saving Service in 1881 awarded her its highest medal for lifesaving heroism and service.

The Life-Saving Service in its recognition noted her rescue on February 4, 1881, of two soldiers, who near dusk were crossing on foot over the ice between their fort and Lime Rock Lighthouse. The men fell through a weak part of the ice, and Ida heard their "drowning cries." Despite the imminent dangers of her also falling through the fragile ice, the intrepid woman raced with a rope over to the two men, threw them the lifeline, and dragged the first soldier from the water onto the ice. By this time her brother joined Ida, and both pulled the second man back to safety. The ice was in a very dangerous state, and a short time afterward, two men fell through the flow in that vicinity and both drowned. The witnesses agreed that Ida's successful rescue carried the risk to losing her own life. The Life-Saving Service awarded her its rare and coveted Gold Medal Life Saving Award.

When she was sixty-three years old, Ida performed her last act of heroism. A close friend of hers had been out rowing, then stood up, lost her balance, and fell overboard. When Ida heard her cries for help, she pushed away in her lifeboat, rowed over to her friend, hauled her on board, and rowed back to the lighthouse's safety. This was the twenty-third "official" person that Ida Lewis had saved. One year later when she was sixty-four, the Carnegie Hero Fund selected her as a life beneficiary and granted her an annual pension of $360. When Ida Lewis died on October 24, 1911, the bells on all the vessels anchored in Newport Harbor tolled in her honor and memory.

The Lighthouse Service discontinued Lime Rock Light after World War I. The Rhode Island legislature next changed the name of the rock to Ida Lewis Rock, and the lighthouse service renamed the station the Ida Lewis Lighthouse. A group of Newport, Rhode Island, residents bought the tower and land later from the government. It is used now as a yacht club and has been called the Ida Lewis Yacht Club since then. In the mid-1990s, the Coast Guard named the first of its new class of Coast Guard buoy tenders for her, with each succeeding vessel in that class honoring a different lighthouse keeper.

A WELL-KNOWN FIGURE in Lake Michigan's history was Harriet E. Colfax, who in the late 1800s worked more than fifty years as keeper, most of them on the Michigan City Light in Indiana. Probably due to the fact that her cousin, Schuyler Colfax, was a member of Congress and vice president under President Grant, the Board appointed Miss Colfax in 1861 as the keeper of this light. The actual lighthouse on shore was a keeper's residence with a forty-foot-high white tower and its fifth-order Fresnel lens.

Long piers graced both sides of the entrance to Michigan City Harbor, and ten years later the Light-House Board built a beacon light at the end of the 1,500 foot long dock on the east side. At the same time that workmen constructed the beacon, they also built a wooden walkway that was supported by metal struts over the wharf. This light was to be maintained by the keeper of the onshore light, and the walkway intended to give some protection against the winter and spring storms that swept over the piers.

The conditions on Lake Michigan during its gales can become nearly as bad as those experienced in the ocean. As the surf crashed over her while she clung to the rope grips, Harriet made her way over the long walkway, just above the seething seas, to check on the lamp and its warning light. The icy water made her footing slippery, and her wet oilskin coat and heavy skirts dragged her down danger-ous conditions at best. The crashing waves from the lake then rose over her head and engulfed her as she clutched the railings. After she filled the lamp with oil, she returned to land over the same treacherous path. Once back in her residence, she had to dry her clothes before the fire and boil hot water for tea.

These storms were gruesome, and the winter gales and storms badly damaged the walkway and the light. During one such storm, the extreme conditions battered the station and then finally extinguished the beacon's lamp. Harriet hired a tugboat to steam to the pier's end and re-light the lamp. Another storm then blew the entire structure into the raging waters. When the destroyed walkway was rebuilt, severe winds in another year arose, shredded sails, and blew four ships into the elevated walkway where it once more broke apart.

Conditions were so bad during the winter months that the harbor was closed. After cleaning the lantern and polishing the lamps, she wrapped the lens in cotton and kerosene, stored the parts in the oil house, and closed the towers. Her responsibilities during these months were to monitor the lake, any boats, and note the weather. When shipping resumed over the lake the following May, Harriet Colfax again lit the lamp in the beacon at the end of the walkway and the one in the tower.

Even while in her eighties, Ms. Colfax insured that her lamp would burn brightly by heating the lard oil on her kitchen stove and running quickly to the tower or over the walkway to pour it into the lamps before the oil could harden. On one terribly windy, rainy night, she climbed up her tower, while it trembled so violently that she had difficulty holding on to it. Blown backward by the winds and stung by the sheets of sleet and spray, Harriet Colfax finally returned to her quarters. She then heard the gale winds blow the tower down.

Harriet Colfax was the keeper from 1861 to 1904, and when she finally retired on October 12, 1904, she had put forty-three years of service into that station. She died five months later. Three women served as assistant keepers before the Coast Guard assumed responsibility for the operations of this lighthouse. By then, the Fresnel lens was moved from the keeper's quarters to the east pier at the entrance to the harbor and the light electrified in 1933.

AT BLACK ROCK LIGHT off Bridgeport, Connecticut, the keepers rarely turned over, with only seven in its 125 years of operation. In 1817, the position went to Stephen Moore, but two years later he was injured and couldn't tend to the light. Although he remained the official keeper for another fifty-two years until his death at the age of one hundred, his daughter, Catherine (Kate), tended the light for all of those years. Kate started assisting her father with the duties by trimming the wicks when she was twelve. A few years after that, her father's health began to fail and Kate Moore from then on was "practically" the keeper. She assumed all the functions at Black Rock Light at age twenty-four and cared for her invalid father and did the work for those fifty-two years. Appointed at age seventy-six as the official keeper after her father's death, Kate Moore continued on until she retired seven years later in 1878 at the age of eighty-three.

Kate said that on calm nights, she slept in the nearby keeper's quarters, dressed "in a suit of boy's clothes" with her lit lantern hanging on the headboard. Her face was turned so that she could see the shining on the wall from the tower light and would know if anything happened. When gale winds could blow out the oil-lamp flames, she stayed in the lighthouse all night and kept the lamps burning. In an interview at age ninety-four, she recalled:

> Our house was forty rods [about seven hundred feet] from the lighthouse, and to reach it I had to walk across two planks under which on stormy nights were four feet of water, and it was not easy to stay on those slippery, wet boards with the wind whirling and the spray blinding me.

She not only kept the light burning, but Kate was also credited with saving twenty-one lives during her sixty-two years at the lighthouse.

During this time, she showed a variety of skills and talents. Tending to their vegetable gardens and raising sheep, cows, and poultry for food, including sheering the sheep, she kept the station self-sufficient. Kate needed to do this because the icy storms and high waves in winter cut the supply access from land. She built up a thriving oyster business. She also taught herself how to read and built a library of one hundred books, as well as learning to carve duck decoys that she sold as souvenirs to visitors and sportsmen. Kate Moore died in Bridgeport, Connecticut, at the age of 105.

ON THE WEST COAST, head keeper Charles Layton, his wife Charlotte, and their four children moved in 1855 into the Point Pinos Lighthouse near Monterey, California. The Light-House Board encouraged families to serve when possible, because the women and children often gave unpaid help to the keeper and they worked together as a unit. Although families also helped out when their father became ill, they still were unpaid unless those members were officially appointed as a keeper or assistant.

Charles left Charlotte in charge of the lighthouse when he joined a group of men trying to capture a dangerous bandit. During a shootout between gang members and the posse, Layton was shot and died soon after he returned home. Despite having to also raise her family, the widow Charlotte kept the station going with help from an assistant keeper.

When the local collector of customs, who then oversaw the area's lighthouses, recommended her and the Monterey citizens supported her with a signed petition, the Light-House Board in 1856 appointed Charlotte Layton as the West Coast's first woman head keeper at the standard salary of $1,000 per year. By the time she was appointed, thirty women had been acting as a head keeper on the U.S. East

Coast, and the reason for the disparity was the much greater number of lighthouses there at the time. Four years later, Charlotte married her assistant keeper, George Harris. Although Board regulations allowed a man to be in a subordinate role to a woman, she stepped down to again become an assistant keeper. After their retirement a few years later, George and Charlotte ran a hotel.

Other female keepers soon followed. Starting when she was a child and continuing through her adult years, Laura Hecox studied the plants, fossils, fish, and animals of coastal Northern California along Monterey Bay. Her father became the keeper of the recently built Santa Cruz Lighthouse in 1869, and this allowed her to continue her studies and help her dad. After her father died in 1883, her brother-in-law, Captain Albert Brown, recommended that the twenty-nine-year-old woman be promoted to the head keeper job at Santa Cruz. She was. This position allowed her to continue her studies there and earn a living. She remained in this position for thirty-four years until her retirement in 1917.

Prior to then, she donated her substantial collections of crustaceans, Eskimo artifacts, minerals, gems, petrified wood, shells, and Indian baskets to the Santa Cruz public library. Laura Hecox was self-educated in many disciplines, ranging from history, geology, botany, and religion to architecture, taxidermy, astronomy, and numismatics. Her collections even today stand out for their detail and breadth.

Another well-known West Coast wickie was Kate McDougal. Charles and Kate McDougal were married, and the seafaring couple had four children. Commander McDougal was appointed the inspector of the Twelfth Lighthouse District in the 1870s, and in 1881 he was inspecting the lighthouse at Cape Mendocino, as well as delivering its gold payroll. Rough surf unfortunately capsized his surfboat as it was approaching the shore, and he drowned. (See chapter 9, "The First Wickies.")

As his widow, Kate was left with four young children and an

inadequate pension, Inspector McDougal's friends in the service watched out for the family. A classmate at the Naval Academy and a future Spanish-American war hero, George Dewey, arranged for the Light-House Board to appoint Kate as the keeper at Mare Island near Vallejo, California, at the eastern edge of San Pablo Bay above San Francisco. Her friends in the Navy also arranged for a telephone as a Christmas gift to be installed at the station.

Since no schools existed on the island and traveling to land was too difficult, she educated her children as best she could. Kate McDougal and her oldest daughter planted a beautiful rose garden in front of the station, and a friend constructed a two-room play-house for the kids that had a wood floor and glass windows. With a Chinese cook preparing the meals, Kate was free to attend to her keeper responsibilities. With no doctors or dentists nearby, she was also the medical attendant. When her son blew off a piece of his ear while "playing around" with dynamite, she sewed it back on with needle and thread. Her children grew up, married, and left.

Keeper McDougal, however, faithfully kept the light for years. When a new light was built across the mouth of the Napa River, the need for the Marc Island light was eliminated. She retired later in 1916 when an automated fog signal was installed. She had served for thirty-five years as its keeper; the station was abandoned one year later and then razed in the 1930s.

A San Francisco Bay woman, Kate Nevins, succeeded her husband as the custodian of Winter Island Light. For forty years, her living room was the ten-by-sixteen-foot cabin of the steamer *Orizaba*, which had stranded on the island in 1891. She was known to sound her familiar warning to mariners during long periods of fog by beating her stove poker against a large tin pan.

When the *Leader* and *Garrett* collided in the bay in 1893, the 150 passengers on board the *Leader* were taken ashore onto Winter Island, when the ship threatened to sink. Most of them were patients from a mental institution that were being transferred to another facility. Kate Nevins's easy, kind approach calmed everyone until another boat could land at the island and retrieve the patients.

EMILY MAITLAND FISH was born in 1843, and at sixteen she traveled to Shanghai, China. Her older sister, Juliet, had married Dr. Fish, who was then in Shanghai on duty as a diplomatic counsel. Juliet died during childbirth, and by the time Emily, the doctor, and the baby journeyed back home in 1862, she and Dr. Fish had married.

They arrived in the United States while the Civil War was being fought, and Dr. Fish joined the Union Army to work as a medical director in the U.S. Army Corp. Joining the predecessor entity to the Red Cross, Emily, with Juliet's child, accompanied the doctor from one gory battle to another and helped attend to the wounded. When the war ended, they moved to Oakland, California, where the doctor established his private practice.

In November 1888, daughter Juliet married Lieutenant Commander Henry E. Nichols, who was the Light-House Board's Twelfth District inspector. After Emily's husband died three years later, Henry and Juliet mentioned to the fifty-year-old widow that a post at Point Pinos Lighthouse would soon be available owing to a retirement and that she might think about taking it. Emily quickly agreed, and the appointment only took her son-in-law's recommendation to get the job. This was three decades after Charlotte Layton's service at the same Point Pinos station.

Emily kept the small Cape Cod lighthouse and its ninety-two-acre reserve in as fine a manner as she had seen overseas. With her Chinese servant Que—who had traveled with Emily and Dr. Fish from Shanghai—she renovated the main house, brought in topsoil, and landscaped the grounds in front of the residence. She transformed the once desolate land into a scenic countryside of flowers, grass, trees, a picket fence, and cypress hedges.

People who saw Emily Fish remarked that she was charming and bright. Tall and attractive, she became a prominent figure with thoroughbred horses drawing her carriage into the town of Monterey. Emily allowed her horses to roam over the expansive property with grazing Holstein cows and French poodles. She managed the light-house with the help of two assistant keepers, conducted a full social schedule, and with Que tended to the gardens and livestock. Emily Fish held teas and dinners at the lighthouse, while socialites and res-idents alike treasured her invitations. Emily later helped form the American Red Cross chapter in Monterey.

When Juliet's husband died in 1902, her daughter wanted to follow in Emily's footsteps and applied for the position of keeper at San Francisco Bay's Angel Island Lighthouse. When the Board awarded her the position, she conducted her duties on Angel Island with the same professionalism and dedication as her mother gave. When a blanketing fog rolled in and the fog equipment failed, Juliet rang the fog bell by hand for twenty hours; when the fog returned two days later, she stayed up the entire night pounding the fog bell with a hammer. The Light-House Board gave her a deserved commenda-tion for those actions.

The two women were on duty at their respective lighthouses when the powerful 1906 San Francisco earthquake struck. That early morning, Emily was in the lighthouse starting her day. When the terrible pounding started, no one knew that it would last for two long minutes. As the earth shook and the building vibrated, she and Que raced up the tower stairs to watch over the light. Even though the intense shaking continued, they attended to the lamp, noting that its flame shot higher due to equipment malfunctioning under the stress. They kept the light under control and then started their inspections to see how severe the damage was.

At the same time, her daughter Juliet felt the rumblings under-neath Angel Island in San Francisco Bay. Horrorstruck, she watched the houses and structures on the surrounding hills collapse, the buildings on the waterfront implode, and the entire skyline become lit with fountains of fiery geysers, thick smoke, and blazing structures. Juliet was fortunate in that the damage to her station was limited; however, mother Emily's at Point Pinos was so damaged that the tower had to be torn down and rebuilt with reinforced concrete.

Both women retired in the early 1910s. Emily bought a house in beautiful Pacific Grove in Northern California, while Juliet lived equally quietly in the hills overlooking Oakland. Emily died in 1931 at the age of eighty-eight.

ON POINT FERMIN LIGHT at the entrance to San Pedro Harbor and Los Angeles, the first keepers were sisters. Although Mary Smith was the named official keeper in 1874, her sister Helen worked with her and helped operate the lighthouse. Deciding that this life was too lonely, both left eight years later. Several men became the keepers afterward for some forty years, until Thelma Austin assumed the duties at Point Fermin in 1925.

When the Service appointed her father as the head keeper, the family of nine (five brothers and two sisters) moved into the lighthouse. Unfortunately, Thelma's mother passed away shortly afterward, and her father then died due to his grief in losing his wife. Thelma wrote the Service requesting that she be given her father's position, in part penning:

Why, the sea and this lighthouse seem to me like a holy shrine, and I'm afraid it would break my heart to give it up. But no matter what happens, I will accept my fate with a brave heart, and just as cheerfully as my parents would have done. When you have been raised in the lighthouse atmosphere, as I have been, it is mighty difficult to change your mode of living and accept any other line of endeavor which does not offer romance and adventure.

Her statement moved the Service into awarding Thelma the position. She had to work as a part-time dental assistant, however, to supplement the low salary. When electricity was finally brought to the light-house, her responsibilities became easier. Instead of spending hours every day filling the lamp, polishing the lens, cleaning away the soot, and trimming the wick, she now only had to turn on the switch and clean the ocean's spray from the lamp room's windows.

Thelma continued her dual jobs of keeper and dental assistant up to December 5, 1941. Two days before Pearl Harbor, the Coast Guard deactivated the lighthouse, replaced the lens with a radar antenna, and placed armed lookouts with high-powered binoculars to roam the outside metal walkways.

Women not only were part of the legacy, courage, and romance of lighthouses, they were an integral part of that life. These accounts also include the stories of their ghosts.

CHAPTER 12

Ghosts in the Towers

Every lighthouse has its own mysteries, strange stories, and peculiar ghost. No other structure built creates the strange sounds, sights, and experiences of a lighthouse, especially when at night on a spiraling spiral staircase, a moaning breeze whirls around one's face with the sounds of the surf crashing far below. Howling winds in lonely towers by the ocean create weird noises anyway, not to mention a shadowy night with a full moon shining through windows while walking alone up a creaking stairwell. Echoing voices and squeaking window frames, slamming metal doors, flashing lights, and unexplained reflections all create their special effects—especially when isolated for hours in a dark place—even if at first one doesn't believe in ghosts.

Tillamook Rock had its own ghost, according to Jim Gibbs, who wrote that it:

> howled like a banshee especially during driving southwesterly storms. It was an experience to stand on the spiral staircase and listen to its shrill cry and then to feel the moist breeze that passed over as if being brushed by a wet blanket.

The early Clatsop Indians viewed Tillamook Rock in spiritual awe and worship. They believed that spirits lived in clandestine tunnels under the ocean that ran out to the rock. The natives wouldn't land their canoes on the reef or try to scale its high rock walls, fearful that these ghosts would be there.

It is said that Muriel Tevenard's spirit haunts the old Yaquina Bay Lighthouse on the Oregon coast. This site had one of the shortest careers of any light station on the West Coast, as one keeper watched over the site from 1871 to 1874, at which time it was abandoned in favor of the larger Yaquina Head station constructed a few miles north. Over a century ago, Muriel and her father journeyed from Coos Bay to the south to Yaquina Bay. He left his daughter with a hotel landlady while he traveled on by sea. Awaiting her father's return, Muriel sketched drawings or walked on the beach below the then abandoned lighthouse, a large, two-story wood house with the tower on the roof.

She met a group of young campers and began spending time with them. One dark night, the teenagers decided to walk through the lonely lighthouse. As a fog slowly pushed in, Muriel and her newfound friends walked slowly into the old station, one of them holding a flickering candle. A circular wood staircase wound its way to the second story, and the girls and boys walked up the creaking, narrow passageway. Brushing aside cobwebs and dust, they discovered a closet on the second landing where a metal box covered a dark hole, more than likely the trunk containing the weights used to drop and turn the lens.

One of the boys began talking in a low voice about what could be inside the trunk, such as the cut-off parts of a dead body, even a decapitated head. The group became nervous when hearing this, especially in this scary place. When a girl suddenly screamed, everyone panicked and ran down the landing into the outside fog and darkness. Muriel had to go back inside, however, to retrieve her gloves that were left behind in fright. When she didn't return quickly, her friends became even more nervous. They then thought she was playing a trick on them by leaving quietly through the back door.

Suddenly, Muriel's high-pitched screams pierced the heavy air, one after another. They tried to open the front door, but it was now latched from the inside. They searched around the abandoned lighthouse, but Muriel was nowhere to be seen. They nervously gave up their search, but later told the locals what had happened. The next day, residents walked over every square inch of the lighthouse, but they couldn't find a shred of evidence that the girl had been inside—except for pools of blood on the spiral staircase and near the trunk inside the closet. Muriel was not found or heard from again.

The Yaquina Bay Lighthouse stood above the house, and wickies have talked for years about seeing strange lights in the lonely lantern house. One Coast Guard keeper said he saw the glow of a swinging lamp floating outside toward his station. He watched the willowy figure holding the light, but when he switched on the tower's floodlight, the apparition was no longer there. Others swear they've seen her specter flowing over the paths behind the lighthouse or even staring out from the dark house.

Similar tales also concern the second Yaquina Head Lighthouse. During its construction, a worker fell in 1872 from the top of the ninety-foot tower to his death between the double walls. As the story goes, the builders decided to leave the body entombed inside and not try to remove the walls where his body fell. They sealed the vents with mortar. Keepers swore later that a ghost was there and that they could frequently hear something enter the tower and climb up the iron staircase. Although experts such as Jim Gibbs discount these stories, he wrote, "Though the story has little foundation, it is no secret that the Yaquina Lighthouse is a spooky place on a windy night and certainly conducive to all kinds of weird imaginations of the mind."

In the same Oregon area, Tom Briggs in the 1880s built a hotel at Monterey Beach. He was married and deeply in love with a very attractive Indian woman, and they had a beautiful daughter who lived with them at the hotel. A gale howled in and whipped up the ocean, as he returned one night to the hotel from a trip by horseback. As Briggs tried to cross a creek that emptied its roiling waters into the ocean, a set of sneaker waves rose up and swept him and his horse out to sea. Neither was seen again. Torn by her beloved father's death, his daughter committed suicide inside her room. Residents in the area have claimed to have seen her apparition walking along the beach on stormy nights in search of her father.

Oswald Allik, who was a keeper at Tillamook Rock Lighthouse, became the last keeper at the Heceta Head Lighthouse in Oregon before it closed. Allik believed there were ghosts at both lighthouses. Keepers saw ghostly figures, rediscovered personal articles lost in different places, saw doors suddenly slam shut and open windows abruptly close, and endured other unsettling experiences.

The abandoned grave of a baby girl lies by Oregon's Heceta Head Lighthouse. The little girl was the daughter of one of the first keepers, and after the family moved away, someone tended to the grave after the loss. Years later, during the mid-1900s, inexplicable things started to happen. Keepers found possessions suddenly moved or they disappeared, closed cupboards were open the next morning, a box of rat poison in the attic vanished, and a 1900s set of silk stockings appeared from nowhere. In the 1970s, a workman was cleaning the windows in the keeper's house. Noticing a mysterious reflection in the glass, he turned and saw the image of a silver-haired woman floating above the floor in a long, dark dress. The terrified man ran away.

Others then sighted the ghost. One night, a married couple in the house heard scraping sounds on their bedroom ceiling. They investigated the following day and found bits of glass that someone had neatly swept into a pile near a new attic window. Some people have seen the Gray Lady, as this apparition is called, at other times.

She has been seen walking the grounds, as if she were searching for someone lost.

A similar haunted lighthouse is Point Lookout in Maryland. The spirit of a woman dressed in a white blouse and long, blue skirt is usually seen at the top of the lighthouse stairs. Some believe that she's the ghost of the wife of the first keeper, who stayed for thirty years after her husband died. People believe that other spirits also inhabit this station, and park rangers swear they've seen apparitions walk around, talk loudly, move articles about, and even open and shut doors.

At nearby Battery Point Lighthouse in Crescent City, wickies said later that they heard the sound of strange footsteps at night in the tower. When bad weather stormed in, several keepers claimed they heard invisible men heavily stomping up the stairs with heavy boots. During this time, the men had to walk frequently up and down the staircases inside a whistling tower in the dark to fill the lamps and check on how they were burning.

One keeper at Battery Point claimed that miniature mermaids had visited him. These small "Tinker bell" figures had pearls for eyes, delicate tiny webbed hands, and lovely green-seaweed hair. He swore up and down that the tiny creatures had visited him and that he had managed to become friends with them. By offering food to the small figures, he tempted the mermaids to leave the sea and come up on land. The keeper claimed that his friendship with the tiny creatures was returned, and that they had accepted his invitation to join him in the living room. Residents apparently took the man later to an area hospital.

For many years, people reported seeing strange lights emanating from California's Point Vicente Light Station. Operational in 1926, one attendant reportedly saw the ghost of a woman who glided gracefully around the lighthouse in a long, flowing gown. A later keeper became very curious about this, especially since the apparition appeared so consistently at certain times. After his investigations, he concluded that the revolving Fresnel lens had been creating the beautiful ethereal form. He said that the light's particular rotation threw off reflections that caused the specter's creation.

This light was dimmed during World War II for security reasons. After the war, however, residents complained about the tower's bright flashes when the light came back to its normal power. The Coast Guard responded by painting the land side of the lantern room's windows in a pearly white color—and the ghost once again became visible. Seen through the opaque windows, some say that the rotating lens created the illusion of a woman pacing the tower's walkway and gave rise to Point Vicente's "Lady of the Light." Others believe that the ghost was a woman's spirit who leaped into the sea when her lover was lost in a shipwreck off the point.

Folklore in the Florida Keys holds that the restless spirit inhabiting Carysfort Reef Lighthouse, a screwpile tower, is of old Captain Johnson. He was a curmudgeon of a man, whisker faced and tough, who died shortly after the lighthouse was built. The wickies who succeeded him heard terrible screeching and moans inside the tower on summer nights. They said it was Johnson's ghost who still hadn't left his position.

A fisherman spent the night at the station, and the lighthouse's shudders and groans made him so nervous that he got up to find out the cause, otherwise he'd never get any sleep. He inspected the station's huge iron girders and braces, finally concluding that the sun's heat expanded the metal with the cool night's air causing this to quickly contract. The sounds of the metal's contractions were what people had been hearing.

According to the legend, Execution Rocks Lighthouse on the western end of Long Island Sound had a dreadful past. Before the Revolution, prisoners who had offended the King of England or advocated any change from his rule suffered a terrible fate. The British publicly executed their prisoners by chaining them to the walls of a large pit and watching them drown horribly when the tide rose and filled the hole. When George Washington and his depleted forces fled from Manhattan, the British were in hot pursuit. As if unseen spirits had decided to enter the fray, the ship transporting the English soldiers suddenly veered onto Execution Rocks and everyone on board drowned. Washington was able to make his safe retreat to White Plains, New York, and battle on from there. Owing to the history of executions on that site, the Light-House Board decreed that anyone who served at the later built lighthouse could serve voluntarily.

Sandy Hook Lighthouse in New Jersey has its own ghost story. During the nineteenth century, a new keeper came to the light. As he inspected the lighthouse, he decided that the structure seemed to have a basement, although he couldn't find any doorway leading there. Over time, his curiosity became so strong that he ripped up the floorboards. The keeper found a way underneath the floor that led to a hidden, dark basement. He crept down. In a scene reminiscent of *Psycho*, the horrified wickie discovered a skeleton that was propped up at a table facing a crudely built fireplace. No one could find out how the skeleton became walled in or solve the mystery of the secret basement.

Destruction Island Lighthouse off the Washington coast is another place where a specter was seen—but only one time. As this spot was once a sacred burial ground for the Indians, residents weren't sure if this wasn't due to the ghosts of Indians who felt that their resting place had been violated, or the soul of a lost fisherman whose body had washed ashore three years before and was buried underneath rocks on the island.

One stormy night, the keeper and his wife were reading in the living room. Their cat lay sound asleep nearby on the floor. The winds moaned outside as a storm approached and blew small twigs noisily against the door. Suddenly the cat leaped to its feet, hissed violently and arched its back. The couple heard dull sounds from the attic and turned in that direction. They heard footsteps then slowly echo down the steps—one by one.

They watched their pet back away as the sounds of the steps hit the landing and crossed the room. An invisible entity opened the door and vanished into the winds, slamming the door behind. While the eerie sounds of the wind continued whistling through the night, their cat curled up and went back to sleep. But the spirit never returned.

Another mysterious story comes from the isolated Hendricks Head Lighthouse that was located near Boothbay Harbor, Maine. The keeper was walking away from the lighthouse when he spotted a "well-dressed lady" who was traveling on the same road. He was surprised to see such a sight because night was approaching and the woman was obviously not from the area. She wordlessly passed by him. When the man returned to the station after his errand, he saw no more signs of his mysterious visitor.

Her dead body washed ashore the next day on the beach near the lighthouse, weighted down with a flatiron. The woman had either been murdered or committed suicide. The lady was never identified, and the wickies buried her in a cemetery close to the lighthouse. From time to time, others saw the beautiful woman in the evening as she walked toward the lighthouse on that lonely stretch of road. She also appeared just above the sea in front of the station, and people stared at the specter that slowly walked over the beach. But it never left footsteps in the soft sand.

THE DEATH of the two men at the first Minot's Ledge Light Station off Boston, Massachusetts, provided even more ghastly tales. The April 1851 storm that struck the New England coast during the night turned Boston into an island, flooded much of the area, and collapsed the lighthouse into bent pilings. The two assistant keepers, Joseph Antoine and Joseph Wilson, were killed.

The construction of the new stone tower started four years afterward, as a lightship stood guard off the harbor. Five years later, the last stone was laid and the light beamed out once again. Tales of strange spirits started soon afterward and continued for years about the strange groans, tappings, and goings-on at the second Minot's Ledge station. Several keepers became convinced that the ghosts of the two doomed assistant keepers still resided in the lighthouse, sending signals to each other and the men about the dangers of Minot's Ledge. Local fishermen reported hearing moans and cries for help echoing from the base of the lighthouse.

When the second Minot light became operational, the head wickie was keeping a lookout from the tower one night. When he tapped his pipe against a table, he heard a series of taps answer back as if trying to communicate in code. The man tapped again and received a similar response. Thinking this was his assistant, the wickie waited and then rang a bell for the man to come on duty. When he finally appeared, the assistant told his boss that the bell had awakened him from a deep sleep and no one else was on the lighthouse. The men shuddered after realizing the tapping sequence was the signal customarily used for relief in the old tower where the two had died.

Mariners on ships passing the new Minot during the night insisted that they heard mysterious noises or saw figures clinging to the lower section of the ladder leading to the lantern-room door. A crew of Portuguese fishermen swore they saw a figure hanging on to an outer ladder and shouting at them in their own language, "Afastar-se! Afastar-se!" ("Keep away! Keep away!") The assistant keeper, Joseph Antoine, was Portuguese.

Later, as the keepers ate dinner, they heard the crashing of the seas against the tower base. A whisper of sea air gave a light moan as it wafted through the lighthouse, and the men then heard the weird tapping again. As one stared at the other, the wickies then reacted and ran up the stairwell to the light tower. Once there, they found the door opened to the gusting winds. They concluded that the sounds were meant to alert them to the impending, dangerous storm.

As at St. George Lighthouse, keepers reacted weirdly to their duty at times and had to fight for their sanity. Another swore that the rounded tower of Minot's Ledge drove him crazy because it lacked corners. One other quietly slit his throat without leaving a note or any reasons why. Wickies came off their duty at Minot and whispered about how they had discovered the lamp and its lens mysteriously cleaned and polished without human help. They passed down for decades the tales of the strange tapping sounds and the spirit that held tightly to the iron ladder.

Close to Minot's Ledge is Boston Light and nearby Georges Island, home of the "Lady in Black." A beautiful Southern woman learned that her husband during the Civil War was being held captive on an island close to the light station. She came there to free her husband, but the troops captured her instead. Condemned to death as a spy, a firing squad executed her the following spring. Wickies talked in low voices about seeing her apparition coming back to the station and haunting it; they heard her soft whispers and willowy apparition—and then it disappeared.

A keeper on the New London Ledge Light Station in Connecticut discovered in 1936 that his beloved wife had run away with a ferry boat captain. He couldn't bear the loss and humiliation, so the man opened the steel door to the lantern gallery, walked out, and leaped to his death. Wickies subsequently said that this door would mysteriously open and they knew the sound of that particular door opening up, which "no wind ever did." Other keepers felt a chill in certain places or heard the sound of footsteps and the lamp-room floor being mopped.

According to the author Elinor DeWitt, the Sequin Light Station on Maine's Kennebec River is the site of a very strange story involving a keeper who brought his bride to live with him. She was a woman who loved music, and the man managed to find a piano and transport it back to the lighthouse. The keeper's wife was ecstatic and played the same tune, over and over, because it was the only sheet music that came with the piano. Even though he brought many different scores and music for her to play, his wife would only play the same tune—becoming a wild-eyed, near-skeleton of a person in the process.

She wouldn't stop. And the man always heard the same music. Night after night, the strange tune echoed from the island. One evening, the piano playing and melody stopped abruptly and never started again. When residents later investigated, they found a macabre sight. The lighthouse keeper had become as mentally deranged as his wife. He had strangled her to death, then used an axe to hack the piano into small wood pieces. Years later, nearby residents insisted that they could still hear the music late at night.

In the early 1900s at St. Simons Lighthouse on the Atlantic coast by Brunswick, Georgia, the Svendsens were in charge of the station. Years before, in an altercation the assistant there had shot and killed the head keeper of the lighthouse. Carl Svendsen's wife each night set dinner on the table when she heard her husband's boot steps echoing down the tower steps after tending to the light. Listening for the same steps, the family dog, Jinx, was in his usual place at the foot of the stairs. As the footsteps became louder and louder, Jinx raised his nose to smell his master. The dog seemed surprised when it didn't pick up the usual scent. When the wife turned to meet her husband, she discovered to her surprise that he wasn't there. Jinx came slowly to his feet and snarled. A near imperceptible form floated through the kitchen and then disappeared as the dog backed into a corner.

Mrs. Svendsen climbed the stairway to the tower to check on her husband. He had never come down. She told him what had happened and the specter that she had seen. A few days later, her husband also heard the spirit's footsteps. The family apparently became used to the frequent sounds of the footsteps, but no one ever appeared, and the Svendsens served that lighthouse for thirty-one years. Jinx never accepted the spirit, however, and growled every time the anomaly appeared. Some believe that the specter was the murdered keeper's restless spirit.

With lighthouses shuttered down and computerized, automated stations now flashing the lights and sounding foghorn blasts, it's easy for people to think that these ghost stories are simply folklore. However, if you ever go inside an isolated lighthouse late at night when the ocean winds moan, or walk up a damp, darkened, spider-webbed tower, you might also hear the sounds of heavy boot steps coming down the stairwell to greet you.

PART IV

THE COAST GUARD
AND ON

CHAPTER 13

St. George Duty and Tales

On the evening of December 7, 1941, after the Japanese attacked Pearl Harbor, the lighthouses on both coasts dimmed their lights or went black. This was two years after the U.S. Coast Guard took over the responsibility for the nation's light stations. The destructive effects of World War II, however, impacted the men on St. George Reef sooner than at most other locations. Two weeks after the sneak attack on Pearl Harbor, a Japanese submarine torpedoed the oil tanker *Emido* twenty miles north of Humboldt Bay. The surviving crewmembers abandoned the vessel, and the ship drifted aimlessly in the currents, finally grinding onto Steamboat Rock at the entrance to Crescent City Harbor. Another winter storm blew in and broke the ship in two, washing one part ashore while sinking the other.

Two days after the attack on the *Emido*, another Japanese submarine destroyed the Union Oil Company tanker *Montebello* to the south and near a lighthouse off Cambria, California. Among other harassment, a Japanese sub shelled an oil refinery near Santa Barbara in February 1942 and added to the fears. Although later in 1942, a fleet of Japanese submarines sunk three more oil tankers between Cape Flattery, Washington, and Cape Blanco, Oregon, the sub attacks on the U.S. West Coast basically ceased. However, these events forced the wickies to be continually on guard, although the long distance between the Japanese refueling bases and the West Coast was too far for most of their submarines. This wasn't the case on the East Coast where Nazi subs took a heavy toll in sinking Allied shipping offshore.

Shortly after midnight in June 1942, a German submarine landed four Nazi spies on a beach near Long Island, New York, to sabotage American defense–related industries. A Coast Guardsman armed only with a flashlight came across the four men on the beach and gave the alarm that eventually ended in their arrest. Four nights later, four more German spies were dropped off at Ponte Vedra Beach, near Jacksonville, Florida, but they were also later found and arrested. America feared that both coasts were now vulnerable, so the military turned its attention to coastal protection. By later executive order, the Coast Guard was transferred to the U.S. Navy until peace was restored, and its responsibility was to patrol the beaches and help guard the coastlines, while the U.S. Army and Navy were there to repel any invaders.

During World War II, St. George Reef Lighthouse operated as another set of eyes and ears for the U.S. military. Its personnel were on a constant, high state of alert, especially given the proximity of the West Coast to attack and the apparent ease with which carrier-based Japanese bombers had devastated Pearl Harbor. Even though homes on land were blacked out, the light at St. George continued blinking through the night to warn shipping, and it was the only light seen from the north for miles.

The Coast Guard's beach patrol was set up to guard the coasts, including hundreds of lonely miles of California shoreline. These beach patrols conducted their tours in jeeps, on horseback, and on foot. The military built lookout towers and barracks at regular intervals along the coast, although most were established at existing lifeboat or light stations. The fears of Japanese spies landing along the Pacific as they did on the Atlantic kept wickies jumpy. On isolated St. George Reef Lighthouse, the men were wary; it would be easy for the Japanese to take over their tower secretly in any initial foray into California and the West Coast. Nothing occurred despite their precautions and the men being armed.

Although landing on St. George was perilous, heading to land could be equally risky. In November 1946, heavy seas carried the St. George launch onto the beach, and the huge breakers pummeled the boat until an amphibious vehicle was able to pull it on land. At another time, the Battery Point Lighthouse keeper, Wayne Piland, and his son, Donald, picked up the outline of the St. George launch drifting off Battery Point. They rushed in their surfboat to the aid of the stranded crew who had run out of gasoline.

LIFE AT ST. GEORGE REEF LIGHTHOUSE continued to be extremely hard on the keepers; dangerous conditions could unexpectedly arise from what was thought to be an "average" storm. During the savage winter of 1952, waves and spray crashed over sixteen stories high to surge over the lighthouse, shattering lantern-room windows in a powerful, dangerous event. Personnel who experienced rogue waves like this were in awe at their impact when slamming against the structure, and over the station's history more than a few soon requested transfer papers.

Duty on St. George was understandably still one of the least sought after assignments. Time spent at the station was inhospitable at best, hazardous at its worst. Families and close companionship even now were not permitted except on "Visitor's Day," and the tower could take on a cold, isolated, and foreboding feeling. Although keepers were rotated on a predetermined basis, the frequent storms didn't lessen its interference with the arrival date of relief crews.

Given the weather's unpredictability, it was difficult to maintain the initial work shifts of three months at the station, followed by two months off. In the early 1970s, the procedures changed and keepers stayed at the lighthouse for four-week periods during one stretch with two weeks of liberty. Five keepers were still attached to the station during Coast Guard times on a rotating basis with generally three on duty and two ashore. The hazardous, back-and-forth trip by small boat to the rock required at least two men in the launch, and it was important to always have three keepers at the station to maintain a double watch when the heavy fogs rolled in.

More than fifty years ago, in 1952, John Gibbons joined the Coast Guard. He was six feet, two inches tall and weighed 160 pounds at the time. Gibby (his nickname) is very personable, tough, and has a quick sense of humor. He can get along with just about anyone—and he would have to on this duty.

When he was eighteen, an officer asked if he was interested in "working in a lighthouse off Portland, Oregon." John was from Colorado, young, and thought it might be fun. Just before his transfer papers came through, he was chatting with another Coast Guard officer. The man asked where he was going, and Gibby told him that he was heading to St. George Reef Lighthouse. The officer said, "You must be kidding. They just killed three men up there (referring to the deaths of three Coast Guardsmen that's described later), and you're going to that forsaken place?"

Gibbons spent thirty-nine months at St. George on two tours of duty: Starting in 1953, he stayed there for twenty months, and then requested a transfer because he was becoming stir-crazy. His transfer was to a lighthouse underneath the Golden Gate Bridge; however, he found this to be so boring with "two old men" that he asked to transfer back and served a second term of nineteen months, leaving in November 1956 at the age of twenty-two. His service was the longest of any Coast Guardsman stationed at St. George Reef Lighthouse.

When he reflected back on his time, he said that it was a "hell hole," "the worst duty in the Twelfth District" (this particular Coast Guard district), and "bad." "You worked day and night," he said, "and here you were stuck on this rock." Despite these feelings, John still found aspects that he liked, such as being left alone and able to do what he wanted.

When Gibby first came to the area on his initial duty tour, the day was rainy, cold, and blustery. He stepped off the bus and looked around at the small town of Crescent City, California, which was a rural, small area surrounded by thick forests. It numbered three thousand hardy folks back then, and the town's prime industries were logging, lumbering, commercial fishing, and businesses catering to the tourists that traveled up the coast highway.

When the prospective keeper walked around Crescent City and saw its Battery Point Lighthouse on a land spit—an easy walk from the mainland at low tide—Gibby said to himself, "Boy, this is good. But why do I have to call them when I can already see the light-house?" Although he shook his head at these seemingly inconsistent instructions, he called the telephone number given to him. The officer who answered just told him to wait, and a short time afterward, Chief Fred Permenter drove up to the bus station in an old pickup and introduced himself.

Permenter was the duty officer in charge at St. George Light-house, and the thirty-five-year-old man had been in the U.S. Coast Guard for fifteen years. Fred was a chief boatswain mate (CBM), as each officer in charge of the lighthouse was also a CBM and designated as chief. A married man with children, he spent his off-duty time and was now stationed on the shore installation at Point St. George with his wife and family.

According to Gibbons, "Fred was a nice guy and well-liked. The people in Crescent City liked him. He was a good friend of the keeper and his wife at the Battery Point Lighthouse and helped out both when they needed it." Permenter was tall, lean, and had dark hair.

Fred drove through the city and headed north along the coast. When Gibby soon saw the Point St. George shore station on land—

a series of white wood buildings in a compound—he thought to himself, "This is okay. I can do this." He then asked Permenter, "Where do I go now?" Without a word, Fred gave him a pair of binoculars and just pointed out to where he should look in the ocean. When Gibbons had his first view of the imposing, isolated lighthouse with the surf crashing over its rocks, he thought to himself, "I'm dead . . . I've really done it now."

When a Coast Guardsman's land leave ended, the men first shopped for groceries, bought their magazines, and readied themselves for their duty tour. One of the girls at the market took one look at their magazines (*"Playboy* types") and said, "You must be from that lighthouse." On the day before Gibby shipped out, one of the burly "old salts" on his shift took him to a local, seedy, smoky bar. The older man sat John down and growled, "Do you want a beer?" The bartender sauntered up, took one look at the younger man, and questioned suspiciously, "Are you twenty-one?"

Before the surprised Gibby could come up with an answer, his companion looked the bartender straight in the eye, pointed away to the beach, and said in a deep-throated voice, "He's out on that lighthouse and he's with me." The barkeep smiled broadly and said knowingly, "That's good enough for me. What do you want, kid?"

That next morning, the station's twenty-six-foot launch was taking John to the rock with Permenter and a second Coast Guardsman. With the whipping winds and choppy waters, Gibby was freezing in the back as he listened to the voice over the radio-transmitter crackle, "ETA in fifteen minutes." He heard the name of the reefs they passed: Star Rock, Hump Rock, Whale Rock, and then South West Seal Rock. As the boat motored along, the air was cold, the fog thick, the water rough, and the visibility only one hundred feet. As soon as the boat came close to their destination, the fog lifted and Gibbons had his first close-up sight of St. George. "It was like a horror movie," he said.

The lighthouse reminded you of Dracula's Castle, and the seas were breaking all over it with hissing foam. I was an eighteen-year-old kid who didn't know what this assignment was going to be like. I kept thinking to myself, "I'm a dead man. I'm really a dead man."

The first couple of hours were something else, and it was hard getting used to that medieval castle. When you finally arrived there, everyone suddenly became really serious, and this started as soon as you landed. The isolation of being on this faraway rock, plus the real dangers of getting on and off, made this assignment tough, hard, and lonely. And isolated duty is isolated duty.

On his first tour, only a few old, torn books were lying around with no magazines, television (this was just starting on the East Coast), or even fishing equipment—"no nothing," as he said. When the men could scrape together the money to buy their first television set, the picture was so bad they spent their time watching the test patterns.

Before he first headed there, the "old salt" on his shift had asked him if he could cook. Gibby had quickly replied, "No, I can't." He explained that he was a second-class engineman and in charge of keeping the engines, equipment, and generators working. The older man said matter-of-factly, "You better learn how to. We all take turns out here." It later turned out that his older acquaintance could only cook steak and frozen vegetables. Gibby remembered how his mom used to cook and started fixing roasts, gravy, mashed potatoes, and complete meals.

He soon was doing all of the food preparations, and the other men traded off washing dishes for him instead of doing the cooking when their turn came. Gibby cooked pizza (which the guys liked), spaghetti, the roasts, chicken, and concluded, "We ate good." Their main meal was dinner; for breakfast and lunch, everyone was on their own.

Each person made cold-cut sandwiches for lunch or ate cereal and cooked eggs for breakfast. Easy, fast meals were the norm. The Coast Guard then gave a food allotment to each man of eighty dollars per month, and each could spend that money as he wanted and bring the food to the lighthouse. This allowance went a long way in those days, which is why the men ate steaks with good cuts of ribeye whenever they wanted.

One time, the other men on his tour kept "bugging" him to get some beans and make a pot of "good" bean soup. Gibby had never done this before, so he bought the beans on his off time and read about how he could make this type of soup. Back on the station, he grabbed a bag of beans and soaked them overnight in a pan of water. He thought about the beans at night and felt that there weren't enough of them to make a meal. When he walked into the kitchen the next morning, he discovered that the beans had swollen up and he had "beans all over the place." He said, "We had beans for breakfast, beans for lunch, and beans at dinner for three days."

The crew asked him another time to make roast turkey. He dutifully read the directions and tossed the turkey in with a towel over it. One hour later the stove was smoking and smelling up the entire kitchen. When Gibby opened the stove door, he discovered that the towel was nearly on fire. He then read that he had to baste the towel, as well. "I burned that sucker out," he said, "and had to start something else."

When not cooking, Gibbons worked in the engine house inside the caisson. He was responsible for the large diesel engines, generators, air compressors (for blowing the foghorns), and the big batteries. The men had to turn the lights off, even during the day, because the batteries were needed to start the generators, which in turn created the needed electricity. Despite Gibby's warnings, a new seaman one day left the lights on and the generators nearly didn't start. This would have meant that the entire lighthouse, including its light, would have been dark—and a major problem. The equipment barely turned over, but he was able to start the systems going.

Due to the installation of electricity-generating equipment and lightbulbs, these wickies didn't have to "fool around" with lighting kerosene lamps, trimming the wicks, or wiping down smoky lenses. All that Gibby had to do was flick a switch or two and start the generators. One night, he turned on the generators and walked out. "Oh, my God," he thought, when he looked up at the tower and saw that the light wasn't on. "No electricity," he fretted as he raced down the stairs back into the huge room of machinery. Gibby then discovered that he had forgotten to flip the switch that turned on the "juice" (electricity) to the lamp.

Although starting the equipment was much easier, this gear was complex in its operations, maintenance, and repairs. The engines and generators were bulky, intricate, and risky if not kept in tip-top shape. The electrical components were a combination of old and new, not to mention that repairs had to be made quickly and on the spot. The batteries were another issue. If someone appeared on the lighthouse with holes in their pants, then everyone knew the person had been working on the huge batteries and some of the acid had spilled over his clothing.

However, the worst job for him was cleaning out the water tank that was inside the deep cistern. Located twenty feet down in the darkness of that damp dungeon at the lowest part of the station, the men had to wash down the slime, use lime to whitewash the walls, and then clean it again. The smells, cramped quarters, and "gook" on the walls made this task a lousy assignment. In later years, the water became contaminated even with this regular cleaning, and the service wisely decided to use rubber bladders (tanks) to store their fresh water. The change worked and the men counted this change as a blessing.

Recreational activities at the lighthouse on off-duty hours took time to develop. Gibby commented:

> For the first years, we had nothing to do with our free time, and we didn't look forward to finishing work. When we finally brought a few fishing rods and equipment to the rock, I couldn't wait to see what we would find. The first fish we caught was a ling cod, and my initial thought was that we had caught a prehistoric animal—and the thing even had a T-bone still inside its stomach that it had eaten.
>
> Another time, we were given the okay to take the lead out of the old storage batteries. We cleaned the lead up, sold it, and built up a slush fund. We then took the money, bought a twenty-two caliber rifle, and used that for target practice. We then learned to stock up on books, magazines, and whatever else we wanted, and to bring that onboard with us in case we had nothing else to do.

The men spotted hundreds of shrimp one day in the ocean by the reef. They lowered buckets with holes inside and captured pounds of the tasty morsels. However, the romantic notion of spending time watching large vessels slowly pass by the reef at sunset quickly evaporated. This didn't occur. Gibbons said, "Fishing boats, yes, but no large shipping. The fishermen, though, were really nice. We'd lower the basket and they'd toss in fresh fish for us to cook and eat."

He later convinced some of the men to start playing cards and he played "good cards." The crew looked forward to the land-based electricians and other technicians who showed up from time to time and did the specialized repair work. These men had different backgrounds and stories and weren't the same people everyone else was with "every hour on the hour." They would also play cards. This activity proved to be fun, especially if you were the one who held the "good cards."

Another time, one of the Coast Guardsmen asked where the chief (chief petty officer) was. Looking around the seas from the pier's catch deck, someone pointed to the waters below and exclaimed loudly, "He's out in the ocean." As the crew crowded over to the railing, the men saw that he and another mate were floating on a raft that was tied to the rocks. He had lashed together large oil drums with ropes, and the derrick had dropped the homemade contraption into the ocean. Dressed in jeans and wearing a life preserver, the chief was riding the drums the way a cowboy rides a bronco.

Gibby invented another recreational activity when he strung a rope from the caisson's large doors down to the boat deck, a "long drop down." At the time, everyone was bored "out of their minds." The men wore heavy work gloves and slid down the rope on the drastic incline at fast rates of speed. This lasted, however, until one heavy seaman tried sliding down and the rope snapped. "He fell hard," said John. "If that had happened further up, he would have killed himself."

Like the others, Gibbons listened at times to the voice chatter over the Coast Guard radio. They overheard the conversations of the men transferring to and from their duty at Tillamook Rock Lighthouse, just like they were doing with the personnel on St. George. Although the seamen never met, the men felt that they knew each other. According to Gibby:

We would try to come up with nearly anything at times to make up for the isolation and boredom. Only a few men enjoyed the solitude, so I must have been weird in that sense. This duty was a training ground for screw-ups: If you screwed up somewhere else, then you were transferred to this lighthouse. This duty wasn't one that anyone actively tried to get to.

After a while, however, Gibby said that most of the screw-ups turned around to become good mates. They had no other way to go, especially on this isolated rock. The other crewmembers didn't care to make up for other people's problems, and they made this fact of life abundantly clear.

FLOYD SHELTON spent two decades in the U.S. Coast Guard, including ten tough months at St. George Reef Lighthouse early in his career. He left just before John Gibbons arrived. Floyd joined the service in November 1949 and after different assignments, the Coast Guard transferred him to their San Francisco Port Security Unit. Totally bored doing this work, when he heard about a seaman's opening on St. George Reef Lighthouse—which he knew nothing about at the time—Floyd requested a transfer. As he had the rank of third classman (above the rank of seaman), his officer in command needed to authorize the transfer. He did without hesitation, and the young man was quickly assigned to St. George.

Floyd in February 1952 took a bus from San Francisco to Crescent City, which landed him in that tiny coastal town. Asking around, local residents directed him to the nearby Battery Point Lighthouse (an easy walk at low tide), but he then discovered as did John Gibbons that his St. George assignment was four miles away over a gravel road across the sand dunes. Shelton walked the distance at night with his duffel bag to get to the St. George land barracks. As luck—or limited luck—had it, Floyd knocked on the door of the first apartment he came upon, and the man who answered was the commanding officer Fred Permenter.

The first question Permenter asked was if Floyd was married, and when he answered in the negative, Permenter became upset, saying that he had specifically asked for a married man. Fred tried to work a transfer back for his new-but-single mate, but Permenter's commanding officer told him to "just leave everything alone." This seemed due to the fact that St. George didn't have people going out of their way to volunteer for such duty, especially if they knew anything about this particular lighthouse.

Due to Permenter wanting married men at this time (presumably because he would have less problems with them on leave), Floyd didn't hit it off with Permenter from the very beginning. It was an inauspicious start, and then Shelton couldn't find any food in the single men's billet. The following morning, one of the wives took pity on the young man and brought him breakfast. Permenter later drove him to Crescent City where he was able to buy groceries. Quickly shipping out to the lighthouse, Shelton's first thoughts at seeing his new assignment were a few expletives and "This is not a good deal."

However, he also had a sense of adventure for the assignment. Shelton had experiences before with lighthouses, as he had previously been stationed on the Coast Guard Cutter *Mallow*, which was based in Astoria at the Oregon border on the Columbia River. The Cutter *Mallow* transferred personnel and off-loaded supplies to stations off the Oregon coast, including Tillamook Lighthouse. In the Pacific Northwest, men and supplies then typically were transferred by a breeches buoy (the circular lifebuoy with canvas breeches for the person's legs) from the cutter's small boat to the lighthouse. On St. George at the time, the men accomplished the transfers by hoisting and launching the station's twenty-six-foot launch direct by a boom from the station—a dangerous undertaking.

The St. George derrick operator used an "outboard" cable and an "inboard" cable, one used to pick up the launches and the other to lower them. The boom was fixed and didn't swing the boat over to the concrete landing, as it had done in earlier days, and the hook only lowered to one set place off the reef. When the boat operator saw the hook descending, he had to push full throttle to be under it at the right time. The Coast Guardsman holding the O ring on the launch with the guidelines had to attach this to the hook at the right time and in less than a minute.

One man's assignment on the launch was to snap the O ring in or out of the boom's cable hook; when transferring up, he had to get on the open foredeck of the launch, reach up, snap the ring on, and quickly turn his head away as the wave retreated. The line "snapped" tight leaving the boat and crew hanging in mid air. Simultaneously the boom operator was signaled to start hauling up, and the crew hung on for the stories-high ride up. This operation was made more difficult by the inability to see and therefore signal the boom operator from the ocean below.

When hoisting, if the crewman didn't get the O ring on as required, then the whole operation needed to completely start over again. However, when launching from the lighthouse, the procedure was even more risky. If the seaman couldn't pop the hook off when the launch momentarily floated, then the boat slid sideways with the wave surge, and as the launch rode the waves back out, it was dragged on its side—still held tight to the boom cable. The ocean surges could rush into the launch, running a high risk of swamping it while the boat was still tethered to the boom. Even though three men had died less than one year before, the transfer operations still hadn't been changed to a breeches buoy operation from a much larger Coast Guard tender. There was no real explanation why the Coast Guard continued afterward to use the same procedure as it did.

If the launching operation wasn't successful, then another fifteen minutes would elapse before the lifting transfer could start again. This time was needed for the air compressor that drove the boom to build up enough pressure again to drive the equipment. Although the north side (away from land) received the biggest surf, rough waves and seas surged around to the opposite side where the boat pickups and landings took place. The men had an average forty-five seconds within which to get a boat down and unhook the derrick ring before the heavy surges rolled in. The short time required to attach the launch was also due to the operator having to quickly reverse the boat.

With the reef usually just twenty feet away, if the launch didn't stop fast enough, the boat slammed into the rocks. If it couldn't hook up quick enough, then the launch operator had to motor away from there and fast. When bringing a boat to the station, the operator deposited the launch on the concrete landing. Since the boat was usually there for only a few hours until the return trip to its Crescent City base, the men then "battened it down" with strong ropes. This operation was all about timing with the waves being the unknown factor—and the procedure always had built-in danger.

Six men plus Fred Permenter at the time comprised the lighthouse crew, which at this time pulled rotating ten-day tours of three men each. As with the others, Shelton received challenging work assignments. For example, he also had the task of wire-brushing, red leading, and painting the cables that attached the boom's crosshatched, steel Eiffel Tower–like apparatus on the southeast side of St. George's stone tower. This job was difficult to do.

Swinging underneath one of the cables "some nine stories" above the rocks, Floyd wire-brushed and painted the cables from an open-throated, snatch block. As paint continually dripped down on him, Shelton had to be careful while swinging high in the air like a trapeze act. The wood block held a swinging bosun's chair with four ropes attached to a four-inch-by-six-inch plank. He and the others had to be wary that the unstable contraption didn't upend and spill the painter away into a fatal fall. A breeches buoy would have been safer with its strong trousers and stronger circling middle ring, but it wasn't around then.

Holding dearly to the apparatus with one hand, Floyd wire brushed or painted with the other. Starting at nearly the top of the stone tower, he made his way down the cable—working tediously and slowly toward the boom. A big problem soon emerged when he reached the end. He couldn't get his hands safely on the crosshatched tower and pull himself onto the structure. With breezes and winds, possible equipment failure, and the crude apparatus, this work was quite risky. Eventually by going hand over hand up the connecting rope and then on to the boom's steel cage, he was able to drag himself onto the boom.

Then another work assignment came his way. Floyd was to paint the steel face of the oil room (also called the lantern room)—the room just beneath the lens room at the top of the lighthouse. He could do part of this job by climbing over the rail from the catwalk above, and then holding to the railing with one hand while painting with the other. For the unreachable areas, he had to tie a rope around his body and swing onto the steel face, as if he were a mountain climber rapelling down a peak. The crashing surf and craggy rocks were stories beneath him as he worked in two-foot sections around the wide tower. One bad move and he would be another casualty on St. George. Floyd observed:

> I can't look at a picture of the lighthouse without remembering the red leading and painting of the boom support cables, all the while hanging from an open-throated snatch-block and working over my head. This still gives me chills.
>
> Then there was the assignment Fred gave me to paint the steel outside face of the oil room. Take a look at the southern side: this is all steel except for one small window. I hung a line from the spiral on top of the lens-room roof and tied the line to myself. I then climbed from the window and scraped and painted the outside face over my shoulder—all the while facing the sea with only my heels on the tiny ledge at the bottom of the steel face. With that straight drop to the rocks, I still can't believe that I did this, as I now think back about it.

With the station's launch usually stored on the boat deck, a concrete pad twenty feet above the ocean, emergencies could suddenly arise. One night, a storm blew in as high waves crested and swept over the rocks to pound the launch. It was clear that the boat had to be hauled up. However, someone would have to work his way down the stories-high steel walkway that circled down to the rocks from the engine room, and then untie the ropes that held the launch to the pad. The selected man: Floyd Shelton.

High-intensity-beam lights illuminated his way down through the whistling winds, as Floyd watched intently for breaks in the incoming wave patterns. Once toward the bottom of the stairs, he saw an opening in the sets of waves rolling toward him. At that time, Shelton raced to the launch that was still awash in seawater. Once at the launch, another large wave rose over him and crashed down. Chilling, green saltwater engulfed him as he held tightly to a rope.

Floyd jumped up on the boat and found some semblance of safety inside the cockpit as another wave swallowed everything. With breakers noisily surging around and over the boat, it took time for him to finally untie the ropes. With the O ring already secured to the hook of the boom's cable-line (a safety precaution in case of storms), when he finished he quickly waved up in a bright halo of light to the operator to start hauling up the boom. Larger waves swept over the boat, and the danger increased. The thundering surf could easily engulf the launch, rip the tie-ring away, and sweep him and the boat away to disappear at sea.

After jumping down from the cockpit, Shelton looked up and saw another set of waves rising over the reef. He crouched behind the boat's chocks (the heavy fitting with two curving jaws that the boat rests on) and held on. Swirling, cold seawater rushed over him, completely immersing him in violent blackness. When these surges passed, he wiped the salt from his eyes and saw that the operator was finally ready to lift. Jumping away, he watched the launch rise.

Floyd raced to the iron stairs that led back to the safety of the stories-high engine room as another set of waves roared in. The wind whipping and ocean hissing toward him, Shelton ran up the stairwell with the seas sweeping up. He made it with the white water nipping at his heels. The men secured the boat to the small steel platform that was off the engine room's massive steel doors. Tying the launch to the platform and railings with ropes, the Coast Guardsmen shoved life jackets in between to safeguard the boat from damage in the high winds.

Along with nearly every other wickie at St. George, Floyd discovered that getting along with one's other mates could be a challenge. As he said diplomatically: "I wasn't on the same page as the other two." This three-man crew had worked out a rotating, three-day kitchen responsibility schedule: cooking one night, setting up the second night, washing the dishes and pans on the third. Floyd liked frozen squash; the other two hated it. On his night to cook, complaints always followed when squash was on the menu. Further grumblings ensued over how well cooked the steak was, the vegetables on the plate, and even over the dining room conversation.

One night, he and another mate fell into a political squabble over the 1952 election when the Republican Dwight Eisenhower ran against Democrat Adlai Stevenson. (General Eisenhower won in a landslide.) Before anyone could stop them, Floyd and the other man were fighting over the kitchen table, pushing, pulling, and punching one another. The third man—appropriately named "Nemo"—pulled the two fighting men apart until tempers cooled. One can just imagine what would have happened today if the two argued over differing beliefs on the relative merits of Senator Kerry and President Bush in such a prison-like setting.

Floyd—like many of the others—couldn't "ever remember taking a shower on the light." However, the men did share bunks in what they called "hot sacking." When the 4:00 p.m. to midnight shift ended, for example, the now off-duty man woke up his duty counterpart. When the replacement left, the tired Coast Guardsman simply hopped inside the warm bed that had just been vacated, complete with the "enjoyable aromas of whoever had just left." The mattresses were rough "blue ticks," or bluish-gray mattresses with equally rough lighthouse white blankets. Most didn't take the time to throw on fresh sheets; these would have been cold and the man tired enough as it was.

Then came the "big storm" of 1952. The winds started blowing. Although he typically had ten days on and ten days off, it wasn't unusual during storm periods for one's duty to be extended by a couple of days owing to the bad conditions. Back in 1952, weather forecasting still was nothing like it is today: no satellite, weather (doppler) radar, or sophisticated charting. It was "very unpredictable" and inaccurate at best.

Floyd was scheduled to end his tour of duty on November 7, 1952. However, because the nation was engulfed by the Korean War conflict, his duty had been extended by another month (the formula varied among servicemen). This put his tour into the storm's full fury. And the perilous conditions kept relief crews from the lighthouse.

For three weeks the winds "were blasting away at forty-five to sixty-five knots (over seventy miles per hour)." Floyd knew that the winds got to "blowing there," but these conditions were bad. When the three-man crew became low on food, the Coast Guard sent its buoy tender, the *Magnolia*, from Eureka to the south. Unfortunately, the conditions were too rough for it to launch a supply boat to the station. The weather prevented helicopters from being launched, and Shelton said that the winds cranked up so much, that this soon became a "surreal experience." The men, of course, were marooned.

Every place was wet with dripping seawater, except for the galley in the tower above the catch deck; the heat from its continuous stove usually dried out the dampness. As the wetness seeped in through the cracks and walls of the entire structure, the men watched the waves "build and build" from its window. The men called this level the "living quarters" with its dining, cooking, radio, and living room facilities where the men "hung out." The next level contained two sleeping beds and a wash basin with a "piss funnel plumbed in alongside." The following floor contained more sleeping facilities, but this was now vacant because Permenter was stationed permanently on land. Windows graced each level, starting with the tower floor beneath the galley.

The wet, windy conditions, however, were "before the big winds came," said Floyd. "The weather had been rough for about three weeks or so, when it really began to blow. We had a couple of nights when we all thought it (the lighthouse) was going to go." The waves began to tower, and the green water smashed over the catch deck seventy feet above sea level and up to the first levels. The men felt the entire structure shake. These vibrations weren't quick, fast hits, but "ominous, deep-throated rumblings" that continuously coursed through the entire station. Floyd felt the "deep power" of the waves, and the Coast Guardsmen didn't know if the lighthouse would be left standing. Every time a wave struck, the lighthouse shook to its very foundations.

As the structure rumbled, mirrors, paintings, dishes, and everything attached to the walls sailed onto the floor. Hearing "water sounds" pounding outside one night, Shelton opened the door and watched incredulously as a waterfall of ocean poured down the spiral staircase. The ocean storm had carried rocks through the lens room—stories above and at its top—and the sea now raced from that top floor down through the structure. Shelton recalled, "There was a waterfall running down the central spiral staircase from the ocean coming in the lens room 145 feet or so above sea level." He later made his way to the top to see if he could stop the flow. This was impossible with the winds, seawater, and ocean spray flying into the room.

The tons of water sloshed down into the very belly of the lighthouse and its engine room. A utility room with toilet and storage capacity lay at the top of the carnivorous engine room. Water now completely flooded it and spilled down into the engine room where the sea sloshed back and forth. More saltwater actually spurted inside the engine room itself, as the waves crashed around the squat foundation and poured beneath the steel doors. The doors never completely closed at the bottom, allowing the sea to flow in. The good news was that with the amount of seawater inside the engine room, the sheer volume of it allowed the ocean to pour out the same way between wave sets.

As in years past when storms cut off hoped-for relief crews, the men reached the point of not even saying "hello" to one another. If the wetness, shaking, and pounding, "hot sacking," and no relief with grumpy men wasn't bad enough, the lack of food added to these tough conditions. When all that was left was milk and pancake mix, the men ate pancakes for every meal, day or night. Everyone became sick and tired of this regimen in no time. They found bottles of vitamins, so the meals then became pancakes and vitamins. And coffee—lots and lots of coffee. Shelton drank so much that he "got buzzing in my head and aches in my stomach." As did the others.

Then the milk ran out. The Coast Guardsmen tried making pancakes with water, but this concoction tasted terrible. The men began to seriously discuss taking flight from the stormy reef at the height of the storm in a small rubber life raft. The winds were blasting from the "southwest, more westerly though—and driving onshore toward the Smith River and Brookings (a close by coastal town to the north in Oregon)." They argued that they were dead if the tower collapsed. They knew if they survived that debacle, the waters would still be deadly. If they made it out in the raft, then "you're dead" also. Finally, given no options that were safe, they decided to stay the course and wait out the storm.

Fred Permenter made a couple of tries to get out to the light in the station's launch, but the terrible currents and waves turned him back. He finally was able to approach the station, and the boom brought the shifting, swaying launch up. The men jumped on board the boat, and the operator (who intended to join the crew by way of the stairway) lowered it to the ocean. Once there, the men couldn't get away, due to the swirling currents. As Shelton relayed: "We hung out over the water for a couple of hours trying to find a calmer sequence of ocean—but no luck. We were forced to return and had to spend another week or so on the light."

As the bad blow lessened, they tried again to make their way to shore. He continued:

When we finally did get off, we were about halfway back and not making much time against the southerly seas and winds. Fred asked the engineman if he had refueled the boat. He said he hadn't. That was a problem, and a big problem.

The seamen shouted back and forth through the winds whether they should return and try to re-land on the lighthouse. Or stay the course and hope there was enough fuel to get back to Crescent City, now some seven miles away. The men by now had enough of St. George and opted to keep going. The rolling swells continued to impede their progress, and the limited fuel was a concern. If they couldn't navigate through the waves, then the currents would sweep them around until a large roller swamped them. As they passed South West Seal Rock, the launch luckily "picked up a little forward progress." The small boat just made it to the harbor before their fuel was completely spent.

Floyd concluded:

Later, someone said that the weather station at Smith River recorded one-hundred and twenty-five miles-per-hour winds on the beach. I can't say what this would be at the light, as our location was six to seven miles seaward of it. I know that I went up to the lens room to see if I could stop the water flow. When I looked out at sea and the mountainous waves, I really thought that we had bought the farm.

As Floyd looked back at his ten months on the rock, he remembered playing hide and seek at night, picking mussels off the rocks, watching the whales migrate, and using the piss funnel alongside the wash sink to avoid cold night walks. He also remembers experiencing the hot sacking, stowing the boat in the storm, cooking the hated frozen squash, and getting wetted down with oily spume from a resting whale under the boom—to name a few.

After his first tour ended that November, Floyd Shelton left to ski and "have some fun," before reenlisting in August 1953. His career spanned twenty years, including skippering "44-footers" in search-and-rescue operations and as the officer in charge of the Coos Bay Lifeboat Station in Oregon. He afterward headed to Portland State University for undergraduate studies and then became director of the Oregon Ports Division for seven years. He was also the director of the Port of Astoria at the mouth of the Columbia River between the states of Oregon and Washington. He later earned his master's degree in maritime law and policy at the University of Wales in Cardiff, and then became the port director of Redwood City in California, before his retirement in 1994.

WHETHER KEEPERS WORKED on St. George in the nineteenth or twentieth century made little difference on this wave-washed rock. Getting along with some men was difficult, if not impossible. The continued headache-causing, earsplitting foghorn sounds and isolation were constant complaints. The men were by themselves until their long tour of duty ended, and they had to find activities to fill their off hours. Fishing, reading, sleeping, hobbies, and other activities were tried to sop up the time, but these were not always successful. Pets usually didn't survive, and gardening or growing flowers was impossible. Meals could become an adventure, especially when the newest recruit was typically the one assigned this task—and these were seamen, not gourmet chefs. Owing to the ocean, winds, and salt moisture, the lighthouse required continual cleaning, maintenance, repairs, and painting. Moreover, it was a risk to life and limb just simply being there.

Whether keepers realized it or not, the dangers at St. George were always around the corner. This risk was not only from sneaker waves and storms, but also from serious problems that arose when you were simply doing your job. One night, John Gibbons was on the midnight to four o'clock shift in the early morning, and his responsibility was to inspect and polish the light. Gibbons couldn't see well due to the strong light that kept flashing on and off, so he didn't watch his step, stumbled, and quickly fell through the catwalk. He plunged ten feet down to the next level. Gibby was very lucky that he caught himself at that level; otherwise, he would have continued falling stories down the rest of the high tower to his death.

Another time, the station's launch nearly sank outside the harbor with the entire crew. Gibby was chatting with another and said, "Gosh, this boat is really riding low." He looked around and saw that the ocean was rising inside the launch. As the men stared at the seawater pouring in, Gibbons thought that someone must have forgotten to insert the boat plug. This opening allows water to drain from a boat when out of the water, but it better be plugged when you're in the ocean. Thrusting his hand into the cold saltwater, Gibby frantically searched inside the sloshing water. His fingers luckily came across the plug and opening. As he quickly plugged the hole, the men next used a bilge pump to suck the water out. Finding that hole in over one foot of water at the stern can be a difficult task under these conditions. Although everyone acknowledged their good fortune, Gibby said that he had "never been so scared."

The landings were always risky. John was holding one time to the O ring as the boom lowered the launch to the sea. As the boat approached the ocean, a large wave tore in faster than anyone had anticipated and smacked into the launch. Just before that happened, however, Gibbons had been able to disconnect the launch from the cable. The boat went one way and Gibby the other, as he held on to the O ring attached to the derrick. He found himself dangling on the cable, mere feet from the cold, chilling swells and sharp rocks. The boat operator hollered for John to hold on to the ring until he could bring the launch back. Skillfully and fairly quickly, the Coast Guardsman maneuvered the small boat back and underneath the swinging man. Before another high wave swelled up, Gibby dropped safely back into the launch's cockpit.

One seaman was quite scared of heights, and he mistakenly stared down one time as the boat swung above the frothy ocean. The man froze as the launch was lowered, even though he held on to the O ring and had to unhook it. Another large wave crested in and broke under the small boat as the swell crashed against the rocks and pummeled the launch. Although the boat pushed dangerously back and forth, the derrick operator was able to winch the launch back onto the boat deck. When the other men ran over to the scared mate, he was so frightened that his hands were icy cold and clenched. His fingers still gripped the boat so tightly that the others had to pry each one away.

Despite the changes or precautions taken over time, these close calls when transferring men and supplies seemed to happen on a near-regular basis. Another time, a mate saw "the sea coming" (a large wave) and yelled, "Hold on, hold on tight!" He grabbed the boat's gunnels on both sides, as the sneaker wave broke over and totally engulfed the launch. His arms buckled from the force of the water that poured over the sides, but the wave didn't smash the launch against the rocks. The boat and men survived.

After more close calls and men dying, the service some time later abandoned the procedure of hooking the entire boat and changed its method to raising and lowering a canvas basket that held people and supplies. For a time, this net was colorfully decorated with different cartoon characters painted on its sides. One of the talented men had painted pictures of Woody Woodpecker, Donald Duck, Mickey Mouse, and Yosemite Sam around the basket.

Owing to equipment and technological changes, the number of men on each station tour was increased later to four. Although their duty was reduced to being two weeks long, living and working in the same cold, damp tower gave little time away from one another. Due to the ever-present water shortages, people could take only one quick, cold shower each week. "We stunk," said John later. "But after a while it made no difference."

After spending time at St. George, although there were exceptions, most of the men weren't afraid of anything. The crews painted the whole lighthouse in 1953 from top to bottom. This meant going over every square foot of a station that was more than fourteen stories high. Gibby's job was to swing over the derrick boom as he painted the guy wires. If he had made a mistake, he would have dropped over seventy feet to the rocks below.

If men had to be on the catch deck during storms to inspect the foghorns, another keeper stayed inside the lighthouse and held to the end of a strong rope. The mate outside tied the line around his middle to keep the powerful windblasts—some up to one hundred miles per hour—from picking him up and sailing him off the lighthouse in a deadly arcing fall. The foghorns had problems operating when oil beaded up inside the bellows, and if in the teeth of a gale, the maintenance mate had to clean it with only this rope holding him to safety.

Like most of the younger men who served on that station, Gibby's worse time was on Saturday nights. He would walk out onto the catch deck that evening and stare at the lights of Crescent City, thinking "Man, would I like to be there having some fun." When on leave, Chief Permenter drove them at times into town in the station's beaten old pickup. They saw a movie, headed to a local bar, talked to residents that they had come to know, and enjoyed themselves. When he returned fifty years later, his wife asked if he recognized anything. Gibby answered, "Yes, that bar over there."

While waiting for the weather to clear, the returning crew sat at the Old Dock Café on the wharf and drank coffee or ate lunch. The old fishermen inside looked at the winds and waves outside and at times said, "You can't make it through that stuff." However, the Coast Guardsmen would take their launch and have close calls, but they would eventually get back to the reef and swear they'd never try that again. But they knew they would.

THE KEEPERS at this lighthouse were tough, and any new person had to adjust quickly; otherwise, his tour would become a long, hard one and worse than most. A "new guy by the name of West" came on one of Gibby's shifts. The young man was eighteen, kept to himself by reading, and talked to no one. One of the older guys on that same shift was a big man, who had worked before in logging camps. Bill stood six-feet, five-inches tall and had been on the rock for a few years. After watching the young man again avoid talking to them, Bill turned to the others and said, "I'm gonna make that kid talk." He grabbed a long kitchen knife, raced around to the young man, and held the knife to his throat. "If you don't talk," big Bill growled, "I'm going to cut your throat." John Gibbons said later, "The kid was white as a sheet, but started talking and didn't stop, although he was always a little nervous."

Gibby sent the nervous West down one day to bring back a bucket of paint, because he wanted to paint the tower railing black. Nearly an hour passed. John walked down to the engine room to find out what was taking the "new kid" so much time on what was a simple task. He found West playing around with the paint can and mixing more thinner into it, saying that he thought the paint was too thick. Gibbons laughed hard and told him that the Coast Guard preferred thick paint for its lighthouses.

Another time, poor West was in the galley on a Sunday morning.

He still was trying to avoid talking to people, and the officer in charge came strolling up. He stopped in front of West and bellowed at him, "Where's the Sunday paper?" The startled youth ran outside the station door. He was halfway down the stairwell to the boat landing before he realized what was going on. He returned "very chagrined."

A new seaman had to be ready for these rights of initiation—regardless of what station—and what was going to be played on him. By this time Gibby was twenty-two years old and a "seasoned salt," regardless of his age. Putting a twisted grin on his face, he turned to another new recruit and said, "You're kind of cute. Why don't you come up and live with me in my bedroom." The young man looked horror-struck. He turned to the closest keeper and said, "Is this guy on the level?" The mate played along by answering solemnly, "Yes, he's been on this crazy rock way too long." The new initiate's face dropped and he went "completely nuts" until someone clued him in.

The mates on any shift came with differing backgrounds and personalities. One Coast Guardsman was from Hollywood and wanted to be an actor. Tim was either "one of the dumbest people around, or totally into some mental state" to get him through this duty. The lighthouse had big steel doors that opened to the catch deck at the pier's top, and the crew one day opened them to let fresh air inside. The seabirds and gulls soon swept into the cavernous space and flung their wet droppings around the rooms. Gibby had more work to do in the engine room and told Tim to take care of the problem. The man quickly replied, "No problem." When Gibbons returned later, he found Tim shooting at the birds with a twenty-two rifle, instead of shooing them out, closing the doors, and cleaning up the place. "Blood and guts were all over the place," Gibby said, "and you could see where the birds had skidded off the walls and floors. I was never so mad at anyone as this one that day."

Another time, Gibby was perched on the far side of the long

boom when it was stretched high over the rocks and ocean. He asked Tim to bring him a screwdriver, thinking the would-be actor would tie a string around the screwdriver, hold one end, and toss the tool over. When John turned around, he saw Tim climbing on his hands and knees over the boom with the screwdriver held tight in one fist. (The boom had guy lines that one could hold to when walking over it.) Knowing that Tim was deathly afraid of heights, and now eight stories above the rocks, Gibbons yelled to the man to go back. He would get the screwdriver from him on the catch deck. Tim soon transferred to another station.

Another crewman who worked on this tour was Joe, and he hailed from the San Francisco Bay area. Joe was a "big guy and really quiet." He stayed on his leaves in the shore quarters at Point St. George and went nowhere except on the last day. On that one day before his scheduled return, Joe headed into town to the local whorehouse that was close to the Battery Point Lighthouse. He'd get drunk, find his favorite partner, do his thing, and return happy. Joe came back one night "drunk out of his mind" and decided he would stop smoking. He threw his cigarettes away. The next day, Joe was on his hands and knees trying to find every "last one of those butts," as he had changed his mind.

Joe moved to San Francisco after his tour ended and became a traffic cop. He had spent enough time at sea and wanted a change of pace. One time crooks robbed a bank within eyesight of his patrol, but Joe did nothing to intercede. When questioned later about this, he replied calmly, "I'm in traffic, not patrol."

One married crewman thought that his wife was running around on him when he was marooned on the lighthouse, and when there, he always trained his high-powered binoculars on land. The seaman thought one day that he saw his wife and her lover "fooling around" in a room. At the time, the man was on the end of the ninety-foot boom, stories high above the ocean. He yelled to the others, "Either get me off or I'm going to jump." When one of the seamen telephoned the chief and told him about the situation, the officer in charge said, "Tell him to go ahead. There's no way I'm coming out from land today." The man didn't jump and soon transferred away.

THE STORMS were as bad as everyone said—if not worse. Gibby relayed:

> The high seas would completely inundate us. They rose totally over and covered the lighthouse. We had six feet of granite around us, and when these waves hit against the tower structure, we could feel the entire lighthouse tremble. There was only one St. George and there will never be another one like it. This one was incredibly well and strongly built. It had to be.

The heavy swells rolled in, fifty to sixty feet high or more in sets that followed one another. Due to the reef's position and the currents, St. George seemed to catch the worst from any storm. When the keepers looked out the galley window, they could see the hissing ocean surging above it. At that level, the station was eight stories over the sea, as the galley windows were one story above the caisson deck. These waves were green seawater from the deep ocean—not white run-ups from a surge that broke against the pier's sides. The winds whistled outside, the seas thundered against the station, and the rains would tear down in sheets. If any seaman was outside on an inspection, only the lifesaving rope kept him alive.

Some watches didn't have storms. This observation depended, however, on what the crew counted as a "storm." If the winds were up to thirty miles per hour, or so, then they didn't count that as being one. When a "storm" hit, the waves, winds, and bad conditions were continual. With these surges, the men could feel the tower vibrate, and the seas were higher than the caisson. Those were storms.

As Gibby said, "The sea was a fierce monster, although calm at first, it could quickly rise to become a beast."

These blasts of wind, rain, and waves forced salty moisture between the granite-block seams, no matter how good the construction was. The windstorms blew saltwater spray and rock chips through window frames, stone cracks, and under the outside doors. The ocean water constantly dripped down and became saltwater trickles that concentrated at the tower's bottom levels. As the water drained down the floors, the plaster in the walls started to peel away. The men stuffed towels under doors, mopped up the stairwell, and put barricades of cloth and wood against the inside streams. A few times, Gibby saw so much water inside the tower that he thought to himself, "I must be a duck."

He and the other Coast Guardsmen on duty believed that the builders of this lighthouse had been "unbelievable" to have accomplished such a building feat so long ago. Gibby observed, "The construction was great, the seams were perfect, and everything was done so well, even after all those years." The men were always thankful of the people who had built the "grand lady," especially when the winds hit one hundred miles per hour and the seas came storming in.

When dense fog blanketed the area and cut down the light's range, the men had another challenge. For days and nights, the foghorn would blast for three seconds, then lapse into silence for two, boom for another three seconds, and then fall into silence for twenty-eight seconds. All talking was in same staccato fashion around the foghorn's blasts, and this continued even when it wasn't operating. His continued closeness to the foghorn's loud noise made Gibby hard of hearing, which he said had its merits at times: he couldn't get into trouble when his wife was mad at him.

Seals always lived on the rocks below, and the men, who were usually looking for something to do, tried to make them pets. A newly born seal stayed around for one week, then became tired of this new world and disappeared. The seals and sea lions were smart as they watched the strange beings above them. They became used to the men's movements on the pier's top, and when a certain motion started with cans, the seals started barking loudly and wouldn't stop. When the crew threw the garbage from the cans to the rocks below, the seals jumped to the spot, quieted down, and ate everything in sight.

The wickies also brought cats and dogs to the lighthouse as pets. These animals unfortunately seemed to disappear if they weren't careful to stay away from the rocks, seek shelter during bad storms, or avoid other dangerous conditions. The flies weren't as much of a problem as at other stations, due apparently because the crew kept the place relatively clean. Worse than at other stations, the birds kept flying "all of the time" into the lens and tower at St. George. The seagulls, gooney birds, and other seabirds continually slammed into the lens, as the bright light seemed to daze them, or they darted straight into the tower walls in trying to avoid it.

THE TOWER ROOMS were all about the same size, approximately fifteen feet by fifteen feet, with a Dutch-door window on two sides and two beds in each room. These two-bedroom levels were located above the galley, while a third bedroom was built inside the radio room, where the land electricians or other specialists stayed when they came. To cut down on the hot sun and give structural support, the walls were recessed inward from the window casements, and the rooms measured some eighteen feet from window to window.

Linoleum now covered the floors, due to the continuing moisture problems, and each room then was painted white. A stove that ran on diesel fuel, chairs, a table, and other furniture were in each room. One night, Gibby lit the diesel stove and fell asleep. He awoke to a pungent smell and discovered that the stove was burning too hot and close to bursting into flames. He never used that stove again.

The galley stove also ran on diesel fuel, but the men seemed to have better luck with it.

Owing to the weather, lack of sun, and constant moisture, the bedrooms were always cold and damp, no matter how the men tried to remedy the situation. During storms, the winds and waves forced saltwater inside and even threw salty spray through the cracks of the lighthouse lamp room. The men had to constantly scrub down the walls and floors because of the continued dampness.

Showering was still limited to once a week on Fridays, and the men set Saturdays as wash day. That is, if they took a shower or washed their clothes. By now, the washing machine, a bathroom, and deep freezer had been installed as a "wash deck" on the tower level just above the catch deck. Although electricity now drove appliances such as the washing machine, oily clothes and rags from the machine shop still posed a problem. Using a technique from decades past, Gibby tied a rope around the oily cloths, lowered them into the ocean from the rock, and let the ocean's currents and saltwater "wash them better than a washing machine."

With the fifteen-foot rooms, window casements, six feet of granite on both sides, and a five-foot stairwell, the tower was approximately thirty-five feet wide. The bedrooms were "fairly big" with the two beds; however, having only one bathroom downstairs was another problem (although later, a second one was installed). Because no one wanted to try and find that bathroom in the dark, the men used glass bottles or headed to the catch deck—designed at first to catch fresh rainwater. By now, the Coast Guard cutters pumped the station's freshwater into storage tanks.

As only one bathroom existed for decades, the wickies became inventive. "People had to pee, no matter what," said Gibby.

As it made no sense to walk all the way down in a cold tower
to hit that bathroom at night, funnels were installed that led

down to the one bathroom. A crewman then came up with the idea of drilling an outside hole through a wood window. They would pee in the tube forced through the funnel, which headed down to the caisson and catch deck. When a surprised officer learned about this, however, he ordered that it be torn out and "now."

One time, Gibbons had a plugged toilet to fix in the caisson, and he told the men not to flush the upside toilet. While he was working on the toilet, someone flushed the one to the topside, and everything boiled over him. Needless to say, he was not a happy camper.

Old files were left inside the lighthouse, but Gibby didn't get around to looking at them. The station had old defense and blackout plans for World War II tacked on one wall. The military had supplied an M-1 gun and a forty-five caliber pistol for defense, but the "powers to be took them away," he said. "They were worried that the crewmen might use the weapons to kill one another."

This duty was extremely difficult on the married men's relationships with their families, kids, and wives. A Coast Guardsman would be home, and then away, as the crew traveled constantly back and forth. Only a special family could get through this difficulty. The bad weather became a real problem when it delayed men from returning home to their families, especially when they were living in stark rooms inside a cold, damp tower with peeling paint.

The men admired the old wickies, as their duty and responsibilities were more severe. During those earliest years, the keepers spent three to six months at a time in continual duty on the lighthouse. They had to catch their fresh water supply (which became salty) from the catch deck, salt their own meat, and even repair their own tools in the blacksmith shop. However, as Gibby pointed out, "At least, that's what we thought the shop was used for."

Although the shop was now inside the engine room, Gibbons

had never looked there. At the very beginning of his first tour, his older buddy told him to leave the door alone. One day his curiosity overcame him, and he worked open the long-ago shut blacksmith-shop door. Flashing a light inside the dark chamber, he discovered inside a workable still that obviously had been used in making boot-leg alcohol. He couldn't believe what he had found, but silently closed the door and didn't say a word about it to anyone.

Due to its high placement and constant hot light, the lamp room became very hot during the summer months. Although curtains could be pulled to protect the lens during sweltering days, the heat was still a problem and the men needed to be careful to avoid heat exhaustion. As to flying the colors (raising the U.S. flag), the keepers did this only when the inspectors or big brass came to the station. There was a commonsense reason for not doing this all of the time: regardless of day or night, in mere hours the constant winds shred-ded any flag that flew.

THE POINT ST. GEORGE STATION had been built on the land point opposite the lighthouse, and the men could stay there when on leave. This facility was a series of wooden, white structures with dark pitched roofs that comprised the Coast Guard's offices, communi-cation facilities, residences, and storage quarters. The single men had their own housing, which was a three-bedroom house with a living room and kitchen, while the married men and their families lived in one of three apartments.

When crews were repairing the facilities on the point, the single men stayed during 1953 in the attic of the Humboldt Bay Coast Guard Station, some seventy miles south of Crescent City. Despite this loft being hot, humid, and without much air, the men thought that they had "died and gone to Heaven," because they were so close to the larger city of Eureka on their leaves. Interestingly enough, although the three young men on Gibby's shift spent all their time together on the rock (from fifteen to thirty days), when they headed to shore, they still stayed together and hung out. This was probably due to John's easygoing nature and sense of humor.

In a huge Christmas storm in 1955, the Klamath River to the south of Crescent City overflowed and inundated liquor stores in the city of Klamath. The floods washed the bottles clear to Humboldt Bay. Pursuant to law, people buried the still-good bottles in the sands. The lighthouse crews came by later and dug them up.

Whether on land or at sea, this bad gale affected many. A married crewmember named Ferguson (whom we will learn more about in a later chapter) said that he wanted to be with his family on the mainland for Christmas. The problem was that his tour started in a few days and would carry through the holidays. He was "crying the blues" about missing Christmas with his family and asked the single men if they would trade with him. To a man, each one said, "No way." The bachelors wanted to have their own tasty dinner on land that special day, especially as each one knew where to get a better meal without having to cook or clean up later.

Just before the crew was to leave, they cleaned the station for the incoming men. As no engine malfunctions, fog, or gales had happened, these Coast Guardsmen looked forward to their holiday time off. Before they knew it, the barometer dropped "like a rock" and as fast as anyone had ever seen—from 30.10 to 28.00 in twenty-four hours. The seas became thirty to forty feet high, and the group was marooned on St. George. One day led to the next, and then their extra food was gone.

On Christmas Eve, Ferguson called them up and said he was very sorry that the others had to spend Christmas on the rock. Good naturedly or not, he started laughing hard. Thanks to the rotten weather, he had gotten his time with the family after all.

For their Christmas Eve meal, the marooned men opened their last can of Spam and ate that with a couple of World War II "C" rations they had discovered. The crew also scrounged up some bread, cut the mold off, and toasted that to go with their rations. The chief on duty even had to ration what food was left, since they had been caught so low, and the weather didn't break until the day before New Year's Eve.

Not only could food become low, but fresh water always seemed to be in short supply. The men pumped the water to tanks above and used a gravity feed to bring it down to the various floors. However, one day the water tasted salty to Gibby. He then discovered the reason why. He had mistakenly hooked the tank with the salty water from the catch deck instead of from the tank that held the fresh water pumped recently from the Coast Guard cutter.

Despite the discovery of a still in the engine room, drinking was not allowed on that lighthouse—or on any other station. This doesn't mean that the rule was strictly enforced. St. George was like the other stations on holidays such as New Year's Eve: the men were allowed to drink "a beer or two," but that was it. Even in those close quarters, smoking was a different issue then and the men lit up whenever they wanted. When one gale hit and stayed for several days, the men had smoked up all of their cigarettes. They tried rolling "some old Bull Durham" that they found and mixed in "some chicory," but this substitution didn't prove to be a good choice—the men nearly gagged when smoking the concoction.

Each crew's mission was to keep the lighthouse clean for the next shift. After another lengthy storm, the place became "a dirty, scraggly hell hole, where your feet stuck to the galley deck." The men were in a foul mood and cared less. A duty inspector came on board on a surprise inspection. Gibby met him at the top of the catch deck, looked him straight in the eye, and said, "Helluva way to start a morning." The officer didn't acknowledge him and walked upstairs. As the officer took one appraising look at the galley, the crew held their breath as they suspected the worst. He instead said surprisingly, "Things are great," and told the men to ready the net and lower him down. The keepers later agreed that the inspector had said this being probably afraid he'd never get off that rock if he had written them up.

Finally discharged, another windstorm blew in and delayed Gibby's departure from the rock for four more days. Although he was due to leave on November 3, 1956, he couldn't get away until November 7. He left the Coast Guard and life on St. George for good. In retrospect, Gibby said he really had enjoyed those times, when he was left on his own and could do things the way he liked. People wouldn't bother him when he wanted to be alone and life there could be adventurous. Totaling everything up, there was something about surviving, even living a life like this that by itself was an accomplishment.

Promotions here did seem to come faster. Gibby started as a third classman and in charge of all the equipment. When he asked the chief petty officer if he could receive another stripe—it soon came. The officer then told him that if he "shipped over" for another tour he'd receive another stripe to first classman. But St. George was a tough assignment. "The prisoners at Alcatraz had a better situation," Gibby concluded. "They had recreation, dry cells, three squares, and cooks that only cooked and didn't burn the Christmas turkey."

Moving back to Denver, Colorado, John became a floral designer in his own florist shop. After running the business for ten years, Gibby then joined the U.S. Postal Service. He worked in Denver for the post office for thirty years and then retired. However, as Gibby always liked being active, he then worked another four years in a fishing-tackle warehouse.

He attended a Veterans Day dinner long after his retirement, and the sailors and soldiers present told the crowd what their duty had been like. Whether during World War II or during the Vietnam War, the military personnel usually had stories about how they had been in fierce firefights with whistling shells, mortars, grenades, and machine-gun bullets. Gibby stood up and told the assembly that his service had been in guarding the California coast before the Vietnam War, and that even though he hadn't taken any fire, he had been in quite dangerous duty: he had been taking care of their girlfriends while they were overseas. Everyone laughed. He was seventy-two years old in 2007, and only eighteen those many years back in 1953.

FROM BROKEN LEGS and near drownings to more serious injuries, accidents happened there and more frequently than one would like. On June 5, 1953, one of the Coast Guard cutters came alongside St. George to pick up a generator. The *Yocona* anchored one hundred yards from the reef, and their small boat motored over to the lighthouse. After the crew lowered the parts into the boat, it headed back to the cutter, and then returned with two, two-inch hoses strung from the vessel to pump fresh water and fuel to the station.

As the men on the cutter began pumping the water, keepers Bill Baldwin and Pat (Red) Griffin tended to the water hose inside the lighthouse. Due to the pressure surging through the line, they watched the hose size increase and the line stiffen to snake toward them. Bill warned the others, including onlookers, to be careful because the pressure moving that much water through any hose had a terrific kick.

It did. About a minute later, the hose jumped into the air and shot water out like a high-pressure fireman's hose. The end of the hose with its brass coupling flew wildly back and forth. The two men turned to run away, as the snaking hose brushed Pat Griffin's head and just missed clobbering him.

Bill Baldwin wasn't as fortunate. The metal coupling slammed him over the head and smashed him unconscious. The blow was hard and left a large opening; blood and tissue flowed out from the wound. Baldwin started having convulsions on the floor.

Pat immediately pressed his palm against the wound to stop further bleeding and tissue loss, wrapped blankets around Bill's body, and placed his foul-weather jacket under Bill's head. The crew called for immediate assistance over the radio, and the cutter's launch quickly returned to pick up the severely injured man.

Griffin tied his friend in a wire basket and roped a bridle around it with which to lower the injured seaman down to the transit boat. Once Baldwin was on board, the cutter sped back to port where a waiting ambulance raced him to a hospital.

Pat Griffin sent a letter to his parents about the accident. Due to the terrible injury, the remaining men had to take on Bill's tasks and work eight hours on with only four off, instead of the standard eight hours off. Pat wrote that he was one "shocked boy" when he saw the unconscious body, ending his letter by writing, "Well that's enough excitement for me for one day. I'm still shaking."

About a month later, Pat located Bill in San Francisco. He wrote that his friend seemed to be making "a lot of progress," but that his speech was shaky and Bill's full recovery would take time. Gibbons said that Bill Baldwin never fully recovered and that he had the feelings and speech of a twelve-year-old.

The risk of duty on St. George was that danger could occur when you least expected it. One of the deadliest in Coast Guard lighthouse history happened here, and this calamity forced exceptional bravery to be shown under very dangerous circumstances.

CHAPTER 14

Uncommon Courage

On April 5, 1951, Fred Permenter was the officer in charge of St. George Lighthouse. The thirty-three-year-old man had been in the U.S. Coast Guard nearly fourteen years since entering the service at nineteen. He started his career at a lifeboat station in Kentucky and next spent time on a buoy tender that operated out of St. Louis, Missouri. During World War II, Permenter had several assignments that resulted in his being decorated various times, including one risky tour of duty on a LST (amphibious landing ship) on the invasions of New Guinea. The Coast Guard assigned him after the war to more buoy tenders before elevating him to command the St. George Reef Lighthouse in February 1951.

At the time, Chief Boatswain Mate (CBM) Permenter spent his off-lighthouse leave with his wife and four young sons—ages eight, five, three, and one—on the shore station at Point St. George Reef Light Station. Owing to his being in the service, Fred and his wife had lived in a number of places since they married. Described as modest and soft spoken, Permenter was wirey and tall but athletic looking. The son of a deputy sheriff in Mississippi, Fred had dark hair and eyes with angular, sharp features and a handsome face.

Two young Coast Guard electricians, Bertram Beckett and Clarence Walker, had finished making their repairs at the lighthouse station. They joined the three-man crew that was being relieved of their duty, and the men were happily awaiting their transfer out. The day was overcast with a brisk wind, heavy swells, and a choppy frothy sea surrounding the rocky reef. As the men waited for the station's boom to be readied and lower the white-painted motor launch for their trip ashore, the incoming ocean's white foam hissed below.

The seaworthy launch was twenty-six feet long with a cabin and one porthole on each side. In stormy weather, the men sought shelter inside the cabin while the operator at the back hunkered down, held on to the wheel, and piloted the craft. The name "St. George Reef" was painted in sharp detail on the stern. A crewman attached the winch-cable's heavy hook to a strong O ring; a cable from that iron ring stretched tightly to the bow while another was taut to the stern in a triangular rig that suspended the boat.

With the boat set on the concrete loading ramp, the five Coast Guardsmen scrambled aboard. One sailor hopped on top of the cabin's roof, while the other four stood in the back cockpit. All wore their bulky, heavy life jackets over sweaters and heavy jackets with white sailor's caps tucked down over their ears for protection against the wind. The man on the cabin roof wore his cap at a jaunting angle in defiance of the gusts.

A picture taken just minutes before the launch was lowered showed the five men standing inside the launch. Coast Guardsman Stanley Costello was at the boat's wheel; a smiling, happy Ross Vandenberg stood on top of the cabin, holding on to the hoisting cable that he would soon unhook the boat from; and Thomas Mulcahy was at the stern handling the mooring line, looking expressionless at the cameraman. Petty Officer Bertram Beckett sat on the inboard side and was talking to Coast Guardsman Clarence Walker, as Permenter operated the boom control to lower the boat. Vandenberg's five-month-old beagle puppy lay happily inside the cockpit.

Costello lived in his off time with his wife and child in Crescent

City. Both Beckett and Walker were stationed at the Eureka Coast Guard Station. While Beckett was single, Walker was married and both men lived in Eureka.

The boom picked up the launch and swung it away from the boat dock to begin the lowering process. The drop into the ocean from the base was a two-story trip from the concrete boat platform, and the view from inside the boat down to the crashing seas was not one for the timid. While keeping an eye on the swells below, Permenter lowered the boat toward the white crashing sea. As the boat swung away from the reef closer to the swelling ocean, Walker was the only person looking back at the lighthouse; the others inside the launch stared at the encroaching surf.

Permenter hesitated at the controls to time the boat's landing after a wave had already crashed against the rocks and was on its way out. Watching intently below at the close swells, the men failed to spot one set of waves building close to the reef. As the launch hit the ocean in the trough of two waves, the first surge prevented Vandenberg from unhooking the launch from the O ring.

As the boat remained attached to the line, the trailing rogue wave that was two-stories high roared in. Caused by two waves meeting at their crest and combining into a higher, deadlier comber, this apparition rose toward the launch as the operator quickly tried to reverse the landing. While the boat remained attached to the cable, the large swell smashed into the dangling launch with tons of bitterly cold water.

The huge rogue wave blasted the launch toward the caisson, and it swung back like a pendulum on the tight cable tether. The boat seemed to disappear from view, as the breaker smashed against the pier with thunderous sounds and heavy foaming spray. The tremendous backwash of white frothing sea careened off the rock to inundate the launch and its captive men, and the boat hurtled away from the reef. The added weight of countless tons of ocean and its force tore away the ring attachment at the bow to which a supporting cable connected. The bow dropped sharply and the cascading avalanche of sea hurled the men into the water.

Regardless of wearing life jackets, the coldness of this water, swift currents, and hypothermia were a deadly threat to the Coast Guardsmen. Held by the stern cable from the O ring and attaching cable to the winch's hook, the swamped launch dangled straight toward the ocean. As the huge wave's powerful backlash swept his men out to sea, Permenter yelled at another crewman to cable the launch back in. Either it or one of its rafts would be of use. He quickly dispatched a Mayday emergency call to the Humboldt Bay Coast Guard Station. A quick look at the ripped-out bow ring next convinced him that the launch was of no use in any rescue attempt, since it couldn't be safely dropped into the ocean.

The currents meanwhile moved the bobbing men farther away from the reef. Three of the men tried the near-impossible task to swim back to the station, while two others tried to get to a buoy. Since running into the equipment room and dragging down a raft pack would take too much precious time, Fred Permenter knew that the closest raft was inside the stricken boat's compartment. Permenter yelled to the operator to get the launch back to the pad, and he quickly scampered down the high iron stairwell to the concrete pad on the rocks. As the launch dangled by its stern, the new operator quickly cabled the swaying boat to the level pad by the pier's base. The launch slid by its bow over the concrete and came to a stop.

Permenter jumped aboard and grabbed a life raft from one of the closed compartments. He heaved it onto the concrete and activated the canister that inflated the raft. The bobbing men meanwhile swept farther away, while two others continued moving in the general direction of the offshore buoy.

Once the raft expanded, Fred untied his shoes and tossed his heavy jacket away, then studied the white surf below. When a heavy swell dashed against the rocks and began washing back, Permenter slid the life raft over the edge into the swirling sea, twenty feet down. He watched it ebb away with the currents. Disregarding another set of incoming heavy waves, which would have dashed him senselessly against the rocks, Fred leaped feet first into the foaming currents that swirled below.

The ocean was cold—damnably cold—and its surprising chill took his breath away. Spurred by adrenaline, he swam with quick strokes away from the reef. Although the raging underwater currents had swept the raft away from him, its force also carried him along. Searching ahead through his saltwater-stung eyes, he watched as the new surges approached. Permenter knew that if he was to survive, he had to get past the continuing swells.

Pulled down by his water-soaked clothing, Fred swam after the raft through the treacherous waters. He didn't want to take the time to take any clothing off and also knew that by knotting a shirt or trouser legs, he could trap air inside and use that as a float if he couldn't get to the raft. Seeing the swells upon him, he felt himself carried up and backward, but luckily this and the next ones didn't break too soon.

With determined efforts, he finally reached the bobbing raft, as another large roller-coaster swell rolled him toward the sky and then down to continue with a crash against the nearby rocks. Fred worked to get inside the raft—an act that would have been impossible for many under these conditions—but finally pulled himself in.

Brushing the saltwater from his eyes, he scanned the choppy seas. At first, he couldn't see anyone. Hearing a yell, he turned toward the sound and saw that two of his men were still moving to the mooring buoy. Mulcahy was following Vandenberg, and the two men were getting closer to it—over three hundred yards or one-sixth of a mile from the lighthouse. As he paddled the raft toward the buoy, he watched the men pull themselves onto it, as the floating, anchored marker surged in and out of view with the waves.

A third man had decided to swim for the float's safety and that was Bertram Beckett. As he tried to come closer to the buoy, the currents began sweeping away and impeding his progress. Beckett came within a few feet of the marker, and the other two urged the man on. He couldn't make it to the buoy and finally said, "I can't make it, I'll drift . . ." The other two were too exhausted to do anything more.

Seeing this, Permenter paddled toward Beckett, but the strong tide and currents soon swept him and the remaining two a distance from the buoy. Fred paddled furiously past the float in pursuit. As the swells continuously rolled past to crash on the reef, his raft lifted high on a top, then soon felt the backwash heading in the opposite direction like a strong rip tide.

As heads bobbed up and down with the waves scattering one away from another, Fred paddled after them. At times, he lost sight of the man due to the roiling seas, hoping that this wasn't because he had slipped under the water. Finally he came across Beckett.

Floating due to his life preserver, the crewman was unconscious with his arms spread out in front. Permenter worked hard to bring the mate up, but even with the heavy body weight and soaked clothing, he finally managed to pull Beckett onto the raft. Turning the man over, he knew that this man was in serious trouble. Beckett—like probably the others—had gulped in water when the wave engulfed them, and hypothermia's coldness was already starting to shut down his life-support system. However, the electrician was still alive and Permenter couldn't spend more precious time on Beckett if he was going to save the others.

Permenter began paddling after the fourth crewman, but the stronger winds whipping against him and different currents made his progress difficult. Weighted down by Beckett who was slumped against the raft's back, Fred tried to move his inflatable toward the fourth life jacket. This one, he thought, was in bad trouble because he also wasn't moving. Permenter felt himself tiring and his arms began to feel as if they were holding up iron anvils. It became more difficult to move through the swells of green and white sea.

Due to the ocean crests that broke at times around the raft and his bringing in Beckett, saltwater slurped inside the inflatable lifeboat. Although tiring from his exertions, Permenter forced his arms to move harder and faster into the ocean. He finally came to the fourth man. Arms also outstretched, the man's face was down in the water. While he worked closer, the undulating sea heaved everyone up and down. Fred threw his paddle into the raft and grabbed the man's clothing.

Try as he might, Permenter couldn't pull the body aboard. The weight, water-soaked clothing, angle, and his exhaustion were too much. Deciding he'd never be able to move the body inside, Permenter pulled the unconscious man as close as he could and draped the arms over the raft. He grabbed nylon cord and lashed the body in an upright position to that side.

The winds still gusted and waves lifted the raft toward the skies and then back into the roller-coaster slides of cold green seas. Fred continued his search for the fifth victim, but he couldn't find any sign of that man. As the ocean pitched him and the others around, Permenter kept looking to ensure that the two heads were above the angry waters. Glancing back at the lighthouse, he realized that the currents and his efforts had taken him a distance away. The large waves continued to thunder against the rocks in rooster-combs of towering sprays, foam, and hissing ocean.

He was exhausted by his efforts and could hardly move. When his body stopped shaking, he knew that the deadly hypothermia was already starting its lethal course. Hopefully, the Coast Guard had acted quickly on his radio call for assistance, because otherwise his efforts to save his men would all be in vain. And he would lose his life as well.

As the raft drifted away in the rolling seas, Fred knew that no one at the lighthouse could help. His body bent over and rocking, he decided to use what strength remained and paddle back to the buoy. The currents changed and whipped the raft around, but Fred kept working through the spray and rising whitecaps toward the bobbing marker. He knew that Humboldt Bay was seventy-five miles to the south, and that it would take valuable time for the station to mount any rescue operations. Permenter knew that help would come, but he wondered if it would arrive in time.

What he didn't know then was that when the group commander at Humboldt Bay received his call, the officer also realized that any delays would be fatal. At the same time that the men were in the water and drifting away, he quickly contacted the veteran Coast Guardsman, Wayne Piland, who operated nearby Battery Point Lighthouse and whose navy son, Donald, was on leave. Hearing the commander's request for help, they quickly ran over the low-tide pathway, jumped into their car, and drove to Citizen's Dock in search of a "good, fast fish-boat."

The first skipper they approached turned them down, saying, "There are too many sheep out there ('sheep' being the term for white caps)." The Pilands next hailed a commercial fishing boat, the large net-dragging-boat *Winga*, and the captain took the men aboard, turned his boat around, and motored quickly toward St. George Reef.

The waters were rough and choppy outside the harbor, and the fishing boat headed with her bow seaward into the chop. Waves and spray nearly overtook the commercial boat, and the poor conditions delayed the vessel in its passage. After a rough trip, the fishing boat finally neared the lighthouse and spotted the buoy. As the vessel smacked against the whitecaps with its whining engine, the crew saw men holding wearily to the undulating buoy and a bobbing raft tied nearby.

The fishermen pulled Vandenberg and Mulcahy first onto their boat, followed in turn by the unconscious, but still alive, Beckett and the fourth man that Permenter rescued. The last one brought onto the boat was the near-unconscious Fred Permenter. The boat motored a distance from the buoy in the direction that Permenter pointed to find the last mate. The crew located another life jacket with the man's head down. They pulled this one also back on board, but the crew never found any sign of Vandenberg's beagle puppy. The fishing boat then smashed over waves and through the hissing sea to the safe confines of Crescent City Harbor.

During the entire voyage, Don Piland without stop tried to revive Beckett with artificial respiration. A doctor and ambulance were waiting at Citizen's Dock when the fishing boat arrived, and the physician rushed aboard to examine the victims. A reluctant Don Piland let the doctor take over and make his evaluation. He declared Beckett dead upon arrival, joining the last two that had been found.

The tragic deaths of the three young Coast Guardsmen brought the total number of St. George men who had died there to at least five. (Adding in other accounts brings this total higher, such as a Coast Guardsman who disappeared in 1965 after only three days on the rock.) When one adds in the deaths of keepers Georges Roux and Julius Charter (see chapter 9, "The First Wickies"), the total comes to at least seven, not to mention the high numbers of severe injuries and illnesses. St. George Reef had proven itself to be one of the most deadly light stations in the United States.

Newspapers carried front-page stories about the deaths with editorials criticizing the Coast Guard's procedures. They questioned why a second boat wasn't in the immediate area in case of problems like this and why a high boom was still used to drop and pick up boats in those dangerous waters. With the numbers of people who had lost their lives at the station and around those waters, St. George Reef Lighthouse became known as the "sentinel of death." For centuries, the deadly Dragon Rocks had waited relentlessly to claim victims, and it did, decade after decade.

The local coroner ordered an inquest into the deaths of the three men. The surviving Coast Guardsmen, Fred Permenter, Ross Vandenberg, and Thomas Mulcahy, all testified about what had happened. Their versions were consistent, sad, and showed valor within very tragic circumstances. The physicians who testified at the inquest said that the three men had died from "shock, exposure, and brain concussion." The rogue wave had been powerful.

Permenter verified the identities of the three victims. His testimony was difficult. Trying to save the men under one's command and then having to identify the bodies can try men's souls. Three had died, but one had put his life on the line for all.

As the newspapers reported, "Fred Permenter, Boatswain's Mate First Class, who was in charge of the station, risked his own life to attempt a rescue." For his heroism, the Coast Guard awarded Fred Permenter the Treasury Department's coveted Gold Lifesaving medal. This award is given once a year for the outstanding example of courage in the Coast Guard—but only if someone's acts that year stand out. The medal was awarded in the office of the Secretary of the Treasury, and he was inducted him into an elite group that included Ida Lewis. Awarded to him during a banquet in his honor, the American Legion bestowed on Permenter its national Medal of Valor and "Hero of the Year" designation.

Self-effacing and giving credit to others, Fred Permenter and his heroics stand out. The savage elements at St. George Reef had again forced common people to reach for uncommon heights while others died. Later, Fred was picking up John Gibbons in the station's beat-up pickup and pointing the lighthouse out to him. Permenter didn't talk about what he had done to try to save his crew. One year after the tragedy, the Coast Guard had to land Wayne Piland and others to physically remove a keeper on St. George who had suffered a severe mental breakdown. Fred Permenter and his family then transferred out the following year.

The seas attempted to claim more victims. One day in 1958 the boom was once again lowering Coast Guardsmen in the launch into what again seemed to be safe waters. Another mountainous wave roared in and caught the boat before it could get out of harm's way.

The towering seas actually flipped the launch as it hurled the three men on board into the ocean. Having learned from Permenter's experience, the Coast Guard had changed its procedures with a cutter now present on all personnel transfers.

The Coast Guard cutter *Ewing* was standing by this time during the operation. The ship's captain immediately ordered the cutter to motor close to the men and the reef. As the men swept out to sea, the *Ewing* was able to safely save all three. Although the rescue was successful, the continuing risk—including the danger of a large cutter sailing too close and crashing against the rocks—continued despite more operational changes.

The ninety-five-foot cutter *Cape Carter* was already stationed at Crescent City, and from this incident on, this vessel was used to transfer the men in place of the boom plucking up a much smaller launch. The *Cape Carter* motored slowly under the long lighthouse boom and as close to the reef as possible. As a swell approached, the personnel scampered into an awaiting "Billy Pugh" net, and the ship then quickly shifted into reverse to avoid steaming into the rocks. (A Billy Pugh net is a platform with ropes tied to a roof; the crane hooks on to an "eye" on the roof and raises or lowers the apparatus.) This cage approach had an eerie similarity to what was in use over a century ago on Tillamook and St. George.

The operator again had to lift or drop the net at the precise time. This had to occur as the cutter was quickly backing away from the reef, the wave swelling past, and the men being lifted up, all at the same time. Depending on the circumstances, a breeches buoy (a pair of rubber pants within a life ring) was used instead of the Billy Pugh net to transfer the men. Depending on the waves, Coast Guard personnel could still be dunked in cold water, but the cable at least was attached to them as a lifeline. As an additional precaution, all of the men wore life vests, and this rule included not only the transferring men but the vessel's crew.

The cutter also accompanied the smaller launch on its trip from the harbor, and the men attached supplies encased in a net to the boom's hook. On other occasions, the Coast Guard's big oceangoing tug, the *Comanche*, or a buoy tender brought men and supplies to the lighthouse. Larger vessels such as these serviced St. George Reef when it was necessary to pump freshwater and fuel oil for the station's generators. Because the larger ships couldn't maneuver as close to the reef as the more nimble cutters could, these vessels needed to lower a small launch over its side that headed to the hook. The crew on board the tug or buoy tender then secured the vessel to a mooring buoy during the operations. But only on days when the seas were calm.

All of these operations were even more time consuming and expensive, but given the unpredictable savageness of these waters, moving men and supplies onto St. George became less hazardous. This didn't mean that these transfer efforts were safe. Operating this station at the time still remained riskier than any other active lighthouse.

DUANE "FERGY" FERGUSON was a career Coast Guardsman, who spent thirty-seven months at the St. George Reef Lighthouse on two tours of duty—second only to John Gibbons's thirty-nine months. (This is the same person who Gibby said wanted to swap his tour so that he could be with his family over the Christmas holidays.) Ferguson retired from the Coast Guard in 1971 and opened Fergy's Fast Lube in Crescent City before retiring.

He was assigned to the lighthouse for the first time in April 1955 as an engineer. "There were six men assigned to the lighthouse. Four on at all times," he said in a later interview. Although St. George was very isolated, the crew was kept busy. Fergy was in charge of repairing and maintaining the engine-room equipment that kept the lighthouse operating. This was the job John Gibbons had before him, and the equipment included the six diesel engines, three generators, and three air compressors. The other men were responsible for the maintenance, operation, and upkeep of the radio equipment, the lens, rigging for the lifting boom, foghorn, and other equipment. Each crew member also took turns on the 24/7 watch command post.

Like many lighthouses, St. George had its own resident ghosts: one of the men who died in the 1951 tragedy. Ferguson said:

> He made his presence known when one of the cups in the galley would suddenly start shaking. We'd give the young fellows a hard time. We'd tell them to give the old boy a cup of coffee. They would watch that cup swing and their eyes would get real big.

Toward the end of his duty John Gibbons was on Ferguson's shift. According to Gibby, Fergy also swore that he had seen those same ghosts and that they had made him nervous. "Fergy not only talked about those coffee cups that moved across a table, but also about whistling sounds and doors slamming for no reason." Gibby then made one of his one-liners: "I didn't believe in those ghosts. I don't think any self-respecting ghost would haunt a God-forsaken, noisy place like that station."

Like many others before him, Fergy felt that the changing of the crews was "really an experience." When the boom lifted the men in a basket "ninety feet up and ninety feet out" to a waiting Coast Guard tender, anything could—and did—happen. He said, "It was like Russian roulette. You never knew what was going to happen." The memories of the three men who died during the 1951 transfer were still fresh when Fergy came on duty, and they kept this in mind when overseeing subsequent transfers.

Fergy particularly liked watching the flocks of migrating geese, schools of killer whales, and the hundreds of sea lions that flocked to the rock. One time, he saw what "must have been one thousand sea lions on the rock," all attracted by the sun, sea, and easy food. When the weather was nice, Fergy fished, and when he was successful, the crew dined on his caught seafood, including ling cod and coho salmon. And this included two full buckets of shrimp when they spotted the shoal of these delicious appetizers.

The crew another time spotted a baby harbor seal on the reef. They adopted the little seal, naming it "Boson Benny." The seal slept in a water tank at night; during the day, the men took him to the reef's edge so that Benny could hunt for food. One day, Benny didn't return. Fergy felt that the seal went closer to shore to get away from a storm.

One day, the chief called Gibby into the Coast Guard's office on the point and said that Fergy wanted to be at the hospital when his wife gave birth to their child. Gibbons said that he would cover Fergy's shift, and in two hours he was on the launch heading to the rock. He worked for forty-five straight days, being his shift, Fergy's shift (when Gibby would be on leave), and then back on his own shift, before heading back to shore. Years later when Gibby saw Fergy's wife, she and her grown son thanked him for what he had done.

As others experienced before, manning the lighthouse was a scary, nerve-wracking experience. One time during a gale, Fergy was on the midnight to 6 a.m. shift on the lens. Suddenly, he heard a loud crash against the glass and jumped in fright. At first, all he could see was blood and feathers, but as he stared closer through the window, he saw it was a bird that the winds had thrown into the glass. Ferguson was shaken by the experience. "I woke up one of the other guys and said, 'You're going to stay up with me for the rest of the night.'"

When the weather turned bad—as it often did—the beneficial leaves became a thing of the past. The men still worked hard, but the harsh conditions and no time off made this even harder. On one occasion the weather was so bad that Fergy and the other men were forced to spend six "long weeks" on the rock. As seen, this was not an uncommon situation.

The enjoyment, trials, and tribulations of the wickies had continued over time at St. George, as the transferring of men and supplies dominated what men recalled when looking back at those
times. Don Nuss served in the Coast Guard from 1957 to 1961. He
was assigned to an "eighty-three footer" that operated from Crescent
City from May 1960 to January 1961. This was a wooden vessel
("Number 83412") that was used in search and rescue and to transfer personnel and supplies at times onto St. George. Don relayed
two stories about these transfers that showed the risk that still continued there, even though new procedures had been instituted.

On one trip, the skipper was nosing the boat into the pickup
point. The procedure used then was that the hoist operator would
lower the Billy Pugh net toward the Coast Guard vessel. When personnel and supplies were loaded on board, the boom operator
brought the net up over seven stories onto the catch deck. The skipper had to again navigate the currents expertly, so that a swell would
raise the boat at the precise time that the operator was bringing the
Pugh net up.

One time, while the procedure was under way, Don felt the boat
"suddenly going in full-stern reverse." The currents had swept the
boat nearly onto the rocks of the lighthouse, and the large supply
vessel was so close that Don could have touched the reef from the
bow. The quick reversal of the engines by the skipper started pulling
the vessel from the rocks. For agonizingly slow seconds, a man could
have still leaned over and slapped the rocks. The propeller finally
took hold and carried the ship out of harm's way.

These currents were swift and capricious. They would sweep
around the rock, join at the point where the supply vessel lay, and
then sweep into the rock. Or depending on the storm conditions
and wind directions, the currents could sweep away from that point.

On another trip, the boat suddenly dropped fifteen feet down
due to the wave action. At the time, a Coast Guardsman was transferring to duty on St. George. The sudden action caught him before

he was into the net, and he was forced to swing his leg in and pull himself up. If he hadn't done this, the man would have been swinging by his arms. The hoist operator had to haul the slack in the cable up quickly; otherwise, the startled person would slam into the boat or the water when the wave swells whipped the boat back up.

In January 1965 a young Coast Guardsman became another casualty on this lighthouse. One wickie heard his screams as he plummeted seventy feet into the "chill" ocean waters. The last sight of the man was in rough seas "four hundred yards northeast" of the station around four o'clock in the afternoon. It wasn't known what brought about the twenty-two-year-old's plunge into the ocean, but capricious blasts of winds, slipping by the railings, inadvertence, and other causes had previously brought tragedy to others. With the technology becoming available to automate lighthouses like these, the dangers in operating St. George could no longer be ignored.

CHAPTER 15

Abandonment—and Renewal

After World War I, the automation of lighthouses began to become technologically possible and indicated that human control would ultimately be unnecessary. The ability to automatically replace burned-out electric lighthouse lamps, warn about the fuel consumption of oil-vapor lamps by a bell alarm, and employ experimental radio beacons brought about this conclusion.

In the 1930s the Lighthouse Service designed a lightship with a warning light, fog signal, and radio beacon that operated by remote control. As electrification came to the more remote areas, the majority of lighthouses by then had electric service, reducing the staffing needs to wind cable weights, trim wicks, and refuel lamps. With shore stations and installations becoming unnecessary, the eventual automation of the light stations began. At the same time, the lifesaving and lifeboat stations were gradually being phased out.

During World War II, the Coast Guard watched over the nation's shorelines. Many lighthouses were employed as spotting stations for military land and sea operations, along with being used as temporary radio stations with portable equipment. With the development of SHORAN (short-range navigation aids) and LORAN (long-range navigation aids), lighthouses were becoming obsolete. One by one, lighthouses became automated or shut down when this longer-range navigational equipment was installed and could cover their former territory.

The keepers left Minot's Ledge for good in 1947 when a modern automatic lens replaced the old Fresnel light. In the early 1980s, the light was converted to solar power. The station's lens and fog bell is now on Government Island inside a replica of the lantern room, and the repaired Fresnel lens is inside that room.

When the U.S. Coast Guard installed a sophisticated $23,000 buoy with light, radar, and fog-signaling apparatus, one-half mile to the west, Terrible Tilly shut down in 1957 and became government surplus. As it cost $15,000 to operate Tillamook Lighthouse each year, the buoy paid for itself in eighteen months with little maintenance. Tillamook Rock Lighthouse was later placed on the National Register of Historic Places.

Keepers watched over Spectacle Reef and its lens until 1972, when the Coast Guard automated this light. Ten years later, a solar-powered optical replaced the Fresnel lens; it was removed and shipped to the Great Lakes Historical Society Museum in Vermilion, Ohio.

St. George Reef was the first lighthouse to be deactivated when a large navigational buoy light could be designed specifically to replace it. The station was the last manned off-shore lighthouse then left on the Pacific Coast, and in 1974 men spent the last Christmas there. Before its deactivation, the lighthouse had a powerful light, radio beacon, and diaphone foghorns. A navigational buoy completely replaced all of these functions.

A large 42-foot high, self-contained navigation aid, the buoy was anchored in 220 feet of water off the stormy reef in 1975, and its cost was approximately $350,000. Located one-half mile away, the lighthouse on most days is clearly visible in the distance. The St. George Reef Large Navigational Buoy (LNB) that replaced the station was a 42-foot diameter "floating lighthouse." It weighed 200,000 pounds and contained small diesel-powered engines that provided electrical power for the seventeen-mile range navigation light, radio beacon, and fog signal. The buoy also contains weather-monitoring equipment for the U.S. Weather Service.

The Coast Guard made its decision to replace the lighthouse with the LNB for both economic and safety considerations. Economically, the buoy was said to pay for itself within a projected eighteen months over the cost of manning and operating the lighthouse. However, the risk of continuing to keep people on the existing light station was another factor that weighed heavily in the decision. The commander of the Coast Guard in Humboldt Bay, Lieutenant Commander Theodore Nutting, said at the time, "The main reason for closing this lighthouse is safety. It is a very hazardous situation out there."

A prime risk eliminated was the dangerous situation existing every time men, equipment, and supplies were transferred, whether they were using baskets, small boats, or nets. The light from the LNB was less, however, as its beam was limited to fourteen miles, and the buoy also didn't pick up the same data that the men on St. George could find and transmit. For example, the keepers called in wind directions, speed, height and direction of seas, and visibility on a continuing basis. Despite this, the decision was an easy one to make.

Anchored in place on April 1, 1975, the LNB was immediately put into operation while the lighthouse was still manned. The station monitored the "super buoy" for several weeks to be sure it operated reliably.

On May 13, 1975, the Coast Guard cutter *Cape Carter* made the last run to the lighthouse to remove the men, eighty-three years after the light station had been constructed. The vessel's decks heaved with the swells as the derrick raised and lowered the Billy Pugh net with the guests and dignitaries, who wanted one last look at the famous station. When the ceremonies came to an end, the people and military personnel left.

The two officers remaining lowered the American flag and operated the derrick boom to drop the last crewmen in the net to the awaiting launch shuttle. The men left everything as it was that day. Beds, chairs, empty file cabinets, furniture, washing machine, and refrigerator were left in place. Pots were still in the oven, dishes in the cupboards, and a 1975 calendar was left hanging on the wall.

Officer in Charge James (J.W.) Sebastian and Petty Officer Louis Salter chained the massive door shut, donned their wetsuits, climbed down the iron staircase to the rocks, and then ferried out in a motorized rubber Zodiac raft to the awaiting cutter. Owing to the sea conditions, the raft bounced heavily over the swells as it raced back to the ship.

The Coast Guard later presented plaques to each member of the last five-man crew and awarded Officer Sebastian the last flag that flew over the station. The crew to work last on St. George Reef Lighthouse comprised Officers Sebastian and Salter with Seamen James Dunham, Gary Newberry, and Rusty Woodward. Chief Petty Officer Sebastian made one final entry into the log that dated back to 1891:

It is with much sentiment that I pen this final entry, 13 May 1975. After four score and three years, St. George Reef Light is dark. No longer will your brilliant beams of light be seen, nor your bellowing fog signal be heard by the mariner. Gone are your keepers. Only by your faithful service has many a disaster been prevented on the treacherous St. George Reef. You stand today, as you have down through the years, a tribute to humanity and worthy of our highest respect. Cut from the soul of our country, you have valiantly earned your place in American history. In your passing, the era of the lonely sea sentinel has truly ended. May another nature show your mercy. You have been abandoned, but never will you be forgotten. Farewell, St. George Reef Light.

J.W. Sebastian—BMC [base military commander]
Officer-in-Charge

The last manned lighthouse on the U.S. West Coast now was abandoned. With hundreds of seals and sea lions being the only lookouts on this small spit of surf-washed rock, vandals were free to shoot out tower windows, rip out equipment from the generator room, and forage through the structure. Without maintenance, painting, or repairs to stem the elements, the constant moisture and storms were free to do their damage.

The lighthouse stood alone and neglected until the early 1980s, when the Del Norte County Historical Society, Bob Bolen with other volunteers, and later the St. George Lighthouse Preservation Society geared into action. The first order of business was to bring the valuable Fresnel lens to land before it could be vandalized. Throughout all of these efforts, Bolen was a key driving force.

A retired airline mechanic, Bolen owned five airplanes; traveled to tens of different countries researching the Aztecs, pyramids, and Mesa Verde cliff dwellers; built thirteen model mockups of old Northern California trains (which he later donated to the Historical Society); and enjoyed a variety of interests—but with a passion for this lighthouse. A retired social worker, Guy Towers, became as interested in lighthouses in the early 1980s. When he moved to Crescent City in 1986, he learned about the condition and state of affairs of this one. Towers quickly hooked up with Bob Bolen and the others to drive forward the efforts of the St. George Lighthouse Preservation Society.

THE DEL NORTE HISTORICAL SOCIETY began working in 1983 to preserve the tower, starting by arranging the transport back of the Fresnel lens to its museum. Bob Bolen was instrumental in designing and bringing about the removal of the giant lens. Before work could be started to move the lens, however, workers first needed to clear a path through the five hundred upset sea lions that had retaken residence on the reef.

As the brown-and-gray mass of sea lions bellowed in surprise at their first glimpse of humans in some years, gulls, terns, albatrosses, and other seabirds squawked or sailed overhead. The group walked up the rusting staircase that led to the large doors leading into the caisson's interior. When the first visitors unlocked the door into the interior and walked in, they saw dark shapes and smelled decay.

Once they turned on their flashlights, the group saw the immense engine-room cavern before them. A high-ceiling, vaulted room with metal steps still clinging tightly to the walls appeared. The staircase was to their left, a row of huge generators through a corridor to the right. Old equipment, rusted hardware, and life jackets were scattered around.

The next sight nearly shocked people out of their shoes. A life-size figure of a man dressed in rain gear and U.S. Coast Guard coveralls dangled from a noose suspended from the ceiling. The last Coast Guardsman to leave eight years before had apparently left this behind as a reminder of what life had been like.

Opening the darkened Bosun's room locker, the men discovered moldy American flags still inside. Gingerly walking up the rusting staircase to the second level, their flashlights illuminated the laundry room with its washer, dryer, old refrigerator, and even a box of laundry soap. Around the corner and a few steps down, they found the huge boom, completely rusted and discolored.

The visitors carefully walked up the spiraling stone steps inside the high tower while filtered light crept in through the wooden window covers, so that when they came to the galley, they saw what kitchen life was once like. Canisters were still loaded with flour, sugar, coffee, and tea bags. An old-fashioned tea kettle still lay on the stove, and old newspapers and magazines were scattered about on the countertop. Coast Guard papers and memorandums were still tacked on one bulletin-board wall.

The crew had left *Newsweek* magazines behind with cover photos of the U.S. withdrawal from Vietnam scattered over the table. Coffee mugs sat upside-down in the sink and a fully stocked cabinet contained corroding metal spice cans. Pots, pans, bowls, and glasses remained just as they had been left. As a memorial to past crew members, an *I Hate to Cook* cookbook was on one countertop with handwritten recipes for steak sauce and pork chops with apples.

The resident lighthouse keepers lived in separate rooms on the next floors. The head keeper, or chief petty officer, had his own room above the galley; the assistant keepers or crew shared the room above it. In each bedroom, people walked into surrealistic shades of darkness and light beams, as chest of drawers, beds, toilets, and showers appeared. Pillows were still on the beds, rolls of toilet paper still hung in the bathrooms, and the bed frames were rusted with stained mattresses.

No matter where they walked, the smell of decay was present and nearly overpowering. In just those eight years, multicolored layers of paint were peeling, wood was rotting, and equipment rusting. Plaster had fallen down in every room, covering furniture and furnishings with shards of masonry. The quarters initially had redwood wainscoting, tongue-and-groove flooring with built-in bunk beds, and shiny brass fixtures. These were now gone, destroyed by the elements into rust and mold or taken by vandals after the lighthouse was abandoned.

In the uppermost, two-level lamp room, visitors stepped outside a metal door to the keeper's walk. Rusted railings edged the narrow iron balcony and its towering views of the ocean crashing over the rocks below. Although the vistas were spectacular, the group noted the room's windows: attempting to clean them during windy days with the ocean being 140 feet below was a courageous act, if not downright foolhardy, they thought.

A Coast Guard buoy tender anchored off the reef to transport the disassembled pieces of the three-ton lens and lighting apparatus. It was six feet in diameter, seven and a half feet high, and consisted of more than five hundred ground-glass prisms set in brass frames on a nine-foot pedestal. Four separate crews were needed to work together to complete the task. One dismantled the lens panels and lowered them seventy feet below to the caisson deck; the second received the panels and carefully wrapped each one; a third "high-line" crew lowered the pieces from the pier deck to the waiting transfer boat; and the fourth transported the prisms from there onto the ship and carefully stored them with the lens equipment for the trip ashore.

The tender transported the parts to Crescent City where they were refurbished, polished, and reassembled to their original shape. The three-ton lens with its magnificent, ever-sparkling ground-glass prisms and brass frames are now housed in a two-story structure constructed at the back of the Del Norte County Historical Society building in Crescent City. For two years, the small town held dances, ice cream socials, and other fund-raisers to raise the $23,000 needed to construct the addition (appropriately named "Bolen Annex") to house the huge lens.

The St. George Reef Lighthouse Preservation Society was officially formed in 1986 as a nonprofit corporation to acquire and restore the lighthouse. The group began working with congressional and state representatives to gain jurisdiction over the lighthouse in a process that took ten years. Since this federal property could not be donated at the time directly to a private group, the government finally transferred the site in 1996 to Del Norte County, which in turn with the National Park Service granted a twenty-five-year lease to the nonprofit entity.

With the assistance of the Coast Guard, the Lighthouse Preservation Society made a successful application to the National Register of Historic Places, which in 1993 accepted the "St. George Reef Light Station" for inclusion on the U.S. National Historic Register. The lighthouse's location was cited as being on "Northwest Seal Rock, approximately six nautical miles off the coast from Point St. George, Crescent City."

Concerned about the huge waves eventually crushing the stored drums of lube and diesel oil and spilling the seven hundred gallons of oil into the seal habitat, the Coast Guard in 1994 arranged for two helicopters from its Humboldt Bay's air station to land five crewmen on the pier top. The men loaded the drums into a net hanging from the helicopters, and the oil was later sent to a waste-oil company for recycling.

THE DEVELOPMENT of the automated, large navigational buoys and use of LORAN led to the replacement of lighthouses in the 1970s, so that by 1990 every one of the lighthouses in the United States was in non-use or automated, except the first one built nearly three hundred years earlier at Boston Harbor Light.

With modern automated beacons, the Coast Guard found it was more cost effective to construct and maintain unmanned navigation aids on a steel structure, buoy, or tower. Under the Coast Guard system, a relatively small number of people can look after the automated stations that it operates today. Acrylic "Fresnel-like" lenses and airport-type "aero-beacons" have replaced many of the classic Fresnel lenses, and solar-powered lights are commonplace.

With the complete automation of lighthouses and no need for the supplemental structures that housed wickies, their families, and supplies, the lighthouses ran into disrepair and damage by vandals. The romance of these structures and their folklore, however, brought about the movement by historical societies and individuals to preserve their history. The Coast Guard then began a process in the 1990s to lease light stations to local historical groups and other organizations that were interested in caring for the structures.

The first lighthouse was constructed in Boston Harbor in the early 1700s, and by 1900 the United States had constructed 1,050 lighthouses with 6,000 located worldwide. By the end of the next century, some 1,800 had been built within and along the U.S. coastlines. Despite these numbers, the United States usually didn't have more than eight hundred lighthouses operating at the same time—still impressive numbers.

Approximately six hundred historic light stations—meaning that a tower may now be missing but the keeper's dwelling and other buildings still survive—exist today in various states of disrepair or restoration in this country. The U.S. Coast Guard has over four hundred of these stations, of which some are leased to local groups, used for military personnel, or operated as active aids for navigation. Under past transfers and various procedures, federal agencies such as the National Park Service, the Forest Service, the Fish and Wildlife Service, and the Navy now own some of these light stations, as do local historical societies, state parks, and even private individuals.

Although the Coast Guard has tried to preserve those under its control, its ability to do so is subject to the funding at hand. The service continues to evaluate its historic inventory and donate more stations to institutions and groups under current law; the Department of Homeland Security now has ultimate responsibility over this process. A major objective of the Coast Guard, however, is to maintain the automated light and fog systems that are active aids to navigation. Since the technology allows people to monitor beacons electronically from great distances, no Coast Guardsmen are needed to work onsite at those stations. In 1998, Boston Light became the last lighthouse to be automated, and a resident civilian keeper, assisted by volunteers from the Coast Guard Auxiliary, now staffs the site.

The Coast Guard's process of transferring its nonessential lighthouses was formalized with the passage of the National Historic Lighthouse Preservation Act of 2000 (NHLPA). This legislation recognizes the value in allowing historic light station properties to be transferred at no cost to federal agencies, state and local governments, nonprofit corporations, educational agencies, and community development organizations. Only those stations that are eligible for listing or listed in the National Register of Historic Places can be transferred under this statutory program; lighthouses that are not eligible for such a listing are disposed of in other ways, including bidding contests. Successful organizations must comply with the NHLPA's conditions, including being able to financially maintain the historic light station and making it available to the general public at "reasonable times and under reasonable conditions."

The U.S. Coast Guard and other federal agencies identify and report historic light stations that are to be "excessed" through the NHLPA. With the General Services Administration (GSA) overseeing the process, the U.S. Interior Secretary makes the final decision on which applicants receive the historic stations. If no applicant is so approved to receive the light station, then the GSA may sell the property under the NHLPA's provisions. Unless a nonprofit group is extraordinarily well capitalized, partnerships and contractual relationships with state and federal agencies are near mandatory in this process.

The State of California and its Department of Parks and Recreation, for example, and county foundations are partnering with the nonprofit Central Coast Lighthouse Keepers, in which more than $2 million has already been invested in the upkeep and restoration of Point Sur Lighthouse. The lantern room and tower, carpenter/blacksmith shop, barn, and replica water tower are among the areas and facilities that have been substantially refurbished with the Central Coast Lighthouse association raising the great amount of the necessary funding. Still an active aid-in-navigation station, the U.S. Coast Guard regularly services the lighthouse. The station and its supporting buildings is now a California State Historic Park.

Other examples of stations transferred include Pigeon Point Light Station in San Mateo County, California, which the Coast Guard donated to the California Department of Parks and Recreation; the Molokai Lighthouse on Molokai Island, Hawaii, has headed administratively to the National Park Service under its Maritime Heritage Program; and the West Point Light Station in Seattle, Washington, was transferred to the City of Seattle's Department of Parks and Recreation. Public and private groups formed a partnership to maintain and preserve the Thomas Point Lighthouse in the Chesapeake Bay. Under these agreements, the city of Annapolis is the lighthouse owner; the United States Lighthouse Society and its Chesapeake Chapter are the lighthouse managers, leasing the structure from the city for all preservation and operations; the Annapolis Maritime Museum is the primary shore-based factor, housing lighthouse exhibits and being the point of departure for public tours; and Anne Arundel County provides "preservation and environmental expertise." There are many other stories of lighthouses, their so interesting history and now preservation, but space limits going into them.

This is the good news. The other news is that the process is slow, entrapped by red tape, governed by politics, and ensnares any recipient in a blizzard of permits, conditions, and obligations that must be met, even after the property is transferred. Additionally, when the Coast Guard and the government decide to abandon a lighthouse, they leave it for good. When the keepers depart for the last time, a lighthouse is left in pristine condition with fresh paint, equipment in good working order, and wood preserved. The problem is that the Service never returns to restart engines, conduct minimum maintenance, pour preserving oil into equipment, or board windows that had given way to the sea. The same experience happened with St. George Reef Lighthouse.

THE ST. GEORGE REEF LIGHTHOUSE PRESERVATION SOCIETY has been working since 1996 to refurbish a lighthouse that had deteriorated terribly. By this time, the destruction by salt air, water, spray, and time over twenty years had taken its course. The engine room's heavy iron doors were so rusted and weather beaten that they couldn't be shut, and the name of the "Coast Guard" was barely visible underneath the rust. Rotten wood floor joists jutted through crumbling cement. The beautifully crafted and ornate wrought-iron handrails that guarded the outside stairwell stairs and pier had rusted and fallen away. Paint and plaster peeled in rolls from the overhead vaulted ceilings, while the fixtures and cabinets were rotted and falling apart. Dark green mold and dark salty corrosion coated the lighthouse's rooms. Inside and out, the station was discolored with dark corrosion and rot.

The huge structure itself, however, is still as sound as when it was first constructed. The rust, corrosion, and moldy rot showed the disrepair, but the core structure was still solid and strong. This Medieval-looking battlement was built like a fortified, solid castle to withstand the hundred-mile-per hour winds and huge stories-high waves. The care and craftsmanship in the design and building of this great lighthouse is evident, despite the continuing gale winds, frigid seas, and heavy rainfall each year.

As part of the Society's preservation efforts, helicopters ferry crews of volunteers, tools, and equipment at designated times to work on the lighthouse. These are massive, concerted efforts to repair, maintain, and refurbish the station. Subject to the weather and fog conditions—which can be so bad that the pilots can't find the site in the dense fog—a helicopter shuttles crews of volunteers and workmen with massive amounts of equipment and supplies for days of work.

In April 2000, workmen unbolted the cast-iron and glass cupola of the lantern room, and a California Air National Guard helicopter carried the suspended structure to the mainland for restoration. The helicopter was supposed to come in at five hundred feet, but approached the beach slightly off course and too low. A flight member said later, "The pilot couldn't see the load while we were in flight. I could see that we were coming in too low and kept telling them to lift up." But by then, it was too late.

The five-ton upper portion of the lantern room crashed over the beach, severing the cables that secured it to the helicopter. The impact smashed most of the structure into pieces, leaving debris scattered over the beach and the dome left upside down. Before people could protect the pieces, some of the onlookers actually raced over, picked up parts of the scattered pieces as souvenirs, and scurried away. With insurance not available or affordable, the nonprofit society didn't have the money to cover the damage.

Two years later, thanks to the donated money, time, and service of local Crescent City residents, the lantern room (as it was now called) was finally restored and transported back. The owner of Fashion Blacksmith, Dale Long, moved the crushed room to his marine construction and repair facility site located one-quarter mile away. The structure stayed there until the repairs were complete, and no better qualified marine-repair firm was around than this one to do this work. Dale Long didn't charge for storage or the use of his equipment, and the repairs took 362 fabrication hours, all of which he provided at no charge. The St. George society paid for the materials ($10,000) and the panels to replace the glass.

When Bob Bolen heard that the preservation society didn't have the necessary $24,000 to transport the lantern room back to the lighthouse, he decided he would help out. Needing a wheelchair to move around, the then eighty-year-old Bolen lived in an assisted-care facility. Bolen decided to sell a house that was part of his retirement income, however, and donated the money needed to bring the room back. His only request was that he could ride in the chase helicopter and watch the lantern room being returned.

Workmen years ago had built the entire lantern room with gray cast iron, which proved to be very sturdy and long-lasting. Cast iron is extremely resilient to saltwater conditions, whereas steel wouldn't have survived as long. The reconstruction used stainless steel to save weight, but the workmen applied a marine epoxy coating to combat rust, salty water, and the extreme weather conditions.

While working on the lantern room, people questioned what the small bronze handles on each window section were used for. It turned out the handles were attached so that the keepers could have something to hold on to when they cleaned the outside windows. With a near-skyscraper terrifying fall to the rocks below, attaching these safety handles made sense, although that job still remained quite risky.

On the scheduled day of the return, April 12, 2002, Bolen didn't want to wait for his ride to the helicopter departure site. He drove his electric wheelchair instead from his Crescent City care facility to where the lantern room was to be hoisted up and flown back—a distance of three and a half miles from where he lived. When a blanketing fog suddenly rolled in and prevented the liftoff, Bolen left in his wheelchair for the nursing home. While on his way back, his wheelchair battery died. Bolen left his wheelchair at a local business and nonchalantly hitch-hiked a ride home.

When weather conditions improved, a friend drove him back the following day. A large Erickson Air Crane S-64E helicopter with a seventy-two-foot rotor flew in from Central Point, Oregon, to haul the lantern room away. When the two helicopters lifted off that morning, Bolen was in the second observing helicopter as the lantern was taken back to where it had been since the 1890s. Ten minutes later, the room was at the top of the lighthouse and placed on top of the pedestal. In another ten minutes, the cupola was lined up precisely over the thirty-two holes in the base plate, each of which was one and a quarter inches in diameter. Workers tied the bolts down. Showing the advantages of modern technology, reattaching the room to the structure took one-half hour. One hundred years before, completing this task took weeks.

The St. George Reef Lighthouse Preservation Society has raised over one-quarter million dollars (and still going) to rebuild the lantern room, install a new solar-powered light, sandblast away corrosion, rebuild the power grid, restore the diesel generators, replace two hundred feet of handrails, renovate rooms, restore the original ninety-foot cast-iron boom, and make other necessary maintenance and repairs. They have cleared huge amounts of rubble from the catch deck, removed tons of debris from the engine room, and removed peeling paint, plaster, and old fixtures.

The volunteers with this public-interest group have labored for years relying on their fund-raising efforts. They have donated equipment and supplies and selflessly given their time to repair the lighthouse. The Army Air Guard has also donated the use of its large helicopters when heavy materials and equipment need to be hauled to the site. Supplemented by donations and membership fees, the profit made from public helicopter tours is the Society's prime fund-raising vehicle. (See www.stgeorgereeflighthouse.us for more information on these tours.) The dedication and sacrifice in money and time by these volunteers stands out.

The lighthouse was relit as a private aid to navigation on Sunday, October 20, 2002—the 110th anniversary of the first lighting of St. George Reef Light. The solar-powered light flashes every twelve seconds, powered by three, 150-pound batteries that convert the sun's energy during the day to battery power that drives the light during the night. The lens structure is three feet tall, and a fifty-watt bulb shines a light that is visible for twenty-five miles.

As the only safe means of transportation to the site is by helicopter landing on the caisson roof, a helicopter shuttled visitors and volunteers to and from the lighthouse during the 2002 anniversary celebration. However, this was also a working weekend. The helicopter airlifted fourteen volunteers and a five-person ground crew to work on the lighthouse that Friday. A large, CH-47 Army Air Guard helicopter airlifted an air compressor and pot (1,400 pounds), three tons of sand for sandblasting, water for pressure washing, and needed equipment. The written "Restoration Flight Number 9" manifest for that work weekend reads with military precision as to what was to be done, by whom, and by when. There was no fooling around.

The goals were repairing the window shutters for the winter, upgrading the electrical, sandblasting and painting the lantern and watch rooms, installing a new water pump, power-washing the catch deck, installing the new solar light, and "the never ending task of cleaning, painting, scraping, and total maintenance." On hand were electricians, a plumber, cooks, medical help, press and media personnel, shore-based communication, and even a Ham radio "special event" coverage to beam the activities around the country. Fifteen people spent the night on the tower on October 18 with eighteen people working and sleeping over the following night.

Written rules were discussed in preflight briefings, including that all passengers must wear life vests, avoid approaching the tail rotor, not slamming the helicopter doors, and other appropriate safety regulations. An unwritten caveat was that danger is always a possibility. One time, Terry McNamara (who has been the "Work Coordinator" or crew leader for several years), his son Nick, and Nick's fiancée, Stephanie, were closing up the lighthouse after a long, hard work weekend. Terry was standing on the tower's south side when he heard a scream. Turning toward the noise, he watched Nick and Stephanie running for their lives with a huge wall of green water right behind them. They joined him on the protected side of the tower, as the giant roller crashed over the caisson deck and roared around the tower's sides. This wave was easily eight stories high. Had the helicopter then been on the catch deck, the massive roller would have destroyed it and drowned anyone inside it. And there have been other experiences like this.

Over time, these volunteers have made striking progress in their refurbishment of the lighthouse. Their members still contribute their time, money, and efforts in bringing this about. For example,

Don Nuss met his wife, Sandy, when he was in Crescent City on his Coast Guard tour. He stayed, married, and settled down in the city. Don established his own metal working/fabricating shop and business (Redwood Welding Service) in Crescent City, while Sandy volunteers with the Del Norte County Historical Society.

Don Nuss also helps with the St. George refurbishment, and volunteers his services. The St. George Preservation Society gave a special award in 2005 to Don for his work as a "master metal worker" in rebuilding the metal railings that circle the catch deck, ring the lantern room, and line other levels. A number of people over the years have similarly volunteered to help preserve this lighthouse. In addition to Bob Bolen and Guy and Alice Towers, others such as Jim and Marilyn McLaughlin, Bob and Jane Faires, Bill and Betty Barton, Gene Olson, Dordi Round, Kay Thomas, Eloise Ware, and Tish Hendrix continually worked on or with the nonprofit board. Unsung heroes such as Terry and Nick McNamara, the McLaughlins, Clark Nuss (Don and Sandy's son), Mitch Gianola, Billy Tedsen, Randy Rogers, Aaron Duncan, and Susan Davis have labored on the numerous work weekends—and there are many others.

However, anytime government regulations come into play, there are sure to be delays and difficulties. One thorny problem revolves around the lease requirement that the nonprofit society maintain a landing permit in order for its helicopters to land on the site. Owing to naturalists' concerns, the permit requires that the society access the lighthouse by helicopter only during non-summer months. Wildlife officials prohibited any travel to the lighthouse between June 1 and October 15, when the sea lions are mating. Helicopter tours therefore can generally only be offered in the fall and spring, weather permitting, from mid-October to June 1.

Due to the Stellar sea lions that reside around the site, concerns later arose as to whether an approaching helicopter might unintentionally injure or disrupt some. The National Marine Fisheries Service became involved and required that the St. George Reef Lighthouse

Preservation Society obtain a "take" permit: if a seal was unintentionally harmed, this license provides that such an act is not illegal and no permit cancellation will result. To gain such a permit, however, requires the concurrence of the Marine Mammal Center. Other issues then surfaced.

For two work seasons, helicopter flights to the site were stopped, making fund-raising difficult and repairs impossible. It was easier to build the lighthouse in the 1880s than it was to land on it in the first decade of the twenty-first century. When the various wildlife agencies and other concerned entities finally signed off, the first helicopters flew again in 2007 with "Restoration Flight No. 19." This work included removing the lens light for repairs, cleaning and painting numerous areas, and completing electrical and plumbing repairs. Volunteers and workers were once more replacing rusted metalwork, repairing equipment, supporting floors, and working to push back the deterioration of the previous years.

When landing in a small helicopter on the caisson deck, visitors have a unique experience awaiting them. Even on bright, clear days, the malevolent ocean crashes in a mind-numbing display of white violence and cross currents against a deep-blue backdrop. The winds whistle on the stories-high walkway outside the lantern room, ripping at jackets and wrenching hats away.

Meanwhile the work of repairing the site continues. The impressive, two-story Fresnel lens and other St. George exhibits are on display at the Del Norte County Historical Society in Crescent City. (For more information, see delnortehistory.org.) The U.S. Postal Service is also honoring the station, issuing a St. George Reef Lighthouse stamp in 2007 as part of its recognition of historic Pacific Coasts lighthouses.

THE STORIES ABOUT LIGHTHOUSES and their reconstruction are, of course, not limited to St. George Reef, despite its history, location, and uniqueness. Hopefully, the history of Tillamook Rock Lighthouse once it closed won't be repeated. After the station was abandoned, the Government Services Administration sold the property two years later in 1959 for $5,600 to Nevada investors. Whatever the new owners had in mind never materialized. Fourteen years later, this group sold the lighthouse and its rock island to General Electric executive George Hupman of New York for $11,000, who had grandiose plans of turning it into a summer resort with helicopter access. The lighthouse interior by now was a total mess. He sent in a crew to begin repairs, but eventually gave up.

Hupman sold it to Max Shillock of Portland, Oregon, for $27,000 in 1978. When Shillock and three others tried to get to the rock, their motorboat overturned in the breakers near Seaside. One man drowned. The other three, including Shillock, struggled to get to the beach and survived, although they suffered from shock and hypothermia.

Shillock in actuality, however, had borrowed the money from someone else. The lenders, including businesswoman Mimi Morrisette and her associates, took back ownership under the name of Eternity at Sea. This group then stripped down the lighthouse's interior and converted it into the world's first lighthouse columbarium!

They created one hundred thousand niches for urns and promised a helicopter ride (provided the weather permitted) to purchasers of the services for loved ones to see the ash-filled urns placed in solitude inside the structure. Very few urns have been placed inside the columbarium, and two of those were stolen, presumably by thieves who must have landed at night in a helicopter.

When keepers reminisce, it makes a big difference whether they worked or grew up with pleasant memories on a land station, like Battery Point Lighthouse, Piedras Blancas Light Station, or the Farallons; or survived on a wave-washed spit like St. George or Tillamook. When on those granite rocks and savage waters, they remember the vicious seas and hurricane winds, waiting for their duty to end, and the highs and lows of this life.

The jarring impact of technology surprised even the most experienced. Electric foghorns with a sharp, single-note blast replaced the old, compressed air diaphone foghorns with their classic, deep, high-to-low sounds. Small lightbulbs in smaller, modern lenses completely replaced the much larger Fresnel, oil-lit lamps. Regardless of the lighthouse they served on, the wickies found it hard to believe that cold, computerized, very small, lifeless equipment could replace their human commitment to the lights and foghorns. Or that the automatic stations could pay for themselves so soon over the cost of running an average lighthouse.

Continued to be owned as private property, only seals are allowed to visit Tillamook Rock Lighthouse. Built so strong and solid, Tillamook languishes as the winds and sea lash it and countless cormorants, murres, gulls, and other sea birds call it home, as they did centuries ago. The bird droppings have turned the place white, and seas still swell and crash against the rock and roar through the cleft on the south side. Huge green waves during the worst storms continue to inundate the abandoned site.

The St. George Reef Lighthouse Preservation Society and its volunteers, meanwhile, labor long hours to gain the necessary permits, raise capital, and complete the renovation. Alexander Ballantyne, Captain Payson, and Colonel Orlando Poe could never have imagined all those years ago, the lengths others would be forced to go to preserve the sacrifice, workmanship, and commitment they had to the most dangerous and expensive lighthouse built in this country.

St. George Lighthouse still stands as an impressive monument to an era that long ago passed. Despite the advent of computers and their powerful technology, however, the dragon's teeth still lay off-shore in wait for the unwary mariner.

SELECTED BIBLIOGRAPHY

"A. Ballantyne, one of the corps of United States Engineers located in San Francisco, will accompany a specially-selected party." Article that begins with cited words, *Los Angeles Times*, January 15, 1903.

Adamson, Hans Christian. *Keepers of the Light*. New York: Greenberg Publishers, 1955.

Associated Press Wire. "Point Sur Lighthouse to be transferred to California State Parks," April 21, 2004.

Barber, L. "Historic Oregon Light Abandoned." *Yachting*, November 1957, vol. 102, 158.

Bathurst, Bella. *The Lighthouse Stevensons*. Hammersmith, London: HarperCollins, 1999.

"Battery Point (Crescent City, CA) Lighthouse." See "Lighthouse Friends.Com," www.lighthousefriends.com/light.asp?ID=58, accessed on October 10, 2006.

Beaver, Patrick. *A History of Lighthouses*. Secaucus, NJ: Citadel, 1973.

Bennett, Laura J. "Classic Casualty: Brother Jonathan Sinking." *Professional Mariner*, vol. 83, October/November 2004, 60–62.

"Blasting at Seal Rock . . ." Article that begins with cited words, *Del Norte Record*, Crescent City, June 9, 1883.

Bowers, Q. David. *The Treasure Ship S.S. Brother Jonathan: Her Life and Loss, 1850–1865*. Wolfeboro, NH: Bowers and Merena Galleries, 1998.

"Brother Jonathan Wreck Is Again Believed Found." *Crescent City American*, December 18, 1931.

Bureau of Marine Inspection and Navigation (National Archives), Steamboat Inspection Service. Report of Casualties and Violations of Steamboat Laws, First District, San Francisco, 1865.

"California Parks See the Light." *Parks & Recreation*, August 2004, vol. 39 (8), 20.

"Cape Mendocino, CA." See "Lighthouse Friends.Com," www.light housefriends.com/light.asp?ID=25, accessed on October 10, 2006.

"Cape Mendocino Light, Cape Mendocino, CA." See "Rudy and Alice's Lighthouse Page," www.rudyalicelighthouse.net/CalLts/CapeMndo/ CapeMndo.htm, accessed on October 10, 2006.

"Captain Ballantyne, Superintendent of the Government Works at Humboldt Bay." Newspaper article that begins with cited words, *Alta California*, March 14, 1885.

"Captain John Olson of Seal Rock . . ." Newspaper article that begins with cited words, *Del Norte Record*, Crescent City, March 5, 1905.

Cates, Karl. "Saviour of the Light." *Del Norte Triplicate*, August 15, 1884.

Clifford, Mary Louise, and J. Candice Clifford. *Women Who Kept the Lights*. Williamsburg, VA: Cypress Communications, 1993.

———, and Elinor DeWire. "Women Who Kept the Lights: An Illustrated History of Female Lighthouse Keepers." *The American Neptune*, 1995, vol. 55, issue 1, 75.

Clunies, Sandy. E-mail regarding background of John Trewavas and stone mason partnership between Trewavas and Ballantyne. Personal communication, September 23, 2005.

———. Various e-mails regarding George Roux, John Olson, work of Ballantyne in Portland, Oregon, A. H. Payson, F. A. Mahan (the Lighthouse Board Engineering Secretary), etc. Personal communication, n.d.

———. "The LH Loop." E-mail about Nov. 1883 letter from D. P. Heap to General Orlando Poe. Personal communication, October 9, 2005.

———. "A Man in the Picture." E-mail about David Chalmers, foreman of the stone cutters. Personal communication, October 10, 2005.

———. "Magruder Dates." E-mail about Theo Magruder's family and the lightkeepers at Battery Rock Lighthouse in Crescent City. Personal communication, October 11, 2005.

———. "Details on Alexander." E-mail about details on A. Ballantyne's hiring, resignation, and re-hiring in 1893. Personal communication, October 11, 2005.

————. "William Henry Heuer." E-mail about background and district engineering experience of District Engineer Major W. H. Heuer. Personal communication, October 12, 2005.

————. "John E. Lind." E-mail about background and life of John Lind, who was a keeper at both St. George and Battery Point. Personal communication, October 12, 2005.

————. "Keeping the Flame: The Life of a Lighthouse Keeper." *NGS NewsMagazine*, January/February/March 2006, 16–19.

Coleman, Jennifer. "Volunteers Putting Old Lighthouse Back on Map." *The Monterey County Herald, Associated Press*, April 21, 2002, B5.

Cox, Phil. "Yes, Angels Do Fly! Dome Returned to St. George Reef Lighthouse." *Lighthouse Digest*, July 2002, 14–15.

"Death and Disaster along the Humboldt Coast." See National Park Service.com, www.cr.nps.gov/history/online_books/redw/history12d.htm, accessed on January 15, 2007.

Defrees, Madeline. *The Light Station on Tillamook Rock*. Corvalis, OR: Arrowood Books, 1990.

Del Norte County Historical Society. Various files, clippings, and information pertaining to the construction, operation, and deactivation of the St. George Reef Lighthouse.

"Design for the N.W. Seal Rock Lt. House [sic] near Crescent City, Cal., by George Ballantyne, ca.1883." See National Archives and Records Administration, Records of the U.S. Coast Guard, www.archives.gov/exhibits/designs_for_democracy/grand_plans_for_a_growing_nation/articles/seal_rock_lighthouse.html, accessed on August 1, 2006.

DeWire, Elinor. "Specters on the Spiral Stairs." *Keeper's Log*, Winter 1986, 8–11.

————. *Guardians of the Lights: The Men and Women of the U.S. Lighthouse Service*. Sarasota, FL: Pineapple Press, 1995.

Dickens, Charles. *American Notes*. London: Chapman & Hall, 1842.

"Disaster Hits St. George Reef." See Lighthouse Digest, May 2000, www.lhdigest.com/Digest/StoryPage.cfm?StoryKey=742, accessed on August 28, 2006.

Ehlers, Chad. *Sentinels of Solitude: West Coast Lighthouses*. San Luis Obispo, CA: EZ Nature Books, 1989.

Enkoji, M. S. "Beacon into the Past." *Sacramento Bee*, June 6, 2005, A1.

"Farallon Island, CA." See "Lighthouse Friends.Com," www.lighthouse friends.com/light.asp?ID=100, accessed on January 15, 2007.

"First-order Fresnel Lens." See California Parks Service, www.parks.ca.gov/ default.asp?page_id=22015, accessed on December 1, 2006.

"Fresnel Lens." See Michigan Lighthouse Conservancy, www.michigan lights.com, accessed on January 15, 2007.

"Full Particulars of the Wreck of the Brother Jonathan." *Alta California*, August 10, 1865.

Gardner, Edw. J. Letter to Mr. John E. Lind. Department of Commerce, Appointment Division, Washington, July 1, 1928.

Genzoli, Andrew. "Granite for St. George Light." *The Times-Standard*, January 19, 1968, 11.

"Getting out of Material." Article that begins with cited words, *Weekly Times-Telephone*, June 7, 1884.

Gibbs, Jim. *Tillamook Light*. Portland, OR: Binford & Mort, 1953.

———. *Sentinels of the North Pacific: The Story of Pacific Coast Lighthouses and Lightships*. Portland, OR: Binford & Mort, 1955.

———. *Disaster Log of Ships*. New York: Bonanza Books, 1971.

———. *West Coast Lighthouses: A Pictorial History of the Guiding Lights of the Sea*. Seattle, WA: Superior Publishing, 1974.

———. *Lighthouses of the Pacific*. West Chester, PA: Schiffer Publishing, 1986.

———, and Bert Webber. *Oregon's Seacoast Lighthouses*. Medford, OR: Webb Research Group, 2000.

Griffin, Pat ("Red"). Letter to Mr. and Mrs. J. W. Griffin, June 5, 1953 (regarding hose nozzle accident at St. George Reef Lighthouse).

"Guest of the Month." *United States Coast Guard Magazine*, June 1952, 20.

Hansen, H. "Tillamook Rock: Beacon of Silence." *Sea Frontiers*, January 1969, vol. 15, 54–60.

"Harbor—Oct. 15, 1895." *Gold Beach Gazette*, October 18, 1895.

"Hatteras Island." See www.hatteras-nc.com/light, accessed on December 1, 2006.

Heap, David Porter. November, 1883, letter to General Orlando Poe, starting with the words, "I send you herewith a revision of the plans of building NW Seal Rock Light proposed by Payson."

Heiser, Sherry. "Beacons May Glow No More." *Del Norte Triplicate*, November 9, 1983.

Henion, Jennifer. "New Lighthouse Museum Would Shine above the Rest." *Triplicate*, December 9, 2003.

Hillinger, Charles. "'Eye' of the Storm Finds a Home at Last." *Los Angeles Times*, August 28, 1983, 1(3).

"History Shines: A Visit with the Guardian Keeper of the Light at St. George Reef." *Curry Coastal Pilot*, August 2, 2003.

Holland, Francis Ross. *America's Lighthouses: An Illustrated History*. New York: Dover Publications, 1988.

Hugenot, Capt. Alan. "Copter Airlifts Five-Ton Section of Offshore Lighthouse." *The Log* (Northern California), April 26–May 9, 2002.

"Inventory of Historic Light Stations, California Lighthouses." See National Park Service.com, www.cr.nps.gov/maritime/light/stgeo.htm, accessed on January 15, 2007.

"Iron Men of the Lighthouse Service." *Popular Mechanics Magazine*, May 1929, vol. 51, 786–791.

Kern, Florence. "Lighthousing in the 1890s." *U.S. Coast Guard Alumni Association Bulletin*, November/December, 1978, 33–38.

Kobe, G. "Famous Lighthouses." *The Chautauquan*, August, 1900, vol. 31, 457–466.

"Landmark of Light." *Marin Independent Journal* (Marin, CA), July 6, 2003.

Leffingwell, Randy, and Pamela Welty. *Lighthouses on the Pacific Coast*. Stillwater, MN: Voyager Press, 2000.

"Lighthouse Digest." See www.lhdigest.com.

"Lighthouse Featured in PBS Program: St. George Reef Featured Nov. 23." *Curry Coastal Pilot*, October 3, 1998.

"Lighthouses: An Administrative History." See National Park Service.com, www.cr.nps.gov/maritime/light/admin.htm, accessed on November 15, 2006.

"Local Department." *Del Norte Record*, Crescent City, July 30, 1892.

Major C. H. McKnistry. Letters to John Olson, Keeper, St. George Reef Light-Station, dated September 12, 1906, and May 12, 1908.

"Maritime Heritage Program." See National Park Service.com, www.cr.nps. gov/maritime/nhlpa/nhlpa.htm, accessed on December 1, 2006.

Marshall, Don B. *California Shipwrecks*. Seattle, WA: Superior Publishing Company, 1978.

McClelland, C. H. "Terrible Tilly." *Keeper's Log*, Summer 1987, 2–9.

McKenzie-Bahr, Mike. "Oil Drums Lifted from Lighthouse." *The Triplicate*, May 27, 1994.

"Minot's Ledge Light History." See www.lighthouse.cc/minots/history. html, accessed on December 2, 2006.

"Minot's Ledge, MA." See "Lighthouse Friends.Com," www.lighthouse friends.com/light.asp?ID=474, accessed on December 15, 2006.

"Moving: Tallest Building Ever Moved." *ENR: Engineering News-Record*, December, 2004.

"Mssrs. Trewavas & Ballantyne." Article that begins with cited words, *Morning Oregonian*, July 22, 1875.

National Archives and Records Administration. *Guide to Records in the National Archives—Pacific Sierra Region*. Washington, DC: National Archives and Records Administration, 1995.

"Next Thursday Night . . ." Article that begins with cited words, *Del Norte Record*, Crescent City, CA, October 15, 1892.

Nichols, H. E., Commander. Letter to Mr. John J. Jeffrey, Keeper, Crescent City. Office of U.S. Light-House Inspector, Twelfth District, December 18, 1893.

Noble, Dennis L. *Lighthouses & Keepers: The U.S. Lighthouse Service and Its Legacy*. Annapolis, MD: Naval Institute Press, 1997.

Olson, John. Various Letters to Major C. H. McKnistry (and others), Army Corp of Engineers. U.S. Light-House Service, Twelfth District, dated June 15, 1906; October 30, 1906; May 11, 1907; October 8, 1907; May 16, 1908; and March 28, 1911.

"Oregon Chapter, U.S. Lighthouse Society." See www.randomb.com/ orelighthouse, accessed on January 15, 2007.

"Orlando Metcalfe Poe." See "Seeing the Light: Lighthouses of the Western Great Lakes," www.terrypepper.com/lights/closeups/ompoe/ompoe. htm, accessed on October 10, 2006.

"Our Military in Service." *Crescent City American*, January 4, 1969.

Payson, Captain H. H. "Principal Report." Letter dated April 4, 1883, Office of Light-House Engineer, Twelfth District, San Francisco, CA.

"Plaque Honors Lighthouse Organizer." *Times-Standard*, August 9, 1995.

"Point Reyes Lighthouse." See "The Point Reyes Light," www.ptreyes light.com/lthouse.html, accessed on January 21, 2007.

"Point St. George Lighthouse Officially Darkened at Age 84." *The Triplicate*, May 14, 1975.

"Point Sur State Historic Park and Lighthouse." See pointsur.org, accessed on December 1, 2006.

Putnam, George R. "Beacons of the Sea." *National Geographic*, vol. 24 (1913), 1–53.

———. *Lighthouses and Lightships of the United States*. Boston and New York: Houghton Mifflin, 1933.

———. *Sentinel of the Coasts*. New York: W.W. Norton, 1937.

Rhodes, H. W. Letter to Mr. J. E. Lind, Keeper, Crescent City Light Station, Department of Commerce, Lighthouse Service, January 16, 1928.

Riley, Joan. "Lighthouse Went Dark in 1975." *The Triplicate*, May 30, 1992.

———. "Bolen Gaining Fame Rebuilding Lighthouse Lenses." *The Triplicate*, October 22, 1992, 1.

———. "St. George Reef Lighthouse More Than a Memory." *The Triplicate*, July 25, 1992, B(1).

"'Rock' Was Dreaded." *Humboldt Times*, May 1975.

Rozin, Skip. "Who Mourns the Vanishing Wickies?" *Audubon*, May 1972, vol. 74, 30–35.

Rutherford, Donald. "St. George Reef Light: Guardian of Dragon Rocks." *Sea Frontiers*, January–February 1985, 31-1, 46–54.

———. "The Guardian of St. George Reef: American's Costliest Lighthouse." *Sea History*, Autumn 1992, vol. 63, 20–24.

"St. George Light and Its Heroic Builders." *The Humboldt Historian*, September–October 1989, 8–22.

"St. George Light Lens Unveiling Set." *Del Norte Triplicate*, May 2, 1984.

"St. George Reef, CA." See "Lighthouse Friends.Com," www. lighthouse friendscom/light.asp?ID=26, accessed January 21, 2007.

"St. George Reef Light." *Del Norte Triplicate* (Redwood Parklander), Fall Edition 1977, vol. 9, no. 3.

"St. George Reef Lighthouse, Crescent City, CA." See Cyberlights.com, www.cyberlights.com/lh/calif/stgeorge.htm, accessed on January 21, 2007.

St. George Reef Lighthouse Preservation Society Website. See www.stgeorgereeflighthouse.us, accessed on January 21, 2007.

Scanlan, J. M. "California Lighthouse Service." *The Overland Monthly*, February 1903, vol. 41, 83–100.

Schell, Susan. "The Fall and Rise of the St. George Lighthouse." *Curry Coastal Pilot*, Spring/Summer 2002, 22.

"Sentinel of the Seas." *The Mentor*, August 1921, vol. 9, 30.

Shanks, Ralph C., and Janetta Thompson. *Lighthouses and Lifeboats on the Redwood Coast*. San Anselmo, CA: Costano Books, 1978.

"She Kept the Reef Light Burning." *The Literary Digest*, April 11, 1925, vol. 85, 46–48.

"Shining Eye of the Lighthouse." See Lanternroom.com, www.lanternroom.com/misc/freslens.htm, accessed on January 15, 2007.

Showley, Roger M. "Keepers of the Flame; Life at Point Loma Lighthouse Was a Mixture of Boredom and Delight." *San Diego Union-Tribune*, April 24, 2005, I-1.

Sienkiewicz, Henryk (translated by Monica M. Gardner). "The Lighthouse Keeper." *The Golden Book Magazine*, July 1934, vol. 20, 99–107.

Snow, Edward Rowe. *Famous Lighthouses of America*. New York: Dodd, Mead & Company, 1955.

"Spectacle Reef Light." See www.terrypepper.com/lights/huron/spectacle/spectacle.htm, accessed on December 15, 2006.

Starr, Penny. "Looking Back at Life on a Lighthouse." *Curry Coastal Pilot*, Brookings, OR, April, 1996.

Stevenson, Ellen. "Lighthouse Heroine: Mrs. Patterson, the Grace Darling of Cape Beale Shore of Vancouver Island." *The Canadian Magazine*, June 1934, vol. 81, 14.

Stevenson, Thomas. *Lighthouse Construction and Illumination*. London and New York: E. & F. N. SPON, 1880.

"Terrible Marine Disaster." *San Francisco Evening Bulletin*, August 2, 1865.

Terry, John. "'Terrible Tilly' Holds Fast to Hard Life in Hostile Sea." *The Oregonian* (Portland, OR), June 20, 1999, C-4.

"The Building of Sea Rock Light." *The Humboldt Historian*, January–February 1983, 13.

"The Lighthouse of St. George Reef." Point of Historical Interest Application, Department of Parks and Recreation, State of California, 1979.

"Thomas Point Shoal Lighthouse." See www.thomaspointlighthouse. org, accessed on January 20, 2007.

Todd, John B. "Last Lighthouse Loses to Progress." *San Francisco Sunday Examiner & Chronicle*, September 29, 1974.

Towers, Guy. "St. George Reef Lighthouse Preservation Society: Restoration and Celebration Activities." *The Keeper's Log*, Winter 2006, 43–44.

United States Coast and Geodetic Survey. *Annual Report of the Superintendent (Benjamin Pierce) of the U.S. Coast and Geodetic Survey, 1869–1870*, Ex. Doc. No. 206, 41 Congress, 2nd Session.

United States Coast Guard. Memo from Commander, Maintenance and Logistics Command Pacific to Commandant, entitled *St. George Reef Light Station Nomination for National Register of Historic Places*, July 1, 1993.

United States Coast Guard—12th Coast Guard District Auxiliary. *The Whistling Buoy*, February 1962, vol. 23, no.1.

———. *The Whistling Buoy*, Fall 1968, vol. 27, no. 3.

United States Dept. of the Interior, National Park Service. *National Register of Historic Places Registration Form (St. George Reef Light Station)*, April 21, 1993.

United States Government. *Annual Census of 1900, 1910, 1920, 1930*. Washington, DC: Government Printing Office, various publication dates.

———. *Seventeenth Annual List of Merchant Vessels of the United States for the Year Ended June 30, 1885*. Washington, DC: Government Printing Office, 1885.

U.S. Light-House Board. *Annual Report of the Light-House Board to the Secretary of the Treasury for the Fiscal Year ending June 30, 1881*. "Report Upon the Construction of Tillamook Rock Light Station, Sea Coast of Oregon" by Major G.L. Gillespie, 13th District. Washington, DC: Government Printing Office, 1881.

————. *Annual Report of the Light-House Board to the Secretary of the Treasury for the Fiscal Year Ending June 30, 1892.* "Construction of Northwest Seal Rock (St. George Reef) Light-House, Seacoast of California" by Major W.H. Heuer, 12th District, including Appendix No. 5. Washington, DC: Government Printing Office, 1881.

————. *Annual Report of the Light-House Board to the Secretary of the Treasury* (various, from 1874–1919). Washington, DC: Government Printing Office, various years.

United States Lighthouse Society. See www.uslhs.org, accessed on January 2, 2007.

Updike, Richard W. "Winslow Lewis and the Lighthouses." *The American Neptune,* January 1968, vol. 28, no. 1, 31–48.

"Visitor Register Log of the St. George Reef Lighthouse." *Bulletin of the Del Norte County Historical Society,* Crescent City, CA, February 15, 1976.

Webber, Bert, and Margie Webber. *Battery Point and St. George Reef Lighthouses (Includes Tidal Wave of 1964 at Crescent City, California).* Medford, OR: Webb Research Group Publishers, 2000.

————. *"Terrible Tilly"; Tillamook Rock Lighthouse: The Biography of a Lighthouse, An Oregon Documentary—Expanded Edition.* Medford, OR: Webb Research Group Publishers, 1998 (1992).

Weiss, Kenneth R. "Hard to Destroy, Hard to Fix and Easy to Love." *Los Angeles Times,* June 21, 2003.

Wheeler, Wayne. "The Keeper's New Clothes." *The Keeper's Log,* Summer 1985, 10–13.

————. "St. George Reef: American's Most Expensive Lighthouse." *The Keeper's Log,* Fall 1985, 2–8.

————. "St. George Reef Lighthouse: A Nineteenth Century Engineering Feat." *The Keeper's Log,* Fall 2003, 2–15.

Yeaton, Bryan. "The Minot's Light Storm." *Weatherwise,* March/April, 2005, vol. 58 (2), 12.

INDEX